HIMALAYAN PILGRIMAGE

HIMALAYAN PILGRIMAGE

A Study of Tibetan Religion
by a Traveller through Western Nepal

David Snellgrove

SHAMBHALA
Boston & Shaftesbury
1989

SHAMBHALA PUBLICATIONS, INC.
HORTICULTURAL HALL
300 MASSACHUSETTS AVENUE
BOSTON, MASSACHUSETTS 02115

SHAMBHALA PUBLICATIONS, INC.
THE OLD SCHOOL HOUSE
THE COURTYARD, BELL STREET
SHAFTESBURY, DORSET SP7 8BP

9 8 7 6 5 4 3 2 1

PRINTED IN THE UNITED STATES OF AMERICA
DISTRIBUTED IN THE UNITED STATES BY RANDOM HOUSE
AND IN CANADA BY RANDOM HOUSE OF CANADA LTD.
DISTRIBUTED IN THE UNITED KINGDOM BY ELEMENT BOOKS, LTD.

LIBRARY OF CONGRESS CATALOGING-IN-PUBLICATION DATA

SNELLGROVE, DAVID L.

HIMALAYAN PILGRIMAGE: A STUDY OF TIBETAN RELIGION
BY A TRAVELLER THROUGH WESTERN NEPAL / DAVID SNELLGROVE.
P.   CM.   BIBLIOGRAPHY: P.   INCLUDES INDEX.
ISBN 0-87773-474-7 (PBK.)
1. NEPAL—RELIGION. 2. NEPAL—DESCRIPTION AND TRAVEL.
3. BUDDHISM—CHINA—TIBET. 4. SNELLGROVE, DAVID L.
—JOURNEYS—NEPAL. 5. SCHOLARS, BUDDHIST
—GREAT BRITAIN—BIOGRAPHY. I. TITLE.
[BL2030.N3S5 1989]   88-18620
915.49'604—DC19   CIP

Dedicated to Pasang Khambache Sherpa

CONTENTS

ILLUSTRATIONS

PREFACE TO SECOND EDITION

The journey described in this book was undertaken in 1956 within a few years of Nepal being opened to foreign visitors. I have the impression however that everyday life has changed comparatively little in the remote northern frontier regions of the Himalayas which are described here one by one from west to east. It is noteworthy too that comparatively little has been added over the years to the limited fund of information about these interesting Tibetan-speaking lands which lie properly within the frontiers of modern Nepal. Thus it is not unsuitable to republish this book just as it is, simply drawing attention below to the few informative works that have appeared in the meantime. I returned via the Kali Gandaki Valley to Dolpo in 1960 and 1961, accompanied as always by Pasang Khambache Sherpa, who is named in the Preface to the First Edition as Parwa Pasang Sherpa, the variation in his name being explained later on in this Preface. I had not been in this area again until the summer of 1978 and then with the same companion, so I would certainly have noticed any remarkable changes which might have taken place in the meantime.

The absence of change in everyday ways of life might seem surprising in view of certain intervening political and economic upheavals, the effects of which have been undoubtedly serious. The most significant of these, the Chinese military occupation of Tibet following upon the Lhasa uprising of 1959, resulted in the disruption of centuries-old trading links between Tibet and Nepal and has had devastating effects upon the prosperity of the T'hakālis of the Kali Gandaki Valley, especially upon the merchant families of the one-time chief trading town of Tukchä. The adverse effects upon animal husbandry in Dolpo were no less serious in their own way. Whereas the villagers of Dolpo had previously grazed their animals, mainly yaks, dzo (the yak-cow cross-breed) and sheep on the nomad pastures of south-western Tibet during the long winter months in total unawareness of modern frontier restrictions, the establishing of Chinese frontier posts along the old border put an immediate stop to such age-old neighbourly customs. When we arrived in Dolpo in 1960 we learned at once of the unprecedented difficulties that the villagers were facing, and there has been since then a drastic reduction in the number of animals that can be maintained during the winter despite the use of alternative grazing grounds found in the lower valleys of Nepal. The Government of Nepal has remained on good terms with the Chinese Communist régime and a limited amount of trading has since restarted under strict Chinese control. But the free social and economic intercourse across the frontier has been firmly stopped. Then a further serious upheaval in these areas was caused by the Khambas, the free-fighting Tibetans, who from 1961 until 1974 effectively occupied large parts of north-western Nepal with the intention of holding a defensive area against the Chinese who could be attacked as occasion permitted. This represented to some extent an occupation of Nepalese territory, much as the Palestinians have been occupying the southern part of Lebanon in order to threaten Israel. There is little doubt that the Dalai Lama's head-quarters in India knew what was afoot, and the chief agent for obtaining outside military help was one of the Dalai Lama's own brothers. It is remarkable that the Nepalese Government should have acted with such patience for so long, but one inevitable effect of this troubled situation was the general exclusion of all travellers and scholars, especially foreign ones, from the areas involved. Inevitably there was also considerable delay in implementing in these remote frontier areas plans for educational and economic development, which the Government of Nepal was already introducing effectively elsewhere. But by delaying such processes these unwelcome political and economic disturbances have now left these regions, so far as everyday life is concerned, very much as they were when we last saw them in 1961.

One recent and notable change, however, is now coming about through the setting up of village schools, a necessary function of which is to foster Nepali as the national language of the whole country while also introducing modern kinds of education. Previously, except for children whose parents, like the merchants of Tukchä, were wealthy enough to send their children to Kathmandu or even to India for education, such education as was available was given by monks and religious-minded laymen through the medium of literary Tibetan. Tibetan dialects are still spoken in the home and in the village outside school (much as German dialect is still spoken in many homes in Alsace despite the strong pressure of French education), but a few youngsters are now qualified to progress to Kathmandu for higher education, even obtaining scholarships still further afield. It came as a great surprise to meet a young man from Dolpo at a lecture that I was giving in New York in December 1977. This is an entirely new development and little as it may still affect the great majority who live in these high mountain valleys, there are clearly major changes afoot. The Lama of Marpha, an important T'hakāli village a few miles north of Tukchä, despite his personal friendly relations with the head-master of the new local school, was lamenting to me this summer (1978) that the new style of education was undermining faith in the Buddhist religion.

One might expect changes in outlook to follow upon the generous manner in which the Government of Nepal has opened up the country to tourists. One of the most popular routes with foreign visitors has been the journey on foot from Pokhara, up to Dzongsam (Jomosom), on to Muktināth, continuing over to Manang and along the Marsyandi Valley down to the new highway and back to Kathmandu. We covered this route in 1956 and again parts of it in 1960 and 1961 when we travelled in and out of Dolpo, twice each way, by the route from Pokhara over the Kali Gandaki Valley. It was this same journey which I made in the summer of 1978 together with Pasang Khambache Sherpa on the way to his experimental fruit-farm at Marpha (of which more will be said below) and we were often asked by old friends what changes we noticed. For me the main changes were in ourselves, such other changes being very localized. The route itself is as difficult as it has always been, and here there is clearly no change except for the worse during the monsoon season, when sections of the old route collapse and even more strenuous ones have to be devised. Nowadays there is a small airfield at Dzongsam (Jomosom) with rather shabby little 'hotels' strung along the side of it. Planes can land there except during the three to four months of the monsoon season, and thus visitors are saved five to six very strenuous days of walking and clambering. The most difficult part of the route is that which ascends steeply to Ulleri and over the Ghorapani Pass to Tatopani in the Kali Gandaki Valley. Here pack animals are scarcely useable and it is remarkable to think that this has served and still continues to serve as one of the main trade routes connecting large parts of north-western Nepal (specifically Mustang and Dolpo) with Pokhara and Kathmandu. Despite the new air-link and the considerable reduction in Tibetan trade, this route is still quite busy and one will meet continually groups of porters carrying merchandise in 80 to 100 lbs loads up to the higher valleys. These loads now include crates of Nepalese beer and bottled fruit-cordials in demand by western travellers. The presence of this kind of refreshment is certainly something new and in its own way a change for the better, but scarcely of local significance. Indeed the tourists affect the area in essentials very little, as very few of them speak any Nepali, let alone a local dialect, so they walk on with their rucksacks, enjoying the magnificent scenery and with minimum contact with the local people. The 'hotels' have learned to put up lists of items in English, to which they can point, and very occasionally there is a son or daughter on the establishment who has learned some English at school. Certainly tourists of all nationalities expect to get by with English, and they usually manage to do so. The villagers expect to learn nothing from them about the outside world, and having grown used to their foreign appearance and learned to appreciate them as a very helpful source of revenue, let them pass without so much as a show of curiosity. Occasionally one meets climbers and walkers wise enough to seek the assistance of local porters who are also usually the best of guides, since they know so well all the routes and all the alternatives in case of difficulty. The advantage of their company is thus twofold: firstly one has so much less to carry that one's enjoyment of the free life of the mountains is greatly increased, and secondly, especially if one has chosen well, one has not just carriers of luggage but firm allies who can bring one into easy contact with the everyday life of the country through which one is travelling and also in case of need save one from very real dangers. Some working knowledge of Nepali is necessary to really benefit from their company, and their companionship when it works out right, is for me one of the greatest joys of travel in Nepal. The long journey made through north-western Nepal, as described in the present book, provided us with the most varied experience in travelling with porters and with pack animals, as they had to be changed again and again, and sometimes we were less fortunate in our companions than in others, but there can be few countries in the world where men would so readily turn to and help others for rates of payment which in retrospect seem to me quite ludicrous. In 1956 we were paying as entirely acceptable rates two Indian rupees or three Nepali rupees a day, to which we added various refreshments in the form of tea or rakshi (local spirits) and a ration of cigarettes. A Nepali rupee was then worth just about an English shilling (or fourteen American cents) and an Indian rupee about half as much again. In 1978 we were paying twenty Nepali rupees daily (rather less nowadays than £1) with the same refreshments and often free meals as well and presents of clothes and new rubber boots at the end of the journey. This too seems a very small amount for the willing and friendly service that one receives, a kind of service without servility, but rendered simply as part of a fairly agreed bargain. Here again there is no essential change, but superficial differences caused by the world-wide depreciation of currency. One should perhaps bear in mind that my memories of travelling with Nepalese porters may have been affected very favourably by the happy experiences of our last journey.

The main changes have certainly been with ourselves and they are especially noteworthy in the case of Pasang Khambache Sherpa, to whom the Second Edition of this book is dedicated and of whom very much more deserves to be written than is possible in this short Preface. I first met Pasang as a young man in Kalimpong (India) in the autumn of 1953 when he was living close to another old friend of mine, the Mongolian Lama Geshé Wangyal, who foreseeing the wrath that was soon to descend upon Tibet, had left Drepung Monastery (near Lhasa) and had settled in Kalimpong. It was he who introduced us over a feast of mo-mo (stuffed dumplings) which he and Pasang prepared one day in every respect, as it turned out, to my benefit. Geshé Wangyal is now well-known among Tibetan enthusiasts in the U.S.A., for he went to New Jersey in 1955 (staying en route with myself and Pasang in England) and established there the first American Tibetan Buddhist monastery. Pasang, a trained wood-carver and block-printer (hence the name *parwa* for 'printer' attached to his name earlier on) belongs to the Khambache clan of the Sherpas of Solu-Khumbu (in eastern Nepal) where he was born and still now maintains his family property. He was educated at rDza-rong-phu Monastery on the Tibetan side of Mount Everest and later at Tashi-lhun-po (Tsang Province of Tibet) where he learned carving and printing. When we first met in 1953 he had recently finished a two-year contract at the Bhutanese Court, where he had been working on a new edition of Tibetan canonical texts, and was in fact recuperating in Kalimpong from an attack of malaria. He was fluent and literate in Nepali and Tibetan and from the time that he joined company with me, he began to learn English. We made a tour of Sherpa monasteries in Solu-Khumbu in the spring of 1954 and in the summer of that year he accompanied me to England as my companion and right-hand

xvi

man. In 1956 we returned to Nepal, making the long journey described in this book. He was again with me in England from 1957 to 1960, travelling also to Scotland, France, Switzerland and Italy. He was of inestimable help to me in my academic work, while studying himself meanwhile. From 1960 to 1961 we were in Nepal again, spending most of the time in Dolpo, although on such visits Pasang found time to visit his home in Solu. When we returned to England in the autumn of 1961 we brought back with us five Tibetans, four monks and a layman, who were all refugees from the Chinese takeover of Tibet in 1959, and our life became far more complicated.

Pasang assisted me in trying to reconstruct the violently interrupted lives of this small Tibetan group, and at first knowing only Tibetan, they could communicate only through us. It was a difficult period and as they became ever more independent Pasang sought the opportunity of branching out on his own. Apart from the wood carving that he had been doing once again to my considerable advantage, we had taken an interest in vines, and in 1965 thanks to our friendly connections with Professor Rolf Stein in Paris, Pasang took up a serious study of vine growing, receiving from the French Government one of several scholarships available to Nepalese students for study in France. He thus followed courses of regular training for two years at Montpellier, where we used to meet. In 1967 he returned to Nepal and received a contract with the Nepalese Ministry of Agriculture, which was just then interested in developing fruit-farming. Meanwhile he took leave to accompany me on a visit to Bhutan, and since then we have met on my occasional visits to Nepal, while Pasang has steadily risen in the administrative hierarchy. He is now Joint-Secretary in the Ministry of Agriculture and Supervisor of experimental fruit-farms in the Mustang, Dolpo and Manang areas. His main operative centre is at Marpha, whence he travels with fantastic speed to Kathmandu and to Pokhara and across high passes to Dolpo and to Manang. Pasang is certainly a remarkable example of the changes which are taking place in Nepal. He has

xvii

been honoured by the king for all the work he has done for economic development, and I take this opportunity of paying tribute to all the help he has been giving me over the years.

As for published research work done in these Tibetan-speaking regions of Nepal since the publication of *Himalayan Pilgrimage,* there are very few works of any substance. I published in 1967 in their Tibetan original and in English translation the biographies of four renowned Dolpo lamas with the title of *Four Lamas of Dolpo.* This was the final fruit of work done during the cold winter of 1960/61 when Pasang and I spent four months snowed up within the Namgung Valley. Corneille Jest, now a well-known French anthropologist, who first accompanied me to Dolpo in 1960 and who has made many return journeys there since, as well as to the Tibetan-speaking regions further east, produced in 1975 a magnificently illustrated ethnological work entitled *Dolpo, communautés de langue tibétaine du Nepal* (Paris). Together with a colleague, J. F. Dobremez, he published in 1976 another volume, more topographical in character, about the regions further east on our old route, entitled *Manaslu, hommes et milieux des vallées du Népal central.* Then we must mention especially Christoph von Fürer-Haimendorf's latest work, *Himalayan Traders, Life in Highland Nepal* (London 1975), which covers in varying degrees of detail some of the main areas that we travelled through in 1956 and also the remote Humla-Jumla region to the north-west of Dolpo, unvisited by us. Reading through our book again, I realize how tired we had become in the latter part of our long journey and how much more might be added even now if one made a return journey. Dr. Michael Aris, whose research work has been centred mainly on Bhutan (his history of Bhutan has just been published by Aris & Phillips of Warminster), visited Kutang and Nup-ri (Nubri) in 1973 and wrote a substantial article afterwards, adding considerable information to our earlier account. This appeared in *Contributions to Nepalese Studies,* the journal of the Institute of (now known as the Research Centre for) Nepal and Asian Studies, Tribhuvan University, vol. II, no.

2 (June 1975), pp. 45–87, entitled: 'Report on the University of California Expedition to Kutang and Nubri in Northern Nepal in Autumn 1973.' Michael Aris also succeeded in making copies of the biographies of a locally renowned seventeenth-century lama, Padma Don-grub and of disciples who succeeded him in the lineage. These have been recently printed in Delhi,[a] and one hopes that an English translation will soon follow. Like my Dolpo biographies these represent a small part of the large amount of Tibetan local literature available in these areas, and demonstrate how much there remains to be brought into the light of day before any Nepalese history of these northern parts of the country can ever be started. It is sad to have to report that Tribhuvan University, which is the main centre of higher learning in Nepal, displays no actual interest in Tibetan studies despite the fact that so many of Nepal's citizens are Tibetan-speaking and many of them thoroughly literate in Tibetan. This comes about mainly because the Government of Nepal tacitly discourages such an interest, almost it might seem in a deliberate attempt to conceal the fact that so many Nepalese are of Tibetan stock. It is noteworthy that since the Chinese Communists took possession of the political entity known as Tibet, that is to say the major part of the Tibetan-speaking world which was subject to the Dalai Lama and his *dGe-lugs-pa* ('Yellow Hat') administration in Lhasa (since 1642), government officials in the remaining Tibetan-speaking areas (viz. mainly Ladakh, Spiti and Lahul, all the northern regions of Nepal, Sikkim and Bhutan) have shown an unwillingness to refer to their people, who are clearly of Tibetan stock for the most part, as in any way Tibetan. Even the identity of language is often denied. While it is true that all these areas have distinct dialects of their own, albeit Tibetan ones, they are united in the use of a common literary language. So far only the Bhutanese have

---

[a] *Autobiographies of Three Spiritual Masters of Kutang,* published by Kunsang Topgay & Mani Dorje, Thimbu, Bhutan, printed at Photo Offset Printers, Ballimaran, Delhi.

attempted to differentiate their written language from literary Tibetan by devising new spellings which accord more with Bhutanese pronunciation, calling this newly created literary form Dzongkha. But if its use is successful, it will have the great disadvantage of cutting those so educated off from all their previous literature, which is in normal Tibetan.

The deliberate avoidance of the term Tibetan (and the corresponding Indian/Nepali term Bhotia/Bhote deriving from the Indian name for Tibet, viz. Bhot) surely arises from an anxiety to separate absolutely these various peoples, who are racially, linguistically and culturally Tibetan but not politically Tibetan, from those others, the majority, who live inside the so-called Autonomous Region of Tibet of the Chinese Peoples' Republic. While one may well sympathize with such an anxiety, it has the unhappy effect of checking any official interest in Tibetan language and culture, especially in Nepal. Nepal and Tibet have been neighbours for centuries, and although so many Nepalese are Tibetan-speaking, no one locally has worked on the creation of a Nepali/Tibetan dictionary. If one looks for a European parallel, it would be as though the French Swiss and the German Swiss lived together in Switzerland without any form of mutual cultural interpenetration. The importance of the German language and literature to so many countries of central Europe is in fact parallel to the importance of Tibetan language and literature in central southern Asia. Austria, which is as independent of Germany as Bhutan is independent of Tibet, possesses its own German dialects just as Bhutan has its own Tibetan dialects, while both Austria and Bhutan over the centuries use the literary styles of German or Tibetan as the case may be. Again Switzerland operates with a plurality of languages, just as Nepal continues to operate, and no Swiss is made to feel any less a Swiss because his native tongue is French or German, Italian or Romance. The situation in Ladakh, historically Tibetan-speaking, corresponds closely to that of Alsace, historically German-speaking although it is part of France. In Europe it is taken for granted that political boundaries do not and cannot coincide with linguistic boundaries where any land-mass is involved (islands are in a different situation); but in Asia there is a strong modern tendency to try and force the issue and to proscribe all languages but that of the majority. In Sri Lanka this is being attempted by insisting that Singhalese should be the only language of the island. In Nepal the situation still remains to some extent open, and one hopes that its University can still become a centre of interest for all the various cultures, in which the country is so rich, as well as the official centre for promoting studies in economic development. Nepal could then play its part in international Tibetan studies with all those other countries that are interested. In July 1979 we held in Oxford the first major International Seminar for Tibetan Studies. Nepal with more Tibetan speakers to its credit than any other country except China and India was conspicuously absent. Those of us who continue to be interested in Nepal always hope for some change in policy.

Kathmandu   David Snellgrove
12th August 1979

PREFACE TO FIRST EDITION

Nepal is a country of such wonderful variety that even the Nepalese themselves have not yet had time to explore the richness of their own heritage. Ranging from about 500 feet above sea-level on its southern frontier to heights of anything between 20,000 and 29,000 in the north, this country inevitably embraces a great variety of human types and cultural patterns. Indeed in the western part, which happens to be the widest, this variety borders on total dissimilitude. What relationship can there be in race, language and culture between the dark T'harus of the southern Tarai, living in simple Indian-style villages of clay and thatch, and the pure Tibetans of the north with their herds of yak and sheep, their stone-built houses and imposing monasteries? Physically too there must be notable differences between men who live at 500 feet above sea-level and those who live at 15,000. But these are extremes and in a sense exceptions, which render all the more remarkable a certain tendency towards cultural unity, which is already characteristic of the greater part of Nepal. The many other races, Newars, Tamangs, Gurungs, Magars, Rais, Limbus, Sherpas, Gorkhas, are not so much different peoples, as variations upon two simple themes, namely Tibetan kinship and Indian penetration, which have been interplaying up and down the valleys for the last two thousand years. The Sherpas have preserved their Tibetan kinship almost inviolate and a very few of the Gorkhas might claim with some justification to be of pure Indian *kshatriya* descent, but the Newars of the Nepal Valley, who historically and culturally are the foremost of Nepalese, represent the most complex interplay of the two fundamental themes.[a]

[a] It is interesting to note that the Newars group their immediate neighbours into two main categories: *Seṃ* (pronounced rather as French 'sain'), who are the Tibetans proper and all people of predominantly Tibetan stock, viz.

Until the end of the eighteenth century the Newars were in fact the only Nepalese, while the whole Himalayan region of which Nepal now consists, still belonged to numerous petty rulers. Then the ruler of Gorkha, a township fifty miles WNW of Kathmandu, seized control of 'Nepal', viz. the three Newar principalities of Bhatgaon, Pātan and Kathmandu, in 1768, and by a remarkable series of campaigns and treaties proceeded to subjugate all the other rulers throughout the Himalayas from Sikkim to Kashmir. It was only the intervention of the British which forced him back within Nepal's present frontiers. Thus modern Nepal took shape one hundred and fifty years ago as a heterogeneous collection of haphazard administrative districts, lacking inner cohesion and still essentially as separate from one another as before. Castles and monasteries were destroyed and villages impoverished, but the 'conquerors' stayed nowhere long enough in sufficient numbers to disturb the established order. In this respect the Newars, whose land they made their home, were the only permanent sufferers. Elsewhere

Tamangs, Gurungs, Magars, Rais, Limbus, Sherpas ; and *Khem*, who are the Gorkhas and other peoples of the lower valleys, identified primarily by their use of the language *Khem-bhay* (Khaskura), which for practical purposes is now identical with Gorkhāli (*alias* Nepāli). A third category, *Marśyā* (a contraction of *Madhyadeśayā*) refers to the people of northern India and Indian settlers in Nepal.

The name Newar itself is simply a phonetic variation of Nepal and so means just Nepalese, but in the limited sense of belonging to the Nepal Valley, to which alone the name Nepal was applied in the past. Thus the terms *Newāri*, referring to the language of the Newars, and *Nepāli*, the language of the Gorkhas and other lowlanders (Khas), are actually synonyms. The latter certainly justifies its claim to be considered the language of Nepal, in that it is now spoken by more than five out of the eight million inhabitants of modern Nepal.

The name Gorkha, as applied to Nepalese soldiers, is actually a misnomer, for these men are primarily Magars, Gurungs, Rais and Limbus; just one regiment consists of Chetris (*kshatriya*), who are Gorkhas in the proper sense. The British established relations with Nepal soon after the Gorkha conquest and so this 'clan-name' came to be applied to all Nepalese troops. In this book I use the word Gorkha in the accurate historical sense of the men of Gorkha, who seized control of the Nepal Valley in 1768, and their descendants, who became the undisputed rulers of Nepal as it now appears on our maps.

the people were able to rebuild their fortunes in part; taxes were paid to officials now appointed or recognized by the house of Gorkha, but otherwise life continued much as before.

Only since the declaration of democracy (still a hope for the future) in 1950 have the Nepalese been able to begin to conceive of themselves as a nation and thus the greatest task which now confronts them is the realization of their responsibilities to one another as fellow-countrymen. Travelling across their mountainous and roadless land, one is aware of an extraordinary variety of peoples, whose concept of 'national unity' is limited to their own village or at most a group of villages. Yet, strangely enough, the chief means towards a wider sense of unity already exist, for the language of the Gorkhas and other lowlanders, now known as Nepāli, is already used throughout the whole length of central Nepal. The other languages, Tamang, Gurung, Magar, etc., although still widely spoken, have been gradually losing their ground. Only Newāri in the Nepal Valley and the Tibetan dialects of the far north remain as strong as ever they were. Thus with just two languages, Nepāli and Tibetan, one can travel with ease almost anywhere in Nepal. Conversely when some of these different peoples, so long as they be speakers of Nepāli (whether as their mother-tongue or as a second language), are gathered together on terms of social equality, a tendency to cultural unity finds spontaneous means of expression. Such circumstances may be rare, for in their own country they are still kept apart, physically by great mountain ranges and artificially by regulations of caste, but whoever has been present, for example, at a Nepalese party in their London Embassy, will understand something of what it means to be Nepalese. There are no people in the world more delightful, and none might be more fortunate, would they but find the means of realizing the same spirit of unity at home.

This book tells of a journey made through the Tibetan regions of western Nepal in 1956. Its title was unwittingly suggested by the people amongst whom we travelled, for used as they are to making pilgrimages themselves, they assumed that we too must be pilgrims. Such journeys are usually undertaken for religious merit, and although we were in pursuit of knowledge and experience, which is not quite the same thing, I would be sad to think that we had deceived our hosts in any way. The Tibetan word for pilgrimage means literally 'going around places' (*gnas-skor*), which describes our activities succinctly enough. To what extent the religious element is present in our case, the good reader must be left to judge for himself. Sometimes I must certainly beg his indulgence, for it is difficult to touch on Tibetan religion without risk of involving us both in a maze of philosophical and theological technicalities. My primary aim, however, is rather to give an overall impression of the peoples, amongst whom we were travelling, and as most of the technical terms have already been explained in a previous book of mine, all that is needed here is just sufficient explanation to allow this account to exist in its own right as a kind of scholar's travel-book.

I have written in *Buddhist Himālaya* about the ways in which Buddhism came to Tibet. Here we are concerned with some remote Himalayan regions, where the people have received their culture and religion at a later stage from the main centres of civilization in Tibet itself. These Tibetans of Nepal (*bhotia*) continue to live in a way which is rarely possible in the modern world. Perhaps great mountains have nowadays become a more formidable barrier than they ever were in the past. When most men had to travel on foot wherever they went, there was merely a difference of degree between travelling across plains and travelling through mountains. Today, when we are accustomed to travelling in fast-moving machines, there is a difference in kind between our travel and that of the true native mountaineers. Meanwhile our lives have become geared, as it were, to the speed at which we move, so that of the few who have the will to cross mountains, even fewer have the time.

Among the few travellers who have preceded me along some of

the tracks there are four to whom I am specially indebted. Firstly there are the two surveyors, Jagdish Behari Lal and Lalbir Singh Thapa, whose work is generally reliable in spite of the great difficulty that must have been experienced in sketching in some of these regions on the basis of too little data. Then I am indebted as always to Professor Tucci, who has made two journeys over sections of my route, one up the Kāli Gandaki to Mustang and the other through Tsharka (*Survey of India:* Chharkābhotgāon), Tarap and Sandul (SI: Chhandul) to Tibri-kot and thence to Jumla.[a] I am indebted further to Mr. L. H. J. Williams of the British Museum (Natural History), who has identified for me the various leaves and flowers which I collected in a haphazard manner. The botanical names which appear on the following pages are the gift of his special knowledge.[b]

Very few foreigners have passed through Dolpo. The first seems to have been the Japanese, Ekai Kawaguchi, who entered political Tibet by way of Tsharka at the beginning of this century.[c] Next to come were the two surveyors, already mentioned, of the Survey of India in 1925–6. Since the last war Dr. Toni Hagen, a Swiss geologist has travelled rapidly straight across from the north-west to the south-east. Then came a British botanist, Polunin, and lastly myself. This region was still largely unknown, for no one had recognized its cultural unity, or even drawn attention to the name of Dolpo and its identity with the ancient western Tibetan district of the same name.[d] Thus it provided the most interesting part of my

[a] His relevant publications are: *Preliminary Report on Two Scientific Expeditions in Nepal,* Rome, 1956, and *Tra Giungle e Pagode,* Rome, 1953.

[b] Western Nepal has been visited by a few British botanists since the war. Williams travelled widely in the regions of Tibrikot and Jumla and as far north as Simikot and Mugu in 1952. Other members of this expedition were W. R. Sykes and Oleg Polunin who wandered over the mountains of eastern Dolpo.

[c] see his *Three Years in Tibet,* Theosophical Publishing House, Banaras and London, 1909, pp. 69–73.

[d] see, for example, Tucci, *Preliminary Report,* p. 55.

travels and so occupies a proportionately large part of this book.

For the time and means to travel I am indebted once again to the School of Oriental Studies in the University of London. For the permission to wander at will through these remote Himalayan regions thanks are due to the Nepalese Government. I acknowledge in particular the assistance given me by Kaisher Bahadur, Secretary of Education, who has acted as a most valued friend on all my visits to Nepal. To many others, whose names appear in this book, I am grateful for help of diverse kinds. Without the assistance of Parwa Pasang Sherpa, whose name appears most frequently, the whole journey would scarcely have been possible. For the success of our venture we depended entirely on the goodwill of the villagers wherever we went. This goodwill was often spontaneous, but it was also sometimes checked by suspicion or even submerged in cupidity. Yet Pasang would still arouse it by a combination of quiet resolution and ingenuous friendliness. Finally from Dr. Colin Rosser I have received innumerable ideas, derived from his own knowledge of Nepal and the Himalayas.

Berkhamsted   David Snellgrove
29th October 1958

NOTE

My method of spelling Tibetan place-names, which is explained in the appendix, is also used occasionally for other Tibetan names and terms. Thus whenever the reader comes upon such a name in roman type, he should pronounce it in accordance with the table given on pp. 277–8. Tibetan classical spellings are indicated by the use of italics. Sanskrit presents no problem in this respect, for there is no such discrepancy between the written forms and the actual pronunciation. I have given the names of most divinities in English translation, followed by the Sanskrit name in brackets if they are of Indian origin and the Tibetan name if they are indigenous Tibetan divinities. A complete list is given in the appendix pp. 286–8.

I

THE START OF OUR JOURNEY

KATHMANDU

At least once in a lifetime one should approach the Nepal
Valley on foot, for this is the simplest way of gaining an
impression of its special historical and cultural significance. It
is better still of course, if one can learn to know its several
approaches, not only from the Indian side (perhaps too short
nowadays to give a really effective impression), but also by the
old Tibetan route leading down into Sankhu, by the western
route from the Gandaki valleys (whence we shall arrive at the
end of the travels described in this book) or even by the route
that leads in to Banepa from the districts of eastern Nepal.

Approaching on foot, one's arrival is the culmination of days
of slow travel with ever mounting expectancy, and that feeling
of calm satisfaction and happy fulfilment, which pervades one
on mounting the pass and seeing the Valley at one's feet, belongs, I am sure, to the very best of human experience. These
conditions of travel have changed not at all, and the many
Tibetan monks and scholars, who went there in search of knowledge a thousand years ago, probably conceived of Nepal in a
way which we are happily still able to appreciate nowadays.

At the beginning of 1956 I approached the Nepal Valley for
the third time, travelling on this occasion by the rapid air-
route from Patna. By mere speed expectation is robbed of its
substance: this is now no land of promise, whose frontiers have
at last been gained by one's own patience and endurance, but
rather an illusive dream-country, delightful while the vision
lasts, but vanishing as soon as the plane touches land, and life
shows itself as prosaic as ever.

One passes through clouds and close over the tops of tree-covered mountains. Then the Valley appears suddenly below with its wooded hillocks and terraced fields, decked with the little red houses of the peasants (Khas); one sees the glistening waters of the Bāgmati, the dark serried rows of houses of those inveterate town-dwellers, the Newars, and here and there a Rāna palace in its pseudo-Italian style; there may just be time to glance at the great stūpa of Bodhnāth, as the plane completes its circling. Then the dream is over and a few minutes later one is fumbling for documents and opening cases under the watchful eyes of officials.

In another way too this arrival differed from previous ones, for certain colleagues of mine had reached Kathmandu before me: Professor Brough, who was working in the libraries, Dr. Baké, who was making precious collections of Nepalese dancing and ritual singing, and Professor Codrington, who roamed the Valley, scintillating with brilliant reflections on the geology, botany and archaeology of the whole Himalayan range. I played my part in these exertions, pacing the streets of Kathmandu and Pātan, noting angles and distances, so that gradually these mazy towns took shape on paper, and temples and shrines of interest, once noted and photographed, could with certainty be found again. For all of us in various ways Nepalese life and culture gained in clarity and interest.

It was in this setting that my plans for a long journey through the Tibetan (*bhotia*) regions of western Nepal took final form. I had worked out a general plan before leaving London; thus Parwa Pasang Sherpa, who had accompanied me to England after our last journey through eastern Nepal in 1954, had now come by sea to Bombay, bringing our camping equipment, mountain-clothes and other essential stores. He had arrived in Kathmandu the day before me, having left the bulk of this luggage in Banaras, where it could be collected at the outset of our journey.

Our general plan was conditioned by the weather, for we would have to visit the districts of interest to us on the southern side of the main Himalayan range between March and May before the monsoon gained force. Then we could conveniently cross over to the northern side and continue to travel there until September, for the high mountains would ward off the storm-clouds and it would be warm enough to cross the higher passes, of which I estimated fifteen between 17,000 and 20,000 feet. Then in September we would cross back into the lower southern valleys and return to Kathmandu. I proposed to start in the far west of the country and the only convenient way of doing this would be to return to India and go round by rail to some suitable starting-point on the Indian-Nepalese frontier. It is quite impracticable to attempt to travel westwards across Nepal beyond the Dhaulagiri massif during winter and spring, unless one keeps so far to the south that nothing would be gained except extra weeks of travel through regions of no primary interest to us. Thus knowing we would have to return to India, we left most of the luggage in Banaras, for great as the distance may appear on the map, we could rely on getting from Kathmandu to any point on the Indian frontier in a matter of days (see maps, pp. 302-3). Except for a few short stretches in the Nepal Valley and for the motorable track that has recently been constructed to connect it with the Indian frontier, there is no road in our sense of the term throughout the length and breadth of Nepal. There are just mountain-paths, which are sometimes suitable for pack-animals, but more often only safe enough for men. Thus all goods and chattels must be carried either on animals or more usually on men's backs. Travel of this kind is always troublesome and far more expensive than any other method since devised by man. Our small party would advance at the cost of about five shillings a mile.

But there were still other problems to be resolved before we need worry about porterage, namely just where we should begin, and of whom our party should consist. I decided the first of these questions in favour of Nepālganj, for this would bring us rapidly into the region of the upper Bheri, the area of greatest interest to me on the southern side of the main range. The other possibility had been Tanakpur in the farthest west, which

3

would have enabled us to visit Jumla and Mugu, but then in the seven months or so at our disposal there would not have been time to reach the Bheri. This Bheri route also appealed to me, as we should be travelling right across Nepal from the Indian almost to the Tibetan frontier and it would be of special interest to observe the ethnic and cultural changes on the way. As for the second problem, Pasang and I were agreed that the party should be kept to a minimum. We would want a general cook-servant, and since Pasang was going home to Shar-Khumbu on a brief visit to his family, we planned that he should bring back with him Takki Babu, a Magar who had proved himself thoroughly reliable and quite indispensible on our travels in eastern Nepal in 1954.[a] I would have preferred to complete the party with another Sherpa, but the Nepalese Government was concerned that I should take a 'student' with me from the Valley, who might profit in knowledge from the journey. Yet there was no 'student' of Tibetan except a young librarian Hemrāj Shākya, whom I was already employing in Kathmandu and Pātan to assist me in the survey of the temples and shrines. He was keen to come, but we were doubtful whether he would be able to bear with the harsh conditions of such a journey. A Newar of high caste and town-dweller, he had left the Valley only once in his life to visit a monastery three days' journey to the north. He had never been in high mountains and had no conception of what was involved. Pasang described our coming difficulties as colourfully as he could, but Hemrāj was not to be dissuaded. 'Though I die, I shall come with you,' he said, and so I had no choice but to agree. Once we had started, there could be no turning back without severely disorganizing the whole party. I could only promise him that if he grew tired, we could arrange for him to return after about four months of travel, when we should be within range of Pokhara. This is what actually happened, and it must be said that Hemrāj exceeded our expectations, for

[a] The Magars are one of the several races which go to make up the political entity of Nepal. See p. xi.

although he suffered much from high altitude, he made no vain laments.

While he and I continued working together in the Valley, making occasional visits to government offices to explain future plans and arrange for an official travel-letter, Pasang travelled homewards—nine days of walking and clambering—and returned in due course, bringing Takki Babu with him. How delighted I was to see Takki Babu again! (pl. IIIc). He looked extremely dirty after five days of travelling at Pasang's forced pace of twenty-five miles a day, but he was soon scrubbed and bathed and dressed in some of Pasang's clothes until we could buy him some of his own on the morrow. He tolerated all this without protest for he knew there was no work for him to do just then, but it was all but impossible to work such a change on him while we were in the mountains. When one is carrying wood and water, attending to fires and blackened pots, it is useless to put on clean clothes, he would argue. We had a suit of good Nepāli clothes made for him in warm flannel, but he would scarcely ever wear them and at the end of our travels they still looked quite new. With Pasang's connivance he bought shirts and trousers of the cheapest material and wore them until they were rags. To keep himself warm he bought a large coarse blanket, which he would wrap round himself when work was finished for the day. Takki Babu is the toughest man I have ever met. Small of build but of unexpected strength, seemingly quite inexhaustible and totally indifferent to whatever load was on his back, he seemed impervious to cold and unmindful of hardship. His real name is Lalita Bahādur, Takki Babu, 'Takki's Dad', being a mere nickname, by which he has been known since his first child, a daughter, was born. He is about forty years old and now has five other children. During his long absence with us, his wife and family would continue to care for his fields and live-stock. While depending entirely on Pasang for his orders, he used to show in return the responsible concern of an elder brother, and on the few occasions when under stress of our difficulties Pasang and I fell into serious dispute, the

most concerned was always Takki Babu, who would shed tears
and beg us to make peace, raising his hands to me in supplication.

THROUGH INDIA

By now it was the beginning of March and time for us to
start. While Pasang, Hemrāj and Takki Babu travelled overland
to Banaras, I went to Pokhara by aeroplane, in order to visit the
lady-doctors there. During the months ahead their hospital
would be our nearest place of refuge in the event of any difficulty. When we reached the upper Bheri and later crossed into
Dolpo, we would be about four weeks journey away from them
and thereafter the distance would become progressively less.
Also I wanted to ask them to receive a mail-bag on my behalf,
which we would be able to collect when we reached Tukchä
early in July. I left on the morning of March 6th and reached
Pokhara in an hour—representing ten days of mountain-travel.[a]
Pokhara is the chief town of No. 3 District West and because of
its aerodrome it is fast becoming second in importance to
Kathmandu. But it is still only a large village with a bazaar of
open shops of Indian style along its main street. Wheeled
vehicles have scarcely made their appearance; there is just one
horse-drawn cart which I shared with a fellow-passenger from
the aerodrome to the village, and also one jeep of which I heard
tell. So short was my time, that I saw too little of this delightful valley, which appears rather like a small replica of the Valley
of Nepal. But the high mountains are far closer and to the
north one can see the whole range of Annapūrna, beyond which
lies the land of Nye-shang (Manangbhot) which we would be
visiting in due course. I drove to the hospital at the northern
end of the town.

The hospital buildings consist of Nissen huts and the medical

[a] This route Kathmandu-Pokhara-Bhairava and the one eastwards Kath-
mandu-Biratnagar are at present the only two internal air-routes in Nepal
(see map, p. 302).

staff lives in little huts of straw, for the Brahman who owns the land on which they live, refuses to allow them to erect permanent buildings for fear that he should somehow lose his right of ownership. What a noble band of Irish and Scottish women they are! Their work is essentially a religious mission and only their faith can sustain them in face of the difficulties they are always encountering. Except by their example they do not attempt to propagate Christianity, for this would bring official sanctions to bear against them and their medical work would become impossible. The senior members of the group are Dr. O'Hanlon and Miss Steele, who started a dispensary and hospital at Nautanwa on the Indian frontier in the days when Nepal was closed to Westerners. After the revolution and the proclamation of 'democracy' in 1950 they were free to enter the country and so travelled over the foot-hills to Pokhara, where they have succeeded in establishing one of the most active hospitals in Nepal. Not only do they work in the surgery and wards but they go out on long journeys into the mountains, whenever villagers ask for their help.

They lent me a hut for the night and entertained me most pleasantly, recalling the visits of former travellers, many of whom were known to me. I took leave the following morning filled with deep feelings of respect for all they were doing. The plane brought me to Bhairava just inside the Nepalese frontier and a few miles from the Indian rail-head at Nautanwa. Pasang and the others would be travelling from Banaras to Gorakhpur, where I had arranged to meet them, so that we could travel together to Nepālganj (map, p. 302). Since their journey was slower than mine, I had time to visit Lumbini, the birth-place of Śākyamuni about fifteen miles distant from Bhairava, and afterwards Kuśinagara (modern Kasia), the place of his death, some forty miles east of Gorakhpur. At both places work was in progress providing rest-houses and shelters for the vast crowds expected later in the year for his 2,500th anniversary; thus there was little of the tranquillity which one would properly associate with these sites.

7

On the evening of March 11th I met Pasang, Hemrāj and Takki Babu in Gorakhpur together with about 600 lb. of luggage amidst all the confusion which is typical of Indian railway stations. Having transferred everything to the night train to Gonda, where we would change for Nepālganj, we went to have a meal and hear each other's news, while waiting for the train to start. Hemrāj was pleased to have visited Sarnāth, the site where Śākyamuni first preached the Buddhist doctrine on the outskirts of Banaras, and Takki Babu was impressed with the largest city he had ever seen in his life. In the turmoil at Banaras station Pasang had lost the wallet containing all the keys of our boxes, but I had another set and my mind was too occupied with other matters to be displeased for more than a moment, so he became cheerful again and told me how well he had been entertained at Banaras University by our friend Padmanābh Jaini, who had been looking after our boxes since January.

The train was slow and reached Gonda too late for our morning connection, leaving us on a hot, dusty station with several hours to wait for the next train. We took a cycle-rickshaw and went to the bazaar in search of beer, impelled by the thought that we would see none for seven months to come. We found two bottles at last and returned triumphantly to the station restaurant to consume them with the meal we had ordered. Since India's national railways must officially disapprove of the consuming of alcohol, a special table was arranged for us outside the restaurant in a concealed corner of the platform. All these efforts however were wasted, for the beer was vile. At last we were in the train again, travelling uneventfully for the rest of the day. It was already quite dark when we descended at the station of Nepālganj Road about 200 yards from the Nepalese frontier and three miles from the town of Nepālganj. It was too late to reach the town at that hour, so we established ourselves for the night in the station waiting-room. An attendant brought us some tea with cakes of unlevened bread (chapatis) and curried vegetables. Our spirits were very high; Takki Babu

8

danced while Pasang played his mouth-organ and Hemrāj clapped his hands. We were nearing the end of all the trouble-some preliminaries and longed to be advancing freely on our own feet.

NEPĀLGANJ

The next morning after the usual bargaining we set out towards Nepālganj in three tangas (small horse-drawn carts with seats facing fore and aft). Having produced our passports at the Indian frontier-post and the travel-letter of the Nepalese Government at the Nepalese post, we rejoiced to be once more in Nepal. But we were still on the plain, less than 500 feet above sea-level; the first low range of Himalayan foothills stretched along the sky-line about twenty-five miles ahead. We would have to pass over these and over the mountains beyond, ascending valleys ever high and higher until we would cross the great ranges of 20,000 feet and from the heights of the remote land of Dolpo see beyond to the vast upland plains of Tibet.

We reached the town and went first of all to pay our respects to the Bara Hakim, the chief official, who proved to be a charming young Nepalese gentleman. He received us in a room furnished in Victorian style and we learned that his home was in Shar-Khumbu, so that he and Pasang knew many people in common. We then made our way to the 'hotel', where we thought we might stay. This was of course sheer folly, as we might well have known. Very small, with a ladder leading up to a top room which was offered to us, it stood right in the middle of the bazaar. Swarms of flies began to encircle us. To the annoyance of the impatient tanga-drivers, we returned to the Bara Hakim and asked his advice, as we should have done in the first place. He very kindly lent us a kind of thatched cottage, which stood empty in his grounds, and there we camped most conveniently during the three days we spent in Nepālganj.

Once settled, we set about supplementing our supplies for

9

the seven months ahead. The bulk of these already reposed in the boxes that accompanied us, but we still needed such items as sugar and soap, paraffin and methylated spirit, pots and pans, an umbrella, tins of milk and packets of tea, supplies of rice and flour. Also I had to obtain large quantities of coin, both Indian and Nepalese, for notes would be of very limited use in the mountains. This added appreciably to the weight of our loads.

PROBLEMS OF PORTERAGE

The other main task was to find men to carry our things. At first there was some talk of horses, but we learned that these would set us out on a circuitous route, whereas I wanted to make direct for Jājarkot (map, p. 295). We went to the coolie-depôt, a long shelter just to the north of the town, and made known our requirements. At first there seemed no hope, for we met only with blank refusals. On a second visit one man showed interest and suggested forty Indian rupees per man-load of one maund (80 lb.) from Nepālganj to Jājarkot. If we were willing to pay this rate, he said, nine men could soon be found. I estimated eight days for the journey and this was a large sum to demand, but we accepted it, realizing that otherwise no one would come with us. The only European who had preceded me through Nepālganj was the Swiss geologist, Dr. Toni Hagen, and he had brought his own porters from Kathmandu. Thus the men with whom we were dealing, were totally unaccustomed to travellers like us; their normal work consisted in carrying loads of merchandise between Nepālganj and Sallyāna. Although I had not yet realized it, we were at odds with one another from the start. I assumed that we would be paying them a high wage for travel on our terms, namely stopping and camping where we pleased, whereas they supposed that they were carrying the goods of some helpless stranger, who parted readily with his money and would be quite content to come along with them at their pleasure. Our only alternative would have been to delay in Nepālganj until some one appeared willing to discuss other terms, but we were anxious to be on our way as soon as possible and to leave this town which now palled upon us. The next morning nine men duly arrived, wanting to see their loads. They insisted on nine exact maunds, so Pasang borrowed a large pair of scales from the bazaar and we set to work apportioning things accordingly. It was all absurdly troublesome, but at last the job was done with just 40 lb. left over for Takki Babu to carry. They agreed to start the following morning, but seeing us replace our camp-beds and other items for use that night they suspected that we would 'tamper' with the loads and said they would want to weigh everything again in the morning. We consented resignedly to this condition and continued hopefully with our shopping and preparations, which included the successful cooking of two loaves of bread in our little tin oven.

Coolies are notoriously late in starting, but on this occasion our worst expectations were surpassed. The men arrived soon after ten and having reweighed the loads to their satisfaction, we left the bazaar by midday, thinking that at last we were on our way. But we found ourselves dumped at the coolie-depôt, where they informed us that they still had some shopping to do. In an attempt to minimize the delay Pasang accompanied them and at their request added another ten rupees all round to the ten they had each been given in advance. They returned after two and a half hours. There followed more discussion. Then two of them disappeared again. We finally left at 4 p.m. and walked for two hours; by then it was already late for setting up camp and we had one of those troublesome evenings, when darkness overtakes one too soon. The coolies expected us to sleep with them on the straw of a little way-side shelter and watched us erecting tents with wonder and alarm, for we were 'tampering' with the loads once more.

That night the heavens opened upon us and out tents strained and shook in the midst of thunder, lightning and driving rain. The coolies came unasked to our assistance and saved some of our boxes from a drenching by carrying them back to the shelter. All this delayed our departure in the morning, but we were away by ten and after more trouble with the loads and with a leaking paraffin tin, we began to make good headway. We passed through Chatār Village where the people are T'harus by race (pl. I*a*), and in the afternoon crossed a delightfully warm stream, the Dundawā, where we were able to bathe; all seemed well at last. We halted soon after five just on the outskirts of Khargawār Village and the evening was well organized. The foothills were now just before us and on the morrow we should be making our first ascent.

Sleep was disturbed by the coolies, who sang a monotonous refrain, and I was awoken at 5 a.m. by shouting and argument. Pasang called me soon afterwards, for the coolies had resolved to abandon us and return to Nepālganj, saying that we were continually altering the loads and not starting early enough. But they added that they would come if we paid eighty rupees per load for the journey. We have always congratulated ourselves on our man-management, but on this occasion no argument was of any avail. There was no question of bargaining afresh and Pasang and Hemrāj merely attempted to recall the men to the terms of the contract. Some were inclined to stay but two excitable ones, who were the main cause of the trouble, at last had their way. Each man handed back to us twenty rupees—for let it not be thought that they were rogues—and they went. Calm returned, the welcome calm of the jungle. We put up one of the tents and while Takki Babu prepared a meal, Pasang went to find what help there might be in the village. He returned with some buffalo-milk and the news that there were only about five people at home and not one able to serve us as porter. He next turned his attention to the passers-by and we agreed to keep secret the tale of our having been abandoned by our former coolies, lest we should be thought to be hard taskmasters. When asked how we had got there, we said that we had brought our belongings in a bullock-cart which had now returned; no one questioned this story. At last we addressed ourselves to a sympathetic listener. He was a Magar, who had been in the army for seven years and seemed overjoyed at the prospect of being of help to us. Both he and his companion promptly deposited their loads at a house in the village nearby and stayed with us ready to carry two of ours as far as their own village of Kurmi, two days' journey to the north. For the next few hours they continued to give support to Pasang in his appeals to all who passed along the track. Thus by late afternoon our numbers were complete and we had agreed on terms of four rupees a day. Once more we could raise our eyes with confidence towards the hills, for tomorrow we would begin to ascend them.

We set out at 6 a.m.; within an hour the open plain was left behind and we were advancing in single file along a narrow forest-track. Then the ground began to rise. Boulders appeared by the way and we heard the sound of a rushing stream. When we stopped for a meal two hours later, we were already in the mountains and I remember being surprised and delighted at the seemingly magical rapidity of the change. No anxious thought for the future disturbed my peace; in retrospect this seems surprising, for the journey before us was sure to be difficult and tiring even at the most optimistic appraisal. We bathed joyfully in a rocky pool beneath a tumbling torrent, while Takki Babu cooked rice and curried vegetables and the porters squatted around their separate fire, tending their own huge pot of rice. Thus invigorated, we continued on our way; climbing now in earnest, we reached, soon after midday, the top of the first ridge, a mere 3,000 feet or so, and turned to look back towards the misty Indian plain. Ahead our view was blocked by the next forest-covered ridge, which we would cross the following day. The summit of our pass was marked characteristically by a pile of stones in which were stuck sticks with rags attached. We descended through the trees to the river below (Babai Kholā), waded through it and established a camp on the far bank. One of our porters was accompanied by his son, who was suffering from a poisoned leg. There was a dreadful sore on his shin and the foot and ankle were badly swollen. His father asked us for medicine and we decided to try our skill at injecting penicillin. I supervised and Pasang operated with seeming success, for the next morning the swelling was very much reduced and the boy left happily for his home.

It was a delightful night with the soothing sound of the river and the gentle hum of insects; we rose gladly in the morning and began the ascent of the ridge that awaited us. Today the climb was appreciably longer and since there was no water on the way, we had to continue to Gurunggāon on the top of the ridge (4,500 feet) before we could prepare our food. The people there were Magars and very friendly to us, especially one old man who had been a soldier and came asking ointment for his eyes. The next range of foothills lay ahead, and after our meal we descended northwards from Gurung along a delightful track where primulas and violets grew in profusion. At the bottom of the valley we came to the village of Charchare, looking most prosperous with its well-nourished fields. Yet we could obtain nothing but unripe mewars (a melon-like fruit) and some sugar-cane to chew. The villagers grow wheat and barley, rice and oats. Vegetables of all kinds would grow, but through ignorance they plant far less than they might. We saw potatoes, cabbages and tomatoes, but unfortunately for us it was far too early in the season. As at Chatār and Khargawār the people are T'harus, who so far have been occupying the low land, while the Magars live on the mountains. We descended to the stream (Jum Kholā) where we had our usual bathe and then climbed up to Kurmi Village just beyond the crest of the next range of hills (about 4,000 feet). It was already dusk, so we paid off our helpers quickly and established ourselves in a thatched outhouse which was put at our disposal by our soldier friend. He lived nearby in a little one-roomed house of clay and thatch together with his wife and daughter, his chickens and a new-born calf. Our shelter proved to be his cow-shed, for the night was fine and he was content to leave his five or six animals in the open. All else was scrub-land and terraced

14

fields and there was no room for a tent except on the track itself.

We spent the next day resting while more men were mustered, for only two of the former party were free to come further with us. Again our medical supplies were in demand; a man with swollen feet appeared, a woman who had fallen out of a tree and was badly bruised, a man with a cough. The goodwill thus established was very useful and we were able to get potatoes and eggs and a chicken. But when we set about making bread, we discovered to our consternation that the wire shelves of the oven had been left on the banks of the Babai Kholā. Pasang drew the village blacksmith into consultation and by evening he had cleverly contrived a new set from a broken umbrella-frame.

The Ascent of the Bheri

The next day, March 22nd, we descended from Kurmi towards the Bheri River some four miles below us. At this point it flows through a wide valley enclosed by gentle forested slopes. It would be a pleasant land to live in, but except for Sahre on the great hills to the east we saw no sign of human habitation. From here the Bheri flows north-westwards for thirty miles or more to join the Karnāli and then these two rivers, uniting as the Gogra, cut through the foothills which we have been crossing and flow down to join the Ganges. By following the course of the Bheri northwards we would come to Jājarkot, Tibrikot, Tārakot and eventually to the southern side of Dolpo. The northern side of that land, the highest inhabited land on earth, is drained by the headwaters of the Karnāli, so that these two rivers which are separated at their source by a watershed of 20,000 feet, are finally united in this pleasant valley. We established ourselves for the night just above the river in one of those roughly thatched huts which are erected for travellers. The place proved to be occupied by fleas, so we put up tents at what seemed a safe distance and Pasang began to make bread. In order to be a success the dough must be prepared in a calm and happy atmosphere, but on this occasion our porters suddenly spoiled everything by announcing that they would take us no further unless we provided them with food for the rest of the journey. This demand was in flagrant violation of the contract, for the high wages we were paying them, covered the cost of their food. They were being quite unscrupulous, for they had deliberately not raised the matter in Kurmi, and although they knew we had four days' journey before us, each man had brought only enough food for one day. Pasang resisted their demand with consequent argument and ill will. They finally agreed to come, but he would have to purchase supplies for them on the way, for we did not have enough rice to feed them from our own stocks; also we were forced to the compromise of deducting only half the cost of this food from their pay. Such heated discussion destroyed the calm of the evening; the dough did not rise and the loaves were blackened with smoke. Moreover we discovered in the morning that even in the seclusion of our tents we had not escaped the notice of the fleas. But that day's march by the wooded banks of the Bheri was so delightful that all troubles were readily forgotten, and even the blackened loaves tasted delicious when we stopped for lunch beside the swirling waters. The valley had now turned northwards; it became narrow and enclosed and we camped that night on a small grassy space close by the river.

The following day we left the Bheri temporarily, for it would have led us too far northwards, and turned eastwards up a side valley (SI: Dudo Kholā), which was wide and terraced for the growing of rice. We delayed a long time, while Pasang went in search of some of last year's crop for our porters. Very few of the peasants still had a sufficient surplus for selling, but at last he returned with a bagful, which was shared equally among the men. Even when they eat together, each man is expected to produce his own ration, which will be poured by mutual agreement into the common pot. Now that this problem of food was finally settled, we continued upstream and camped high up above the right bank. An unusual event was the appearance of a man hawking bananas and to his great surprise we purchased the whole of his stock. The next day we continued climbing northwards out of this valley, leaving behind us a circle of forest-covered hills, which dropped with the neat steps of careful terracing to the stream far below. We soon reached the top of the Neto Pass (4,500 feet), whence we could see the valley of the Bheri below us once more and the misty outlines of higher mountains far ahead. Then we hastened down to Kahinikanda Village just below the pass. The people are Magars, all Nepāli-speakers, but although Tibet is so distant, the first sign of some connection appears, for the houses have flat roofs made of clay and strengthened with wooden lathes, which gives them a certain Tibetan appearance. But the frames of the doors and windows are still quite Nepalese in style. Our efforts to procure eggs and potatoes met with little success, for the people took us to be officials and feared that we might refuse to pay for what they gave us. One young man came to our assistance, however, and pointed out a house where we could get honey (pl. I*b*). The old woman there reminded me of Chaucer's 'povre wydwe somdeel stape in age' and Chauntecleer strutted about her yard. After some persuading and much delay while she went to borrow a measure from a neighbour's house, she at last filled one of our large saucepans with honey in exchange for two rupees. It was very dark and tasted deliciously of mountain herbs. We continued down by a stream (Marma Kholā) and set up camp.

The following morning we were soon walking again by the high bank of the Bheri, now a younger and slightly smaller river, tossing furiously along its rocky bed. We were now entering the Jājarkot Valley and were impressed by its luxurious appearance, for the rich red clay was everywhere overgrown with wheat which would be ripe for harvest by the end of April. The main villages are Kudu to the south-west, Lāmīchhāne to the south-east, Gharigrāma in the centre and Tātāgrāma towards the north. Further north the fortress-town of Jājarkot, which in former times must have dominated the whole valley, is poised high above the far bank of the river. We paused in Gharigrāma to watch the women working a cumbersome revolving press, from which mustard-oil was oozing. A woman approached and begged us to come and see her son. He lay on a wooden couch in their house; one side of his neck was a great running sore and his whole face was swollen in a ghastly fashion, while flies were swarming about him. His mother said that he had been lying ill for three months. We washed away the remains of filthy paper which was stuck to the wound and applied Cetavex ointment and a bandage, wondering how long he would continue to look so clean. We also gave him a penicillin injection and hoped that this attention would be sufficient to check the infection, for we would never see him again. In return his grateful mother sold us some 'black' rice, the kind that grows without standing in water. Our rice-eating coolies complained of its quality, but Pasang merely reminded them that they should have brought their own with them. People who are used to rice, take unwillingly to other foods; even Pasang was anxious to prolong its use as far as possible, but we were now entering lands where rice becomes increasingly difficult to cultivate.

We crossed a deeply eroded stream-bed and made our way across the fields in scorching heat. Two women were busy threshing lentils by driving oxen round in a small circle, thus trampling the stalks beneath the animals' feet. We passed through Tātāgrāma and then followed a path high above the left bank of the Bheri, which has cut its course through the flat alluvial valley-bed (pl. IIb). Just below Jājarkot it twists slightly west of north and then turns sharply west. In this dry season before the coming of the monsoon great expanses of pallid sand lie revealed on one side of the gorge. We descended through trees and crossed to the right bank by what was once a fine little suspension bridge. A small plaque announces its Scottish origin to the few readers of English who pass this way. We set up camp just beyond the bridge in a lonely grassy place with Jājarkot on its dominating ridge some 1,000 feet above us. As

18

usual the coolies disturbed our sleep with their coughing and spitting; it was a consoling thought to know that we should be rid of them in the morning. They had been particularly trouble-some, begging things the whole time and then making our reasonable refusals a cause for contention. With so many months before us in the mountains, I refused to give them any more of the cigarettes brought for Takki Babu and our more friendly helpers. But we remembered to show our thanks to the two who had been with us since we were stranded down at Khargawār.

The next day, March 27th, we were completely at peace, able to wash clothes and bathe in the river, cook palatable food and record notes and photographs. In the evening we climbed up to JĀJARKOT. It must once have been an all but impregnable fortress and even now the track is difficult enough. The people are mainly Chetris and T'hakuris by caste, all Nepāli-speakers, and their affairs are controlled by an official (*ditta*) appointed by the Nepalese Government.[a] The higher rank of *suba* is held by the descendants of the former ruler. For Jājarkot was once a petty Himalayan kingdom, deriving its comparative wealth from the rich soil deposits which cover the wide valley below. It is like another 'Nepal Valley' on a far smaller scale. But here there are no signs of early culture and the only temple is a rather poor affair dedicated to Durgā, who is a recent Gurkha importation. The local divinity is Masta, a mountain-god, whose cult extends up to Tibrikot (p. 27) and Rohagāon

[a] The problem of race and caste in Nepal is a very complicated one. Chetri, derived from skr. *kshatriya*, the second of the brahmanical castes, suggests originally the rank of knight. T'hakuri, derived from skr. *thakkura*, meaning 'deity', 'lord', was originally a title claimed by warriors of lordly rank, specifically the Rājputs. These people of Jājarkot would therefore be theoretically of pure Indian, viz. Hindu, descent, valiant fighters who have established a small kingdom for themselves in the mountains. In fact they have intermarried in the past with the earlier inhabitants. If one may judge by features, some of the Brahmans still appear as true Indian types. See also p. 29.

(p. 57). This was the first we had heard of him and although we saw no shrine here, we were told that they existed in the villages round about. His chief attendants are the *jākrī* (priests), who are possessed by the god during the period approaching the full moon, when they can prophesy and soothsay. The people told us that Masta had thus foretold the Gorkha victory in the wars with the Tibetans in 1788 and 1791 and so the soldiers had brought back among their trophies temple-banners and trumpets, conch-shells, ritual vessels and implements, which are still preserved in Masta's shrines. We did not see them, but presumably those very articles have kept the villagers mindful of past events. The spirits of departed Brahmans (*bhaju*) are propitiated as well as those of ancestors generally. The *yeti* has his equivalent in the *lamkana* ('long-eared' monster) and dreadful stories are told about its doings.

The *ditta* of Jājarkot received us with great friendliness, read our official letter of commendation and undertook to provide us with eight porters. But the traders were away that evening and there was no food to be bought; it was only thanks to Pasang's persistence that we were able to obtain some white rice and unripe mewars at a house on the way down. We had enough wheat-flour for the present and could rely upon buying more later on; we also felt justified in opening our stores, where we had packet-soups, dried fruits and vegetables, tomato purée, biscuits and chocolate, all to be rationed for the months ahead.

We spent two more days at this camp and then on March 30th, Good Friday, resumed our travels, assisted by eight cheerful T'hakuris. The track followed close to the river and after about one mile of slow progress we came upon a party of fishermen, busy in the water with net and hook. They sold us three fishes, which Pasang carried on a string sheltering them under our umbrella from the fierce rays of the sun. But it was quite impracticable to clamber over rocks in this way, so when we came to a pleasant little sandal-wood grove about a mile further on, we sat down and cooked and ate the fish, which fulfilled all our expectations and was the one meal of high quality that we enjoyed in seven months. Pasang thoughtfully reserved some for a curry in the evening. Our porters meanwhile disported themselves in the river, showing their splendid prowess. We continued happily for the rest of the day and camped once more by the Bheri.

The following day was a very hard one, for we were forced to climb 4,000 feet higher in order to bypass a difficult section of the river. Moreover there was no water until we reached the far side, so it was impossible to prepare food until well after midday. This is a great hardship for the porters who are anxious to start before 6 a.m. in the expectation of stopping for a meal within three hours or so, but they bore this without undue protest. These T'hakuris were probably the best set of men we have ever had; they accepted their wages without demur and the extra which we gave them, with thanks; they progressed at a steady pace and never gainsaid us in the choosing of a site for our halts. By evening we had reached the Bheri again and on the morrow we crossed to the left bank and passed the junction of the Sāma Kholā. After a hot and tiring day we camped belatedly in the middle of Gusalkhola Village, where a European had never been seen before and wondering crowds surrounded us. This was Easter Sunday.

Monday was a pleasant day for the sky was slightly overcast and the track followed the river fairly closely. From now on the Bheri began to change. The slopes became steeper and the trees less dense. Euphorbia was abundant. There were the large pink blooms of *Bauhinia variegata,* the yellow blossom of *Caesalpinia sepiaria* and most delightful of all, the deep-red combs of the leafless coral tree (*Erythrina suberosa*), which gleamed against the blue of the sky above and the milky green of the river below.

It began to rain as we approached Tallon, which delayed the porters who all took shelter. Meanwhile Pasang and I hastened ahead to investigate the possibilities for the morrow. From Tallon there are two possible routes to Tibrikot; the main one continues due north and joins the track from Jumla which we had been advised to follow, while the other continues to ascend the Great Bheri (Thuli Bheri) seemingly direct to Tibrikot. In fact it is no shorter for advance is so much slower, but the idea of keeping to this river attracted me. When we had asked about it in Jājarkot, we had been told that our porters would fall from the rocks and that no one in his senses would follow such a route. It was certain that our T'hakuris would not go that way, and if we wanted to do so, we would have to find other men. So in Tallon we tried to pursue enquiries. We learned however that a villager had recently died and all the responsible men of the community were engaged in cremating his body far away down by the river. A decision was urgent, for it was already late and by the time the porters caught us up, we had to know which of the two tracks we intended to take, the one towards Aulgurta and the north or the one down to the river and across to Anā. Just then a responsible-looking peasant appeared and we put our problem to him. He was a man of Gotām, he said, and was just now on his way to Anā. He had been to Tibrikot many times by the river-route and could easily find eight men willing to go with us. What were the wages? Two Indian rupees a day. That was agreeable, he said.

While Pasang waited for our porters, I went on to Anā with Takki Babu as escort and this stranger as guide. We crossed the Bheri in gathering dusk and drizzling rain by a slippery bridge of natural rock and hastened along the muddy track into the village, where with the stranger's assistance we settled in an empty shed. By the time we had procured wood and water and made tea, Pasang and the porters arrived. It was now dark and pouring with rain; our little shed was chaos for a while, but our lamps were lighted, everyone served with tea, a tent erected outside, and cakes of bread were cooked. Except in such difficult circumstances, these T'hakuris would not have consented to eat food cooked on the fire which we were using, but far from complaining at anything whatsoever, they were in the best of humour. We explained our changed plans and gave them their full bonus. By the time I awoke next morning they were

gone. I was sorry to see them no more. Takki Babu brought tea
to the tent and it seemed pleasantly luxurious not to have to rise
forthwith and dismantle bed and abode in haste. It had been
too dark and wet the previous evening to survey even our immediate surroundings, so when I drew back the tent-flaps it came
as a surprise to find three women seated on the open veranda of
their house a few yards away, calmly passing a short pipe from
one to the other and quietly watching the show. I let fall the
flaps, set the camera and emerged once more, this time taking
them by surprise (pl. IIa). The houses are in the form of sturdy
shacks, built of stone with an upper storey of wood and roofed
with thatch. We found ourselves right in the centre of twenty
such dwellings. They are grouped together just above the right
bank of the Bheri, which flows now at about 5,000 feet above
sea-level. The larger neighbouring village of Gotām stands on
the mountain-side two miles to the south and about 1,000 feet
higher. There are Brahmans, T'hakuris and also people of a
nondescript mixed type, presumably part Magar, part plains-
folk who have gradually penetrated up the valleys. By caste they
are *sarki* ('leather-workers') and *kāmi* ('blacksmiths'), but these
are mere labels indicating no more than baseness of birth. In no
way are they a depressed people, for the land they occupy is
very rich. They grow wheat in the spring, and after an early
harvest they flood the terraces and plant out the rice. In summer
they harvest the maize which is their staple food and in the late
autumn their buckwheat. They have few cattle and so rely
mainly on seed-oil. We saw no shrine in their village but they
acknowledge the existence of Masta and of lesser beings known
as *siddha, gupta, citra* and *saikāmri,* though they were very vague
about them all, simply adding that milk and incense should be
offered to them thrice a year at a full-moon season. These
villagers were always amused when we asked about their gods,
answering light-heartedly as though the question were of little
moment and turning the conversation to other more practical
subjects. How different from Tibetans!

The headman, a Brahman, let us have some milk, and a *sarki*

23

woman sold us eggs which proved to be half-hatched. Pasang bought more honey and a supply of wheat, which Takki Babu turned into flour at the water-mill. We expected to delay one day while our would-be helpers got ready for the journey, but excuses were made and we had to wait yet another. We continued to stay in the middle of the village, although from morning until evening flies swarmed over everything. Nevertheless it was not worth while organizing the removal of all our loads to a site outside the village. I wandered afield taking bread and chocolate in my knapsack. The coral tree (*Erythrina suberosa*) still bloomed and everywhere were olive trees (*Olea cuspidata*) and huge clumps of euphorbia. The Himalayan musk rose (*Rosa brunonii*) was not in bloom, but St. John's wort and *Reinwardtia trigyna* were covered in yellow flowers and *Woodfordia fruticosa* in small clusters of red blossom. The barberry bushes (*Berberis asiatica*) were hanging with sprays of purple berries and *Colebrookia oppositifolia* with close clusters of catkins. There are little strawberry plants (*Fragaria indica*), yellow anaphalis and little pink blooms of *Clinopodium umbrosum*.

I met Takki Babu on his way back from cutting wood. We returned together and set about baking bread with some of the flour he had ground the evening before. Bread-making always seemed to him far too complicated a process, for he comes from a land where people eat rice. He shook his head and said: 'Who could eat it, when it takes so long to make?'

We left on the third morning, April 5th, with a Brahman, a T'hakuri and six low-caste porters making up a complement of eight. Having followed the course of the Bheri for about three hours, we halted for a meal, only to discover that the bag containing all our cutlery had been left behind. Takki Babu was momentarily quite disconsolate; then he resolutely set out on the journey back, while we cooked and ate as best we could and waited. He returned hungry and happy three hours later, bearing the missing bag, and having covered the distance unladen in just half the time. He had found the children of Anā sitting in the dust, playing gleefully with our spoons and forks. When Takki Babu had finished his meal, we continued on our way. The track kept very close to the river; we passed below Jamra Village and camped beyond it on the river-bank.

It was on the next day, as the route turned eastwards, that the first difficulties appeared. The valley had now become a narrow gorge and the track a series of rock-climbs. By British mountaineering standards the route might have been graded *moderately difficult* and certainly *exposed*, but it must be remembered that our porters were climbing with 80 lb. on their backs and five of their loads were in the form of bulky boxes. Their performance was truly amazing. Pasang and I assisted them with a hand from above now and then, but they showed no appreciation for this help and would doubtless have managed just as well without it. They spurned the proffered nylon rope, but suggested that now we had seen the route, we might perhaps pay them an extra Nepalese rupee a day, to which we readily agreed. They complained that their feet were being torn, but it must not be thought that they were bleeding, for never was skin so thick. It splits to a depth of a quarter of an inch and blood is still not drawn. They carry sandals of plaited grass, but seldom wear them and never where the route is difficult. They were surprised that our boots should hold so well, but then they know nothing of *vibram* soles and *tricouni* nails. We passed below Shimi and looked down upon the junction of the Bheri and the Thuli Bheri ('Great Bheri'). It was a long and tiring day, for halting places had become rare in the gorge. We came eventually to a boulder-strewn bank and established ourselves under some large overhanging rocks. The night was hot and oppressive with blood-sucking insects on the prowl. We were now amidst cedars and pines, where we could use the resinous wood as flares and so save our paraffin.

We followed the left bank all the next day until we came to a bridge about two miles below Pālāng. This provides a choice of routes and so after conferring with the porters we decided on the more difficult but shorter route along the right bank.

We camped that night on a delightful site just opposite Pālāng Village. At this point two tributaries poured into our river from the south and the south-east; a snow-clad peak (SI: 17,685 feet) closed the view up the south-eastern gorge. Boulders lay all around and careless monkeys sent stones hurtling down from the crumbling crags above. We chased them off with shouts and cleared spaces large enough for the two tents. The porters slept in a nearby cave.

From this point the track becomes difficult again but by compensation fantastically beautiful. Euphorbia grows from the rocks. There are little trees with copper-coloured foliage (*Celtis australis*) and others with the leaves at the end of their branches turned red, so that from a distance they appear as great red flowers (*Pistacia integerrima*). Fig-trees (*Ficus palmata*) grow no higher than bushes and the olives (*Olea cuspidata*), so common at Anā, have become noticeably smaller. We clambered on along the gorge, forded two streams and found ourselves at last below Tibrikot. Here the river has cut its way through a bed of compressed stones hardened into coarse cement, which towered like a great wall fifty feet above us. A track led out of this abyss up to terraced fields and high above we could just see the tops of temple-flags. We ascended a steep path to the village and went at once to find the headman. He was friendly from the first and offered to help us in any way possible, so long as we paid for what we received. We have heard this condition stated so often, that we can only conclude that many who travel with government sanction seek to press the villagers into supplying their needs free of charge. He suggested we should stay up by the temple, but it was a bleak and waterless place, so we descended to the stream that flows down from the north and set up our camp not far from the bridge over which passes the Jumla track. When we came to pay off the porters, they refused to accept paper money. It was the first time that this had occurred. We wanted to conserve our stocks of coin and so refused to give in to them, for we knew that the headman of Tibrikot would accept notes from us. We finally agreed on a compromise of half coin and half paper, but they were so disconsolate, that I ever after-wards regretted our firmness, for they had come with us valiently. I had brought less than 1,000 rupees in coin and to be confident with regard to the months ahead we needed quite four times as much. Because of the undue weight I risked the chance of finding someone who wanted paper-money and would exchange it for coins. In the event I was justified, but at this stage of the journey we were very uncertain about the future. If no one wanted paper later on, we would be in a hopeless plight and I remember my anxiety when these men posed the problem in this cogent form. They were in fact the last of our helpers to receive paper money.

TIBRIKOT, a village of some fifty houses, stands at about 7,000–8,000 feet and represents the limit of 'Hindu' penetration. The leading families are Brahmans and Chetris with the Chetri sub-caste of Gosaingiri, all of whom live in an upper section of the village. The *sarki* and *kāmi* live below the summit of the temple-hill and this is presumably the older part, for where the temple now stands there was certainly a fort in former times (pl. V*b*). The temple was commended to us as being a 'government temple' and that defines it well enough. Having destroyed the fort, the Gorkhas presumably built this temple in its place. It is dedicated to the goddess Tripura-sundarī, whose image is attended night and morning by Brahman *pujārīs* (shrine-attendants). The walls of the inner shrine are crudely painted and Śākyamuni appears in miniature rubbing shoulders with the Hindu gods, Nīl-kaṇth, Nārāyan and Bhairav. It is significant that the low castes and not the Brahmans and Chetris live just below this temple, for one may presume that they were the original inhabitants, when Tibrikot was still a petty kingdom. Moreover they are not really 'Hindu' at all. Their gods are Masta and Jākrī Babiro, whose shrines are down by the bridge close to the Jumla track. In one shrine there are just sticks with rags attached. Outside there are roughly carved poles arranged in sets. The central set consists of a tall flag-pole with four medium-length poles and one short one all bound together. The sets to either side consist of one longish pole, two medium ones and one short one. The other shrine contains a large flat stone and by its side a cairn-like structure which is hollow and open to the east with the usual rags hung inside. It is guarded at the entrance by three roughly carved wooden effigies of grotesque human shape (pl. IV). These are known as *dhauiliya* or *dok-pa* and they were described by the villagers as protectors from harm of all kinds.[a] Similar effigies are set up all over the village, on house-tops, on walls, in pathways and in fields, but no one had any precise information to give about them (pl. V*a*). They are an established custom and that is enough. The headman, an orthodox Brahman, had none on his roof-top, and spoke of them slightingly, but other Brahmans and Chetris certainly had them on theirs. Masta and Babiro have two attendants of *sarki* caste and also one from among the *gosaingiri*. This latter caste also has its own shrine, a small stone temple beneath a pipul tree just about half-way between the upper-caste and the low-caste quarters. It is dedicated to Bhairav-nāth. In the place of an image there is a small heap of large black pebbles and lumps of rock-crystal, surmounted by the usual sticks with bells attached.

There is no doubt that Masta and Babiro represent indigenous beliefs, while Tripura-sundarī and Bhairav-nāth are in a sense foreigners; yet local tradition maintains that their cult too was established in pre-Gorkha times. The villagers told us how a former 'king' of Tibrikot had one day been told by his servants of a miraculous doubling of the rice they were thrashing. Ten seers of rice-crop should after thrashing produce five seers of grain, but to their wonderment there were found to be ten to every ten. As this miracle was repeated persistently, the king ordered that the ground there should be dug up. When this was done, they discovered images of Tripura-sundarī and eight attendant goddesses. Thus they built a temple for these images in the fort, and when the fort was destroyed the cult still con-

---

[a] *dok-pa* may be the same word as Tibetan *ldog-pa*, for it is pronounced in the same way and has the meaning of 'opposer'.

tinued. As for the cult of Bhairava, it is related that the villagers had dreadful dreams, in which fearful beasts and monsters appeared to them. They consulted the *jākrī* (presumably Babiro's attendant), who said that Bhairava required to be placated and they must build him a shrine. This was done and a Brahman was placed in charge. But since this Brahman was continually inflicted with misfortune, it was concluded that this caste was displeasing to the god, so a member of the *gosaingiri* was appointed instead and all has been well ever since.

One may regard these stories as mere excuses made by the later arrivals for the importing of their gods. The whole area, through which we have passed so far, is treated officially (in government publications) as being Hindu, but the only Hindu shrines we have seen are the small Durgā shrine at Jājarkot and these two temples at Tibrikot. Moreover we have followed a river-route where one might expect to find Hindu penetration. Yet even in these villages the old mountain-gods, Babiro and Masta, hold sway. Up on the mountains dwell the Magars and one will find there scarcely a trace of Hindu religion. In no real sense can one refer to these people generally as Hindu. The Brahmans and Chetris may be properly called so, but they are only a small minority. One becomes acutely aware of the absence of Hindu culture on this southern side of the main range in contrast with the all-pervading Tibetan culture to the north.

Tibrikot gives an impression of importance quite out of relation to its actual size, for it is a great trading centre. It occupies a dominant position on the trade-route from Jumla to the upper Bheri, which is the main east-west route through western Nepal. It also links the Tibetan regions of the north with the valleys to the south, through which we have passed. During the summer months the pass north of Tibrikot is open; wool and salt, traded from Dolpo still further north, are brought over by the men of Pungmo (SI: Pudāmigāon) and exchanged for the grain of the Gotām Valley, of which the chief villagers of Tibrikot and Tichu-rong buy up large stocks. Rice, wheat and maize grow on the terraced slopes below Tibrikot, but the cultivable land is very limited.

We left on the third morning, April 11th, together with eight fresh porters, arranged for us by the headman. He had been most helpful, providing us with rice and dhaal and milk. He came to see us off at the village-gate, expressing the wish that we should meet again in this life and if not, that we should at least remember well of one another (pl. VI*b*). We descended eastwards from Tibrikot, crossed the Bheri and continued along its left bank. The character of the valley changed perceptibly, reminding me of the Chandra Gorge on the way to Spiti. There were now few trees, chiefly stunted olives and pines. Soon junipers appeared and the river returned to its rocky bed. Looking back, we saw two shepherd-boys resting on the bank while their goats nibbled the short coarse grass. About six miles along the route we took a right-hand fork and followed a smaller track leading over a rise and round to Motipur Village. On the top of the ridge were two cairns for the mountain-gods with the normal opening to the east for offerings, which consist of incense in the form of smouldering juniper and on some occasions dishes of blood and milk. The view back to the west is stupendous for it is ringed by a whole range of snow-peaks (pl. VI*a*). In Motipur there are temples to Masta and Babiro and we noticed a small 'protector' on one of the house-tops.

Pasang and I hastened ahead of the porters and suddenly came face to face with a small party of T'hakuris, consisting of three men and a little girl, who followed the others sobbing. We stopped to ask them where they were going and why the child was crying; she at once sat down in the middle of the track and moaned in a most pitiable way (pl. VII*b*). We learned that she was being taken by her father and the bridegroom, a man of twenty-four, to her new home in Motipur. The men, not in the least concerned at her unhappy plight, were anxious only to question us about our affairs. Who can speak on this matter? The difference in age was far less than in other similar

cases we met with and perhaps this child will grow up to discover she has a good husband.

After another four miles we passed the junction of the Suli
Gād, which flows into the Bheri from the north. It is up there
that lies the route to the Phoksumdo Lake and beyond to
Dolpo. We reached Dunyer (SI: Dunaihi), where the villagers
have built a spacious temple for Babiro and a tiny one for the
Hindu goddess Sarasvatī; thence we continued another two
miles to Upper Dunyer, where there is a frontier check-post.
We set up camp below the village and had not long to await
our official visitors, who came curious to know who we were
and whither we intended to go. Our letter from the Nepalese
Government allayed all suspicions and Krishna Kumar, the
officer in charge, proved a most helpful friend.

Now twenty-seven days since leaving Nepālganj, we were at
last on the threshold of the lands of Tibetan culture. Our real
travels were in fact about to begin. I planned a visit eastwards
to the Tārakot area (Tichu-rong), after which we would return
to Dunyer and resume the journey northwards. For this we
would require large stocks of wheat and rice. We also needed
butter, not for our bread, but for all our cooking. The alternative was seed-oil, which is unpalatable to those unaccustomed
to it. We had erred in not bringing supplies from England, for
it was another two months before Tibetan butter became available to us in unlimited quantities, much later in fact than we
had expected. Except for two chickens and now a third at
Dunyer, we had had no meat since we started. But after this we
sought them out no more, for I disliked to see the wretched
creature imprisoned under a basket awaiting the death to which
it was sentenced—decapitation at the hands of Takki Babu.
We might have eaten goat on the same terms, but our party
was too small to justify this slaughter, especially as Hemrāj
would not eat meat at all. The T'hakurīs of Dunyer and the
check-post officials were all vegetarians and we lived well
enough on the potatoes and turnips, eggs and milk, with which
they supplied us. The men would come down to visit us and

then stand discreetly spinning wool, while they watched our strange methods of preparing food. We realized at Dunyer for the first time how tired we were, so we rested for two days, occupied with washing clothes, writing up notes, gazing at maps and checking place-names against local knowledge.

Chöten
(*see* p. 34)

I.

a. T'haru youths of Chatār Village. (p. 12)
b. House in Kahinikanda Village. (p. 17)

II.

a. Women of Anā, smoking a pipe which they hand from one to another. (p. 23)
b. The Bheri just below Jājarkot, looking south. (p. 18)

III.
a. Pasang.
b. Hemrāj.
c. Takki Babu.

IV.

Masta's shrine at Tibrikot. (*p. 28*)

V.

a. Dhauliya *effigy on a* sarki house. (p. 28)

b. *Tibrikot from the north with rice-fields in the foreground.* (p. 27)

VI.

a. Cairn of a mountain-god. View looking west towards Tibrikot.
(p. 30)
b. The headman of Tibrikot and other villagers. (p. 30)

VII.

a. *The entrance-chöten of Tārakot.* (p. 34)
b. *T'hakuri villagers travelling.* (p. 30) *The bridegroom is behind the girl, and her father is beside her.*

VIII.

Tichu-rong, looking north over Tārakot, back the way we had come. (p. 33)

II

TICHU-RONG AND THE
PHOKSUMDO LAKE

TICHU-RONG

At noon on Saturday, April 14th, having deposited most of our chattels in the headman's house at Dunyer, we crossed the bridge below the village and continued up the Bheri with just two local men as porters. Tārakot is only ten miles distant, but it was already evening when we saw another bridge below us and Tārakot beyond on the summit of a ridge. We had travelled all the afternoon along a rocky gorge, concealed from the mountains on either side, but now the valley opened once more and we saw other villages besides Tārakot high up on the slopes above. Tārakot itself is known locally simply as Dzong, 'the fort', and doubtless there was such a building there originally, where dwelt the 'king' of this little land of Tichu-rong[a] (pl. VIII). There are three other villages, all higher than Dzong, known as Ba, Tup and Dri-k'ung.[b] Dzong, which stands at about 10,000 feet, was the chief of them, because it completely dominated the valley at this point. No one could have travelled in the past without the good will of its master. A community like this, consisting of several separate villages, one of which dominates by its strategic position, is typical of these high Himalayan valleys. Later in our travels we found just the same pattern at Tshuk (p. 170) and Dzar-dzong (p. 199).

We camped that night below Tārakot and rose eager to make contact with the fringe of Tibetan culture which we had now

[a] This name is unknown to the SI. The Tibetan classical spelling is probably *dri-chu-rong*, meaning 'Valley of Fragrant Water'.
[b] The Nepāli names for these three villages are Sartara, Tupara and Densa.

33

reached. A track winds round below 'the fort' and ascends from the north-east, passing through a large white entrance-chöten (pl. VIIa). The chöten, meaning literally 'support for worship' (*mchod-rten*), is the typical Buddhist monument, derived originally from Indian models.[a] In every Buddhist country it has developed a distinctive pattern, but its significance remains essentially the same. Primarily a shrine, in which relics were enclosed, it came to symbolize universal buddhahood. Texts, representing perfect wisdom, and images as symbols of buddha-forms, often replace actual relics. Just as the noble aspiration of buddhahood is conceived as embracing the whole of existence, so the outward form of the chöten is identified in its different parts with the five elements, which represent schematically the sum total of phenomenal existence. The square base is identified with earth, the dome with water, the tapering upper section with fire, the lunar crescent with air and the solar disk with space (p. 32). The entrance-chöten, known locally as 'ka-ni chöten', may not quite conform with this pattern, for the dome is sometimes replaced by a double tier. Architecturally it is just an entrance-porch conceived as a chöten. It is usually painted inside on the ceiling and four walls with sets of divinities, representing the school of Tibetan religion which is practised locally. Thus as soon as we entered this Tārakot chöten, we could identify the local religious practice as the 'Old Sect' (*rnying-ma-pa*) of Tibetan Buddhism, whose worship centres around the 'Lotus-Born' Buddha (*Padmasambhava*). He is an historical figure, who assisted in establishing Buddhism in Tibet in the eighth century. He came to be regarded by his followers as the all-powerful manifestation of the Great Saviour 'Glancing Eye' (*Avalokiteśvara*) and both are held to be

[a] In most English travel-books the Tibetan word appears as 'chorten'. The old Anglo-Indian word, now little used, is 'tope', deriving originally from the Sanskrit term *stūpa*. The Singhalese word 'dagoba' is also current in English. In India and Nepal the word 'chaitya', an early alternative to *stūpa*, is commonly used. The best term for general use is undoubtedly 'stupa', for it is the correct original term and is now used by archaeologists in Europe and India.

34

of the essence of the Supreme Buddha 'All Good' (*Samanta-bhadra*). Among Buddhists only the' Old Sect' has reserved this name for the supreme buddha-body; thus when we see 'All Good' represented in the centre of the ceiling with 'Glancing Eye' on one side and 'Lotus-Born' on the other, we are in no doubt about the type of Buddhism represented. Also depicted are 'Horse-Neck (*Hayagrīva*), a fierce defender belonging to the same family as the three tranquil buddha-forms, and a set of five goddesses (*ḍākinī*) who are the transmitters of mystic doctrines and represent the five sacred families into which prac-tisers of the doctrine may be divided. On the western wall are shown the three great 'saviours' (*bodhisattva*), who are in a sense the prototypes (literally 'protectors', *rigs gsum dgon-po*) of the three primary families: 'Glorious Gentle One' (*Mañjuśrī*) of the *tathāgata*-family, 'Glancing Eye' (*Avalokiteśvara*) of the *lotus*-family and 'Thunderbolt-in-Hand' (*Vajrapāṇi*) of the *vajra*-family. On the eastern wall are the three Buddhas of past, present and future, 'Light-Maker' (*Dīpankara*), 'Sage of the Śākyas (*Śākyamuni*) and 'Loving-Kindness' (*Maitreya*). On the northern and southern walls are the Five Buddhas, who are heads of the five families, and the Buddha Master of Medicine.[a]

One sees many smaller chötens, all clearly Buddhist in in-tention; they are not surmounted with sticks and rags like the cairns of the mountain-gods. We climbed up to the village and were surprised to find that it consisted of only twenty-five houses or so. These are built of stone with flat mud roofs and are all surmounted by prayer-flags. There was no sign here of the wooden effigy of a 'dhauliya protector', the last of which we had noticed at Dunyer. We sought out the house of the headman and went to make enquiries about food-supplies, but we were primarily interested in the villagers themselves. They

[a] In discussing the significance of Tibetan divinities one is easily led into a maze of abstruse metaphysical patterns, which can only be explained in terms of a general historical and religious study, such as I have attempted to give in *Buddhist Himālaya*, a book which for this reason is far more technical than the present one. I must beg those readers, who remain dissatisfied with the brief summaries given here, to refer to the index there.

are Magars, but so far tibetanized as to speak Tibetan, wear Tibetan clothes and practice Tibetan religion. However, so strangely perverse is human nature, that they choose to consider themselves of higher caste than the real Tibetans to the north, with whom intermarriage would be rather scandalous. Their staple food is buckwheat, barley and potatoes. The wealthier villagers possess stocks of wheat and rice, which have come from Gotām. They rely upon seed-oil, such little butter as they use coming from Dolpo. It is sewn up in skins, quite rancid and most unpalatable even for cooking.

An hour of steady climbing brings one to Dri-k'ung a village of about fifteen houses. The main temple of all Tichu-rong is situated here, so this place is referred to locally as just Gomba (dgon-pa) 'the monastery', just as Tārakot is called 'the fort'. The name of the temple itself is Dar-sa, which probably means 'Spreading Place (of the Doctrine)'. An alternative pronunciation is Densa and this seems to be the recognized Nepāli form. In this transition area it is very difficult to sort out some of the names. There are often two quite different ones for these places, one Nepāli and one Tibetan, of which the latter is the more intractible, for no Tibetan-speaker here is sufficiently educated to give the spelling reliably. A woman unlocked the temple for us, which revealed itself as rather a poor affair. The walls are plain and the floor is just bare earth. The main image is that of 'Lotus-Born' and he is flanked by 'Glorious Gentle One' and 'Glancing Eye'. There is a 'Defenders' Room' (srung-khang) containing an image of the four-armed 'Great Black' divinity (Mahākāla), who is hideous to look upon and is flanked by the 'Lion-Headed' Dākinī (senge gdong-ma) and the 'Raven-Headed' one (pho-rog gdong-ma). In most monasteries there is a small separate temple such as this, reserved for divinities which were once hostile to the Buddhist doctrine but have now been converted and coerced into acting as 'defenders'. The chief ones, such as Mahākāla, are of Indian origin and had been adopted in this way long before Buddhism came to Tibet, but the process has continued in Tibetan lands, for it is clearly a

36

convenient way of keeping faith with the old gods while acknowledging the superiority of Buddhist religion.

All the images at Dri-k'ung Monastery were new and we learned from the keeper of the temple that the whole place had been rebuilt just five years ago through the enthusiasm of a certain Tibetan lama, the 'Precious One of Shang' (*shang rin-po-che*). (This name was then quite strange to us, but we were to hear of this lama again and again until eventually we met him.) At the far end of the temple and at a higher level is a kind of inner sanctum, which one may enter by a door to the left and leave by a door to the right, thus performing the regular right-about circumambulation of the images, which is an ancient Indian gesture of devout respect. The central image in this sanctum is a fine bronze of the Buddha 'Imperturbable' (*Akshobhya*), seated cross-legged and about seven feet high. Akshobhya is one of the Five Buddhas and head of the *vajra*-family. His characteristic gesture is that of touching the ground with his right hand, thus calling the earth to witness the perfection of his accumulated merit. All the Five Buddhas represent so many idealized aspects of the historical Buddha Śākyamuni. Akshobhya may be identified originally with Śākyamuni at the moment of enlightenment, when he was being challenged by all the forces of evil. Thus he was known as 'Imperturbable'. He may be still further differentiated iconographically by a *vajra*, sacred thunderbolt, symbol of divine power, which is sometimes shown on the upturned palm of his left hand.

The 'Old Sect' favours the *lotus*-family, whose head is the Buddha 'Boundless Light' (*Amitābha*), identified with their Supreme Buddha 'All Good'. Thus this image of Akshobhya, which is undoubtedly earlier than the period of the later eighteenth century when this whole area was conquered by the Gorkhas, suggests the existence of another order of Tibetan Buddhism, which must have flourished here in earlier centuries. It was probably that of the Sa-kya-pa order, a form of religious practice based on that of the great Tibetan monastery of Sa-kya, which was founded in the eleventh century and subsequently did a great deal of proselyting throughout the regions which we were now about to enter. These orders of Tibetan Buddhism differ hardly at all in their essential beliefs and religious practices but they vary in their traditions, some concentrating on the liturgies of one buddha-family and some on those of another. Likewise they have developed their own literary traditions, writing their own histories and accumulating separate collections of extra-canonical works. The canon itself (Kanjur) and the early commentaries (Tenjur), which were translated from Indian originals, are of course revered in common by all orders of Tibetan Buddhism.[a]

There can be no doubt that the doctrine has been sadly neglected in these frontier areas during the last 150 years, but one observes now the beginning of a revival and the most popular form is that of the Nying-ma-pa ('Old Sect') with 'Lotus-Born' (*Padmasambhava*) very much to the fore. This is the most adulterated form of Tibetan Buddhism and has several important affinities with the doctrine known as p'ön (classical spelling: *bon*)[b] which claims to be the pre-Buddhist religion of the Tibetans. Much more will be said about this below.

Hearing that the Lama of Pungmo (SI: Pudāmingāon) had been invited to perform a ceremony in the house of one of the villagers, we went to pay him a visit. It was not a success. The house was filled with merry-makers, all the merrier for the barley-beer (chang) which flowed so freely. Followed by a crowd, we entered a small dark room, where the lama was seated beside the sacrificial cakes (torma). Two lay-folk sat beside him, passing from one to the other a bottle of local spirit (arak). This was pressed upon us, but we declined. Conversation

[a] They belong to four main groups: the Nying-ma-pa = 'Old Sect', (*rnying-ma-pa*), the Sa-kya-pa (*Sa-skya-pa*), the Ka-gyü-pa = 'Order of the Transmitted Word' (*bka'-rgyud-pa*), and the Ge-luk-pa = 'Virtuous Order' (*dge-lug-pa*). The first three are grouped together popularly as the 'Red Hats' and the last, which was founded by the great reforming lama, Tsong-kha-pa at the beginning of the fifteenth century, is referred to as the 'Yellow Hats'.

[b] It should be pronounced like the English syllable 'pern' in a deep tone (Phonetic Table, p. 277).

was quite profitless and we left as soon as good manners per-mitted. We later visited this lama at his own monastery and found him to be a pleasant and intelligent man of about forty years (see p. 67). Forbearance is one of the virtues which a lama of good intentions requires to the full.

The general situation of Dri-k'ung is superb, for the village is seen against a background of pine-covered slopes and massive snow-mountains to the south, which rise ever higher eastwards to form the great Dhaulagiri massif. The following day we continued up the valley of the Bheri. Little white roses (*Rosa sericea*) bloomed along the track and here and there were clusters of leafless *Buddleia tibetica,* known locally as the 'flower of a hundred heads' (*mgo-brgya-me-tog*). Junipers were growing to an enormous height.

SANDUL

Sandul Monastery (SI: Chhandul Gömpa) is about five miles beyond Tārakot and stands at the junction of the Bheri and the stream that descends from Tarap. Thus one has to cross the Bheri to reach the temple; the track leads down by crazy steps through the rocks to a tree-trunk bridge which spans a deep and narrow gorge. All the rocks beyond are incised with the spell OM MAṆIPADME HŪṂ and one feels as though one were about to enter some hidden and idyllic valley, of which Tibetans love to tell, where men and animals live in peace and harmony.[a] This was doubtless the intention of the monks who first settled here and named their hermitage Sandul (*sa-'dul*), 'Tranquillizer of the Land'. Yet but for the zeal of the Lama of Shang it seems there would be now no temple here at all; it is he who has

[a] This Buddhist spell is in the form of a Sanskrit invocation translatable as 'O thou of the Jewelled Lotus'. The divine name is given a feminine form, because such spells (skr. *vidyā*) represent the feminine aspect of the male divinity, in this case 'Glancing Eye' (*Avalokiteśvara*), to whom they belong. This problem is discussed in *Buddhist Himālaya*, p. 116.

collected funds and rebuilt it as well as present circumstances have allowed. There are traces of the older building in some carved wooden beams, which display more expert craftsmanship, and one can see the stone foundations of other buildings behind the present temple, indicating that this site must once have been of far greater importance. There is nothing to suggest its age, but one may presume that it was destroyed when the Gurkhas occupied this region and so fell into decay. The central image in the main hall is 'Lotus-Born' (*Padmasambhava*) flanked by his fierce manifestation, 'Fierce Master' (*gu-ru drag-po*) and the Lion-Headed Ḍākinī (*senge gdong-ma*) all modern *terra-cotta* work of the craftsmen of Tarap. 'Lotus-Born' is placed just to the left of the table of offerings; behind there is a grill, through which one looks up at an enormous image of Maitreya, Buddha of the Future, seated in the centre of an inner sanctum similar to the one at Dri-k'ung. The wall to the right of the table has paintings of Tsong-kha-pa, founder-lama of the 'Virtuous Order', and of the Buddha 'Boundless Life' (*Amitāyus*), who is another form of 'Boundless Light' (*Amitābha*). When one enters the sanctum, one sees that Maitreya is flanked by small inset images of the sixteen arhats.[a] On the far side are the 'Great Black' divinity (*Mahākāla*) and the lion-headed and raven-headed ḍākinīs; next to them are the effigies of three former lamas of Sandul. On the far right is an image of Śākyamuni and against the right-hand wall is a set of the thirty-five Buddhas of Confession painted in miniature on stones and fixed in wooden frames.

It is apparent that this temple receives little or no support nowadays. The nearest village is Ka-ne (SI: Khānīgāon), half an hour's climb up the mountain-side to the west, where the people are Magars and nominally Buddhist. On one occasion recently they had sacrificed a goat to Mahākāla inside the temple in spite of the resistance of the old lama and the two monks there. Later this was reported to the Lama of Shang, who

[a] The arhats ('worthy ones') are the early disciples who gained nirvāna. The set of sixteen is a conventional one.

40

threatened them with calamities if they committed such an act again. We set up our camp in a grove just near the monastery and then climbed up to Ka-ne in the hope of increasing our provisions. The headman was a truculent fellow, but willingly sold us a lump of butter sewn up in skin, some rice and some potatoes. He told us that he had recently returned from a journey to Calcutta and was intending to go trading northwards before long. Learning that there was a p'ön monastery at the village of P'ar-lä (SI: Baijubāra) about six miles further on, we resolved to visit it.

P'öN

The next day we climbed up to Ka-ne again and followed a track which continued high up round the mountain-side with superb views of the snows across the valley to the south. We saw the villages of Dzong and Ba and Tup looking very small on those vast mountain slopes. As we approached the little village of Chauri we came upon a prayer-wall and noticed that the invocations carved upon the stones were unfamiliar ones. There were only two which were repeated again and again:

A A DKAR SA LE 'OD A YANG OM
OM MA TRI MU YE SA LE 'DU

We realized at once that they were p'ön-po and not Buddhist spells, the second one being the popular p'ön-po invocation, which corresponds to the OM MAṆIPADME HŪṂ of the Buddhists. From now on we were going to see OM MATRI MUYE SA LE 'DU innumerable times, but on this first encounter we tarried and mused on the meaning. OM is the ancient Indian mystic syllable. MATRI MUYE meant nothing to us. SA LE 'DU is Tibetan, meaning presumably 'in clarity unite'. In spite of our persistent questioning later on we learned nothing more about this spell, which is just taken for granted by those who recite it. We were told that MATRI MUYE was in the language of Sh'ang-sh'ung, which means in effect that it has no meaning at all, for this language is largely pretence.

A A DKAR SA LE 'OD A YANG OM can be interpreted a little more satisfactorily. 'A' has mystic significance as representing the fundamental vowel-sound. DKAR is Tibetan, meaning 'white', and is followed by SA LE 'OD, 'in clarity unite', then 'A' again, then YANG (? gYang), 'blessing' and finally OM. I am sure that no Tibetan ever stops to ponder on the literal meaning and one would be very naïve to expect such an interpretation from any lama however well read. The potency consists in the sounds themselves, for they are the spell of Shen-rap, the divine teacher of p'ön (see p. 47). To recite them continuously brings one to unity with him and saves from rebirth in the spheres of existence.

Within another half-hour we reached P'AR-LÄ and cast around in vain for somewhere to pitch a tent, for the village was built down the mountain-side and apart from the track itself there was not a foot of level ground. We therefore called on the headman and asked if we might use his house. He was up at the temple, we learned, where a ceremony was in progress, but his wife led us willingly on to the roof and said we might stay there. So steep was the ground, that the house was two storeys high at the front while just two steps led on to the roof at the back. Two more rooms were built there, which we were able to use, sharing them with another lodger, an old woman from Mustang. There was also space for a tent on the flat earth roof and so we used the Mead tent, which could be erected without hammering in pegs. When these arrangements were completed, we climbed up to the monastery, which is built just beneath the summit crags at a height of about 14,000 feet. It stands above a small grove of juniper trees and is called the 'Swastika Monastery of the Juniper Grove' (gYung-drung shug-tshal dgon-pa).

The swastika is an ancient Indian mystical sign for good fortune, which was adopted in Tibet very early on. The Buddhists use it with the bent arms of the cross pointing clockwise, but the p'ön-pos use it anti-clockwise. In the same contrary manner they spin their prayer-wheels left-about and circumambulate prayer-walls, shrines and temples with their left side towards the object of respect. This practice must have developed in the first instance out of deliberate opposition to the Buddhists, for to circumambulate a Buddhist image or temple left-about would be a sure way of showing one's contempt for it. No such rancour exists nowadays. I remember especially a row of prayer-walls leading into the village of Tsharka, first a Buddhist one, then a p'ön-po one and then again a Buddhist one. Every villager I saw pass those walls, would instinctively leave the first on his right, the second on his left and the third again on his right. We noticed on many occasions how our porters would first glance to identify a wall as we approached it, whether it was 'of the doctrine' (*chos-pa*) or p'ön-po (*bon-po*), so that they might keep to its proper side.

The p'ön-pos claim to represent the old indigenous religion of Tibet of the pre-Buddhist days, but some of them have since adopted so much of Buddhist teaching and religious practice, that they might be considered a special sect of Tibetan Buddhism, albeit a very odd one.[a] They may well be adjudged the world greatest plagiarists, for they have rewritten the whole Tibetan Canon (Kanjur), giving it a supposed p'ön-po setting instead of a Buddhist one and attributing it to their founder-teacher Shen-rap. There is a very early tradition that the original p'ön-po teachings came from the Land of Sh'ang-sh'ung in West Tibet.[b] Thus by giving the 'original' titles of all the many hundreds of their supposedly canonical texts in the

---

[a] These are the 'white (viz. virtuous) p'ön', with whom we shall be concerned. They are contrasted with the 'black p'ön', practisers of black magic. (For types of such practice see René de Nebesky-Wojkowitz, *Oracles and Demons of Tibet*, O.U.P. London, 1956, pp. 481 ff.) There is, however, no final and clear-cut distinction between white and black p'ön, just as there is no essential difference between p'ön magic and buddhist magic. Some of the canonical Buddhist tantras and their Indian commentaries contain prescriptions for harmful rites of all kinds.

[b] More about this will be found in B[uddhist] H[imālaya], pp. 292–3.

language of Sh'ang-sh'ung, they imply that they have been translated from that language in just the same way as the Buddhist canon was translated from Sanskrit. We were later able to look through these works at our leisure (p. 120) and there is no doubt of the falsity of the claim. Yet such is the lack of critical interest among these good-natured people, that no one bothers to dispute the matter and the Buddhists remain content that the p'ön-pos are after all so very similar to themselves.

At the same time their traditions remain distinct in other respects. As we climbed up that afternoon to the 'Swastika Monastery of the Juniper Grove' we passed a large number of prayer-walls and also a ka-ni chöten with strange paintings on the inside walls. Of the ten divinities portrayed we could recognize only three, who resembled the Buddhas of the Three Times. All the symbols, however, were familiar and the thrones, which were distinguished by different animals beneath them, elephants, lions, peacocks, etc., suggested at once that here was a set of the main p'ön divinities, similar to that of the Five Buddhas. We would certainly see them again and in due course learn to identify them, so we went on to the monastery. We entered the dark hall and found the ceremony still in progress. The lama, a young man in his early twenties, was seated at the head of a row of men and boys, just seven of them, all intoning invocations which were interspersed with crashes of music from cymbals, drums and trumpets in the regular Tibetan manner. We sat down on a low platform on the other side of the temple and awaited a break in the performance. The walls were all painted and I recognized the figures which we had seen in the chöten on the way up, but here there were many others besides to intrigue me. The main image above the table of offerings seemed to be Śākyamuni which was surprising, for why should he hold place of honour where p'ön prevails? As soon as there was a break in the ceremony, the men asked who we were and whence we had come, so I was able to counter their enquiries.

'Who is the central image there?'

44

'It is the Teacher (*ston-pa*).'
'Do you mean Śākyamuni?'
'Yes.'
'But where is Shen-rap?'
'They are the same.'

These brief questions pleased them immensely and they were amused to think that anyone should seem to doubt the identity of Śākyamuni with Shen-rap. We asked them what text they were reciting and they told us it was 'The Prayer for the Fulfilment of Directed Thought' (*gsol-'debs bsam-pa lhun-'grub-pa*). Before starting again they lent us one of their copies. It was a manuscript written in the headless form of Tibetan with numerous verbal contractions. In all these regions printed books are very rare indeed.[a]

'E MA HO—In the realm of the Great Blessed One, the Sky-Goer (*mkhas-spyod*), may the welfare of living beings be achieved by the Doctrine which knows neither birth nor death. In this last age of 500 years we entreat the Sky-Guide Gyer-Pung,[b] the supreme guide of living beings, that he may bless us with the instantaneous fulfilment of our directed thought.

'In this age we, the last afflicted beings, are tormented by sickness and disease and there is no occasion for the happiness of Ö-gyel's realm.[c] O regard us with compassion, Gyer-pung, Best of Guides! Keeping the three entrances (bodily, verbal, mental) closed (against distraction), in faith do we entreat you, that you may bless us with instantaneous fulfilment of our directed thought.

'When afflicted beings are suffering from illness, may we

[a] By printed books I refer exclusively to Tibetan printed books, viz. xylographs (see p. 151). Printed books in European style are quite unknown.
[b] *gyer-spungs dran-pa namkha: dran-pa* is the p'ön term for the 'Great Beings', corresponding to the Buddhas. The word was interpreted to me as meaning 'Guide' and it may reasonably be associated with the verb '*dren-pa*, 'to lead'. *Gyer-spungs* may mean 'chant-accumulation'.
[c] Ö-gyel is the mythical ancestor of the early Tibetan kings. It is interesting to observe that the p'ön-pos associate him with a golden age. (*BH*, p. 128 ff.)

make our entreaties with devotion and unwavering one-pointedness of mind. May the Guide Master of Medicine and the "One Inseparable" (*dbyer-med-pa*) remove with certainty all sufferings and disease. We entreat the Sky-Guide Gyer-Pung that he may bless us with instantaneous fulfilment of our directed thought.

'When we are threatened by the demons and spirits of the Bardo (intermediate state between death and rebirth), unwaveringly and with devotion we entreat the Blessed One, that the Guides together with the company of tutelary divinities (*yi-dam*) and godlings may tranquillize the demons and spirits, despatching them to their proper place. We entreat the Sky-Guide Gyer-Pung that he may bless us with instantaneous fulfilment of our directed thought.

'When we are suffering from hunger and thirst, from poverty and plague, unwavering and with devotion we entreat the Blessed One that the Guides together with the company of gods of wealth and phantom forms may clear away all suffering, poverty and weakness. We entreat the Sky-Guide Gyer-Pung that he may bless us with instantaneous fulfilment of our directed thought.

'When our life is ending and death approaches, may this devout entreaty be made unwaveringly for us, so that the Guides and Knowledge-Holders[a] together with the gods of life may surely grant extension of our days. We entreat the Sky-Guide Gyer-pung that he may bless us with instantaneous fulfilment of our directed thought.'

The whole tenor of this invocation resembles that of any Tibetan Buddhist ceremony, yet some of the beings addressed bear very different names. The reference to the mythical king, O-gyel reminds one of the pre-Buddhist beliefs of the Tibetans,

---

[a] These are the *vidyādhara* of Indian tradition. They represent the perfected yogin of the type of the eighty-four *Siddhas* (*BH*, pp. 85–7). Popularly they were believed to be capable of transmuting their physical body into an immortal '*vajra*-body'.

46

centring around a supreme sky divinity who manifested himself as the king on earth. It is this sky divinity who is invoked here as the 'Sky-Guide' (*dran-pa namkha*). Under Indian influence he became known as the 'All Good' (*kun-tu bzang-po* = *samantabhadra*) and this name continued to be used by the 'Old Sect' of Tibetan Buddhism (Nying-ma-pa) as well as by the p'ön-pos. For the Nying-ma-pas this represented yet another epithet for ineffable buddhahood and so 'All Good' (*Samantabhadra*) is identified by them with 'Boundless Light' (*Amitābha*), head of the lotus-family, to which they belong. When the p'ön-pos use this name, however, they still conceive of him as primarily the sky divinity and it is interesting to find the notion of divine kingship persisting in the p'ön god, 'Ancestor King of Phantom Forms' (*gong-mdzad 'phrul-gyi rgyal-po*), whose image we saw for the first time in Par-lä Monastery.[a] Iconographically Samantabhadra is represented as a naked ascetic seated cross-legged with hands together in the posture of meditation. His nakedness would associate him with Jain rather than Buddhist tradition and it is indeed possible that the p'ön-pos deliberately adopted a style that was not Buddhist. He may be painted either blue or white, for both are celestial colours.[b] He has four supreme manifestations:

TEACHER SHEN-RAP (*ston-pa gshen-rab*),[c] who sits on a throne marked with jewels while his right hand makes the 'earth-witness' gesture (p. 37). He may also be holding in this hand a magic dart (*phur-pa*). His left hand lies on his lap

---

[a] I derive the association from the name itself. *Gong mdzad* means literally 'made first'. The early Tibetan kings were given the title of 'god of phantom form' (*'phrul-gyi lha*).

[b] The Nying-ma-pas use the same iconographical form, but Samantabhadra is usually shown as blue and clasping a feminine partner (Samantabhadrī) who is white.

[c] Shen (*gshen*) is the term used of a type of priest in pre-Buddhist Tibet. Shen-rap would therefore mean 'Best of Priests. A résumé of his fantastic biography, a parody of Śākyamuni's, is given by Helmut Hoffmann, *Die Religionen Tibets*, Freiburg/München, 1956, pp. 76 ff.

palm upwards. He is crowned and wears regal garments and the colour of his body is either blue or white (pl. XXVI).

SHEN-GOD WHITE LIGHT (*gshen-lha 'od-dkar*), who sits on a throne supported by elephants with his hands on his lap in the gesture of meditation. A curved knife (*gri-gug*) protrudes over his right shoulder. He is dressed in regal garments and the colour of his body is either white or black (pls. IX*c* and XXVII).

PURE 10,000 TIMES 100,000 (*sang-po 'bum-khri*), who sits on a throne supported by peacocks with his left hand on his lap palm upwards and his right hand holding a white parasol. He too is dressed regally and his body is white.

SA-TRIK IMMACULATE AND PURE (*sa-trig yer sangs*), who sits on a throne supported by lions with her hands before her heart in the gesture of preaching. Alternatively she may be holding a garlanded rod across the right shoulder. Lotuses grow on either side of her, one of them supporting a swastika and the other a crossed vajra. She is dressed regally and her body is yellow (pl. X*a*).

Although iconographically 'All Good' and these four supreme manifestations often seem to correspond with the Five Buddhas, in no true sense are they equivalents. 'Teacher Shen-rap', the supposed founder of p'ön, is consciously identified with Śākyamuni. 'Shen-God White Light' is given the title of 'god of knowledge' (*ye-shes-kyi lha*); in p'ön rituals he occupies a place corresponding to 'Glancing Eye', so fulfilling the function of 'Lord of Compassion'. 'The Pure 10,000 times 100,000' is the chief of the 'gods of existence' (*srid-pa*), but so far he has impressed me with no special character in the rituals. 'Sa-trik' the p'ön mother-goddess, is equated with the Buddhist Goddess of Wisdom (*Prajñāpāramitā*). None of these Buddhist equivalents fits into the fivefold scheme.

The idea of the supreme being as fivefold has been adopted explicitly by the p'ön-pos in a divine form known as the

'Composite Conqueror' (*rgyal-ba 'dus-pa*), who is said to be the primary manifestation of 'All Good' (*Samantabhadra*). This divinity has five faces and ten arms. The top face is blue, the next one red, the central one below is white, the left one green and the right one yellow. These are the colours of the Five Buddhas and there is no doubt concerning the Buddhist origin of this god. In the same way the Buddhas of the Three Times have been adopted and although new names have been found for them, they are still naïvely referred to as 'buddhas' (*dus gsum sangs-rgyas*) as well as 'conquerors'.

Time	Buddhist	P'ön
Past	Light-Maker (*Dīpankara*)	Acme Conqueror Omniscient (*rtog-rgyal ye-mkhyen*)
Present	Śākya-Sage (*Śākyamuni*)	Shen-rap (*gshen-rabs*)
Future	Loving-Kindness (*Maitreya*)	Torch of Purity (*thang-ma me-sgron*)

As soon as the ceremony was finished for that day, we befriended the local painter, who willingly assisted us in these identifications. This temple at P'ar-lä was the first p'ön-po one we had seen and fortunately it contained all the more important divinities either as images or paintings. Later on we were able to meet them again and again, so gradually becoming familiar with all these iconographical forms.

Corresponding with the 'Composite Conqueror' as the primary *tranquil* manifestation of 'All Good', there is a *fierce* manifestation with nine faces and eighteen arms, known as Wäl-sä (pl. XXXIII).[a] The topmost face is of the mythical bird

[a] In all the liturgies this name is spelt *dbal-gsas* and translatable as 'Summit Prince'. I wonder if he is to be associated with the *wal-wal sras-po*, who head the divine lineage of the mythical ancestor-king of Tibet. The relevant passage is quoted in *BH*, p. 130, where I translated the name of these obscure divinities quite provisionally as 'Sons of Clarity'. But *dbal* and *wal* are both pronounced '*wäl*', and *gsas* and *sras* both as '*sä*'. *Sras*, the honorific word for 'son', which is still in use, may reasonably be associated with the ancient word, *gsas*, meaning 'leader' or 'prince'. As for the correspondence of db- and

49

khyung (*garuḍa*), the next two are of a dragon and a crocodile (*makara*), the next pair are tigers with a leopard in the centre and the lower three are grotesque human faces, red, blue and white. In his two upper hands he waves aloft a banner of victory (*rgyal-mtshan*) and a human skin; with his two lower ones he clasps his partner 'Vile Outcast Mother of those who progress towards Bliss' (*gtum-mo bde-'gro yum*) and holds a magic dart (*phur-pa*); in the remaining fourteen he holds weapons of various kinds. His body is dark blue and hers is green. In her two hands she holds a ritual vase and a dish of offerings. Whatever the origin of Wäl-sä's name, it is certain that iconographically he has been conceived in the pattern of fierce divinities of buddha-rank (*Heruka*). There are two other beings of like nature, 'Supreme Chief Gaping-Mouth' (*gtso mchog kha-'gying*) with three faces and six arms, and 'Wild God Topper' (*lha-god thog-pa*) with four faces and eight arms.

Of the other tranquil divinities we must mention the 'Victorious One' (*rnam-par rgyal-ba*) who is blue and clad in regal attire with his left hand in the 'earth-witness' gesture and his right raised high in the gesture of dauntlessness.

There is a monk wearing red garments and seated in the posture of meditation. He is known as 'Secret Epitome of Scripture' of the A-sh'a (*'a-zha gsang-ba mdo-bsdud*) and is supposed to have been a disciple of Shen-rap's.[a]

There are also some miniature paintings of 'Sky-Guide' (*dran-pa namkha*) represented as a yogin together with his two 'sons', 'Lotus-Born' (*Padmasambhava*) and 'Life-Empowering Knowledge-Holder' (*tshe-dbang rig-'dzin*). Later on we obtained the complete works of the latter and learned that he is regarded as the first formulator of p'ön doctrine, just as 'Lotus-Born' is

w- in the other word, one may observe that the name of the mythical ancestor-king, pronounced 'Wö-gyel' is written *dbod-rgyal* in these later p'ön texts and *'od-rgyal* in the early literature (*rgyal-po bka'i thang-yig*).

[a] The A-'sha were a tribe on China's western frontier, who were defeated by the Tibetans in the seventh century. See F. W. Thomas, *Tibetan Literary Texts and Documents concerning Chinese Turkestan*, Luzac, London, 1951, vol. II, pp. 34 ff.

popularly regarded as the founder of Tibetan Buddhism. It is interesting to observe that the p'ön-pos treat them as brothers.

On the back wall of the temple there are depicted five divinities of secondary rank, who are commonly invoked as protectors. Most important of these is the 'Tiger God' (stag-lha), an horrific red divinity, who has been adopted by the Nying-mapas as 'Fierce Master' (gu-ru drag-po), a supposed manifestation of Padmasambhava. Then there is the mythical bird khyung (garuda), whose attributes reveal his Indian origin. There is Jambhala, the god of wealth, and the 'Destroyer' (rnam-par 'joms-pa), who is a p'ön-po imitation of the Buddhist Vajrapāṇi. Lastly there is a monstrous green divinity with ten heads and twenty arms. The topmost head is that of a khyung and the remainder are grotesquely human. In his lowest pair of hands he holds a skull-cup and a banner of victory while the rest hold gruesome weapons. He is known as 'Bond-Keeper Gaṇacakra' or more usually as the 'black-green god of 100 heads and 1000 arms' (ljang-nag dbu brgya phyag stong), although I have never seen him depicted with so many.[a] At Par-lä he has an entourage of four lesser divinities, known as 'kings of existence' (sridrgyal), white, blue, red and black.

The ceremony continued the next day and we followed it with some difficulty because of the unfamiliar nature of the texts. We were present for the summoning of the divinities and the presentation of the offerings. These are arranged in the same manner as in Buddhist ceremonies and are of both tranquil and fierce variety. The three main tormas (sacrificial cakes), which stood on the highest shelf were those of the 'Composite Conqueror', the 'Tiger-God' and Ganacakra. The 'Tiger-God', as tutelary divinity of the monastery, was the centre of the ceremony; he was being invoked for the protection of the village.

[a] The 'bond-keepers' (dam-can) are properly non-Buddhist divinities who are under a bond to defend the Buddhist doctrine. Thus as a title for a p'ön-op divinity it seems especially incongruous. Gaṇacakra (Sanskrit pronounced: ga-na cha-kra) means 'circle of offerings'.

51

This was the last day of the invocations and we were indeed fortunate to be present, for the performance ended with a ritual dance, which takes place but once a year. The dancers formed a circle in the temple, reeling this way and that and gradually making their way through the door. Then having encircled the chöten in the courtyard outside, they turned down to a grass slope beyond. A great torma was placed on the ground in the centre of the group and they wheeled around it, invoking the 'Tiger-God' to be present once more, for this torma was intended for him (pl. IXa). Two fearful masked figures, representing the red and black 'kings of existence' of Ganacakra's troupe, now approached holding a mystic diagram (maṇḍala) drawn on paper, in which all harmful demons were forced to incorporate themselves. The dancers, having opened their circle to allow it entry, continued wheeling around it. The lama was then handed a bow and arrow, with which he shot the mandala to its heart. Cries of victory and joy ensued and in these the villagers enthusiastically took part. A small torma was flung to the winds as an offering to the spirits who intended no special harm and the Tiger-God's torma was consumed in fire. This whole dance took place in a snow-storm, which greatly increased the effect of the scene, although it spoiled photography. I often reflect that the best things can seldom be photographed without distortion. If one could capture the expressions and gestures of the performers while they are chanting inside the temple or the rapture of the crowd as the ceremony reaches its climax! Our research can all too easily appear as a lifeless structure, because so much evades our scholarly diagnosis.

The villagers were undoubtedly proud of their young lama, saying that he must certainly be an 'incarnation' (p. IXb). They told us how he had shown a devotion to the religious life from childhood and that his father had sent him to a wise lama at Samling Monastery, a week's journey to the north. He alone in the village has taken the vow of celibacy, living in private quarters over the main temple. His father is a wealthy villager, who seems to have provided most of the funds for the reconstruction and decoration of the temple, which has been carried out during the last few years. All these villagers are Magars, but they speak Tibetan as their native tongue and some of them might well pass as Tibetans, among them the young lama himself. The following morning we visited him in the temple, where he was intoning prayers with four of the villagers. He gave us a manuscript copy of the p'ön version of the 'Liturgy of the Tranquil and Fierce Divinities', a most welcome gift, and urged us to visit Samling. In this we needed no persuading, for I had already worked out its probable location on our map.

When we left P'ar-lä, the paintings inside the ka-ni chöten on the way up to the monastery were no longer a mystery to us. We had been correct in identifying three of them as the Buddhas of the Three Times. The four supreme manifestations were now familiar to us and so was the monk 'Epitome of Scripture'. There was also a painting of another monk, named 'Banner of Wisdom' (*shes-rab rgyal-mtshan*), who is said to be the p'ön equivalent of Tsong-kha-pa. These villagers were aware of no incongruity in thus associating their heterodox beliefs with the lama who is chiefly renowned for his zeal in purifying Buddhist doctrine and practice. The last painting of the ten seemed to be a duplication of Shen-rap portrayed like the Buddha 'Imperturbable', but seated on a throne supported by lions instead of elephants.

We continued westwards along a track which led down steeply towards the Bheri. About half a mile below the village there were two more ka-ni chötens, both beautifully painted inside and providing yet another test to our recently acquired knowledge. The ceiling of the first one was divided into nine squares.

1. The mandala of 'All Good' (*Samantabhadra*) with the four supreme emanations to the four directions (pp. 47–8).
2. The Supreme Being, 'All Good'.
3. 'Composite Conqueror'.

7	5	6
2	1	4
9	3	8

4. 'Ancestor King of Phantom Forms'.
5. Shen-rap, Conqueror of the Present.
6. 'Acme Conqueror Omniscient', Conqueror of the Past.
7. 'Torch of Purity', Conqueror of the Future.
8. Garuḍa.
9. 'Tiger-God'.

Around the four walls were painted the four supreme manifestations with elaborate entourage (pls. IX*c*, X*a*). All of this served to confirm our newly acquired knowledge. In the smaller chöten very little of the painting remained on the ceiling, but we could make out circles of garuḍas in pleasing tones of red and black and brown.

THE SULI GĀD

There was nothing further to delay us along the track until we reached the river-bank again and found some goosefoot, which we gathered into a rucksack for our evening meal. It began to rain a little and while we sheltered in a cave I remember talking to Pasang about Chinese restaurants in Calcutta. How weak is human nature!

We reached our camp-site below Dunyer Village and soon everything was well organized. We would have to delay several days before continuing our journey up the Suli Gād; not only was there much new material to write up, but we were also rather tired and entirely destitute of cereals. The headman was able to let us have a little rice and wheat-flour, but it was in very short supply in Dunyer, where the people live mainly on maize and buckwheat. Further north barley would become available, but of wheat there was no certainty. We decided that we must accumulate 100 lb of rice and 100 lb of wheat. So the next day Takki Babu set out with the headman to see what could be purchased from the stocks held by the villagers of Motipur. Thanks to the assistance of the officials of the check-post we had bought up in two days as much as we required, and Pasang set about the task of rendering the grain fit for our consumption. The rice had to be cleaned and winnowed. The wheat was far more trouble. First it had to be picked over very carefully in order to remove small stones, stray husks, and droppings left by rats. Then the greater part had to be ground at the village water-mill, a very slow process, occupying in all about twelve hours. Some of the wheat we turned into tsamba by first parching the grains in a large flat pan and grinding them afterwards. This 'cooked flour' can be eaten simply by mixing it with buttered tea. We were also able to bake bread and cake, for eggs were available and there was dried fruit in our stores. Although we were on a sort of pilgrimage (and this is how Pasang always described our intentions), we would have welcomed a joint of meat, but that was not available. The last ten pounds of the large Langtang Cheese, which we had brought from Kathmandu, was carried off by a dog one night.[a]

All was ready six days later and we estimated that we would require nine porters. There were two heavy boxes containing tea, coffee, cocoa, chocolate, dried vegetables, soups, tins of tomato purée, jam, marmalade and honey, dried fruits and milk, Marmite and Peek Frean's biscuits.[b] These had to last for four months at least, but they would gradually decrease in

[a] This cheese is made by a noble band of Swiss, who are trying to teach the Nepalese to take an appreciative interest in dairy products.
[b] The Marmite and Peek Frean's biscuits were presents from the makers most gratefully received.

weight. There was one man-load of sugar and spices, two and a half of grain with one of the tents to make up the half load. Yet another of paraffin and petrol, cooking oils, butter and camp-beds. There was a load of bedding-rolls and clothes and lastly one load consisting of my box with typewriter, papers, medicines, films and photographic equipment, all brought up to weight by the addition of the second tent. This still left a large basket for Takki Babu, filled with pots and pans, enough food for the day and whatever rain-capes and blankets were bundled on top.

So we left Dunyer on Friday, April 27th, after a farewell meal with the officers of the frontier check-post, who had been so very helpful to us during our stay. But while we were talking with them up in the village, we lost control of events down at our camp-site. Only seven of the nine porters presented themselves and these decided to share the two extra loads and the two missing men's pay between themselves. Had we known in time, we would have obtained two more men, for the loads were already heavy enough. Thus we left belatedly with over-loaded men, who perforce advanced so slowly that we were destined to reach our destination long after nightfall. We crossed the Bheri by the bridge at Lower Dunyer and ascended the mountain-side opposite, continuing in a generally northern direction so that eventually we found ourselves high above the left bank of the Suli Gād. By keeping to the course of this river we could expect to reach the Phoksumdo Lake in three to four days' time. Pasang and I hastened ahead as far as the empty houses which are used by the villagers of Rohagāon as winter-quarters; here we waited for three hours until the porters at long last appeared. Then I continued with Takki Babu, while Pasang stayed with the rest of the party so as to reduce delay as much as possible. Little gentians, violets and primulas grew by the track and tall spruce began to close in around us. On we went, hoping to find a place to camp somewhere short of Rohagāon. But the slopes along the valley remained as steep as ever and we found nowhere to accomodate a tent, until at last we reached the flat roof-tops of Rohagāon itself. Since there was no tent to erect until the porters arrived, we could do nothing but seek out the headman's house, sit on his roof and wait and wait. Dusk fell and then night and we continued waiting, until faint lights appeared on the mountain-side beyond the torrent which cuts its way down steeply to the Suli Gād just south of Rohagāon. It was well past midnight by the time we were at rest; even then we could sleep little, for the village-dogs were too disturbed by the presence of so many strangers.

Pasang was astir betimes and arranged with the headman for nine men to accompany us, since the others would be returning to Dunyer. Meanwhile I looked around the village. It consists of about twenty-five houses, the people are of mixed race and all of low caste (*sarki, rokāyā, ukero, budhaṭhīki*). They speak Nepāli but also understand some Tibetan. There is not a trace of either Hindu or Buddhist culture and their only temple is the empty shrine of the god Masta. But they observe one interesting custom, namely that of setting up resting-places along the track for the merit of deceased relatives. In some cases the central stone is inscribed with the date and a few words of blessing; above the inscription is a crudely drawn 'protector', clearly similar in character to the roughly cut figures that appear on the house-tops at Tibrikot. They refer to this image as 'Ju-she', but are quite vague about it, except for the fact that it protects. The Nepāli script is as crudely cut as the effigy, and since the surfaces of the stones have not been properly prepared, even the recent ones are scarcely legible. The houses are mostly of the plain stone type, which is common throughout this whole area, but a few of them have an outer coating of clay decorated with red lines and carved windows in the manner of the houses of the upper castes at Tibrikot.

The track, adorned now with white roses as well as with the gentians and violets of yesterday, continued more or less level across the steep valley-side until it was running side by side with the higher reaches of the Suli Gād. We followed it contentedly, regretting only that it was too early in the day to make use of the pleasant green swards and the shade of the junipers and spruce. Then the gorge became narrow again with great cliffs of rock towering on either side and we were forced to climb high above them. Thus when the time came to look for a camp-site, we found ourselves once more on steep mountain-sides. Takki Babu and I looked ahead in vain and then retraced our steps to a small sloping grassy ledge, which we had rejected as unsuitable when we passed it before. By levelling the ground it was possible to make room for one tent, and since there was no fear of rain the rest of the party slept confidently under the trees.

The next morning we continued across high ground be-strewn with mauve primulas (*Primula denticulata*). We found an occasional daisy-like erigeron (*Erigeron bellidioides*), a few irises (*Iris kamaonensis*) and here and there a cluster of the star-like flowers of *Stellera chamaejasme*. We were now about 11,000 feet above sea-level; when we next saw this plant, we would be 5,000 feet higher at Samling Monastery, where it bloomed in such profusion (pl. XXIV*b*). After two hours walking we found our-selves once more beside the Suli Gād. Here too there was an excellent site for camping, but night would certainly have over-taken our porters if we had attempted to reach it the previous evening. The sun had not yet reached us and it was bitterly cold on the east side of the gorge; we lit a fire, warmed ourselves and cooked the morning meal.

Two more hours of pleasant walking beside the river and through the close-set pines brought us to a river-junction. Here one stream descends from the NW beyond Pungmo (SI: Pudāmigāon), which we would be visiting in due course. The other descends from the NE and the Phoksumdo Lake. There is a bridge just above the junction and by crossing over to the right bank of this stream one can ascend through Palam, the winter-quarters of the lake-side dwellers, and on by a steep track up to Ringmo (SI: Ringmigāon), their lake-side village, which they call by the Tibetan name of Tsho-wa (*mtsho-ba*), 'lake-side'. But our porters refused to go so far and kept us to the left bank of the stream, so that by ascending gradually for another two miles we came to Murwa, the summer resort of these same people. We were now separated from Ringmo by a massive ridge towering 2,000 feet above us and beyond this was the giant waterfall, no longer visible from Murwa, which drains the lake above. The sight of this on the way up the valley fully compensated for the trouble of the longer route (pl. XIII*b*). By now it was evening and while we set up camp, Pasang argued persuasively with our porters, urging them to come with us the following day. But they would not, so he paid them off and pursued enquiries amongst the houses, where by good chance he found a villager with five yaks, willing to assist us. There were very few people about, for most of them were up at the lake-side village; but for this fortunate encounter we would have been forced to delay here until we could get helpers down from above.

PHOKSUMDO

The change of transport in the morning involved us in the troublesome business of repacking our loads, for these had to be arranged to suit the backs of our new helpers. But it was worth the trouble, for they were so well behaved that never have we had so trouble-free a march. There were no complaints, delays or arguments. We crossed a small tributary stream and climbed the mountain-side opposite by a steep zigzagging track. This brought us high above the waterfall and from the ridge we saw our first view of the lake, filling the northern end of this upper valley and gleaming blue within a basin of brown precipitous rock. We descended gently towards Ringmo at its southern end. The land around the village is cultivated, growing potatoes, buckwheat, mustard and also a little wheat. There are small herds of yaks and goats. The south-eastern side of the lake is forested with pines and junipers. All around rise high rock-crags, in May still sprinkled liberally with snow, while the view back to the south is closed by the snow-peaks which rise beyond the lower valley.

The banks of the lake are flat and grassy at the southern end and here we set up camp, feeling that we had come at last to the paradise of the Buddha 'Boundless Light'. The water is edged with silver birch and the gleaming whiteness of the branches against the unearthly blue of the water is one of the most blissful things that I have known. Across the lake at the south-eastern corner is the monastery, built on the last piece of shore beyond which the rocks become sheer precipice (pl. XIa). In such a scene one loses all sense of urgency and practicability and Pasang's first suggestion was that we should make a boat. The villagers themselves seem never to have thought of doing this, for they are stolid, unimaginative folk, intent on their daily tasks. We went to visit the headman to warn him of our need for porters and to find out what food might be available. We passed a woman who sat in the sun at her loom, weaving a length of woollen cloth of many colours, a man who was chipping quietly away at prayer-stones and another who was drying meat in the sun. We found the headman together with his wife and daughter, ploughing a small field behind his house by means of a simple wooden share tipped with an iron point. He promised to arrange for porters if we would wait a few days, to which we readily agreed, and made us a present of a few potatoes.

There is a plentiful supply of wood, but these people possess no finer tool than an axe. Although they have a fast-flowing supply of water, they grind their grain laboriously with hand-mills. There used to be a water-mill, they said, but it had fallen into disrepair and no one had troubled to rebuild it. One could therefore scarcely expect them to direct their thoughts to the building of boats. Arable land is very scarce, but they have built the fifteen houses, of which this upper village consists, all over the better parts. They live mainly on buckwheat and potatoes and brew a sour kind of beer from their wheat. They eat the flesh of goats, sheep and yak, but treat themselves to it only very occasionally. The flesh we had seen being dried, was that of a goat, which had been killed by a yak just before our arrival; instead of making a feast of this tragedy, the owner was attempting to practise an economy for which the weather was generally far too warm. We bought some of his meat that day and it was palatable, but when we bought some dried pieces two days later, not even Takki Babu was prepared to eat it. They had no milk to sell us during our stay, but they are able to make some butter during the summer months, contenting themselves with mustard-oil the rest of the year. Racially they seem to be a tibetanized mixture like the people of Rohagāon and Tichu-rong, but they like to consider themselves superior in caste and will only marry among themselves or with partners from Pungmo (SI: Pudāmigāon). They spoke deprecatingly of the people of P'ar-lä and Tichu-rong as eaters of pork and chicken. They keep neither pigs nor chickens themselves.

One might expect people who own three sets of houses, to show some signs of material prosperity, but in fact there is none. They possess small stocks of food, cooking utensils, clothes and that is all. They weave their own clothes and are all dressed in Tibetan style. They spend the spring near the lake, planting their crops in early May. In the summer they descend to Murwa and do their planting there. In the winter they cross over to Palam, where they are sure of grazing for their animals.

It is about a mile in all across the fields and round the lake to the monastery, which consists of a small group of ten houses. There are two 'lamas', one a local man (pl. XIIa) and the other a Tibetan from Kham Province, who is married to a local woman and has been living here now for twenty-six years. There are twelve other men, some married, some unmarried, who interest themselves more or less in the religious life. They do so simply because they have inherited this interest from their fathers together with collections of texts, paintings and images. Only the two lamas seem to be really literate, although the others are quite capable of reciting the liturgies and so taking part in the ceremonies. Their collections of texts and images suggest, however, that their forefathers must have taken a serious interest in the p'ön doctrine, which they all still profess. The texts are all manuscripts, copied from those at Samling and perhaps from other places unknown to the present generation. Only the Kham Lama was still adding to his collection and possessed several quite passable thankas which he had had painted in Tarap. His clay images were not so good. The others possessed bronze images, brought from the Nepal Valley some time in the past. Their religious possessions are arranged in their private chapels, all equally dark and dusty. By overwhelming contrast one could climb up onto the roofs into a blaze of sunshine and gaze across the blue waters of the lake to the great snow-mountain beyond (SI: Kānjirobā, 22,880 ft.). There is also a separate temple for general use, but so neglected that it will fall down before long. The frescoes on the side-walls were of the main p'ön divinities, with which we were now familiar. At this stage we were still engaged in noting new iconographic forms and fitting names to them, but there was nothing that remained unidentified in this monastery except for some lamas and yogins, whose paintings covered the back wall of the temple. On the thankas the main divinities, 'Composite Conqueror', Wäl-sä, the four supreme manifestations, Shen-rap as Śākyamuni, the 'Victorious One', appeared again and again. The bronze images in use were generally Buddhist, mostly of Akshobhya, identified with Shen-rap, and Amitāyus, identified with 'Shen-God White Light'. These images had all been brought from the Nepal Valley by former generations; p'ön images proper could only have been obtained there by special order. The only four of such a kind were in the possession of the local 'lama' and were clearly identifiable as the four supreme p'ön manifestations (pp. 47–8). It was a great surprise to me therefore, when the owner informed us that they were just goddesses, especially since all four were clearly masculine. Presumably the original owner, this old man's grandfather, must have known what images he was ordering. But nowadays, such unreflecting ignorance has become all too typical of this area. The most interesting person here was certainly the Lama of Kham. He received us in an hospitable manner, offering us tsamba and buttered tea; the next day he visited us at our camp, answering questions concerning unfamiliar abbreviations in the texts and giving information about the locality. Thus we learned that in ancient times there was a village where the lake now is; it was flooded and submerged by a spiteful demoness, fleeing from the wrath of the buddha-magician 'Lotus-Born', when he was intent of converting Tibet. She gave the local people a turquoise, making them promise not to tell her pursuer that she had passed that way. But 'Lotus-Born' by his superior powers caused the turquoise to become a lump of dung. The people were angry at what they supposed to be the trickery of the demoness and revealed where she had gone. She in her turn took revenge by causing the flood. While he told this tale, the lama sat by one of our tents, wrapped in his coarse red homespun, his hair, part natural, part false, twisted up in p'ön-po style to form a great topknot, in one hand a small copper prayer-wheel and on his lap a few pages of text. He sipped buttered tea from one of our polythene cups and conversed with perfect ease and decorum (pl. X*b*). He was the first cultured Tibetan we had met on these travels, and his company pleased us immensely. He manifested no surprise at meeting travellers like us and no wondering curiosity at our tents and equipment. He just met us on equal terms as fellow-beings.

We spent three days by the lake, delighting in our surroundings and visiting the village and the monastery. There were several chötens along the track from the lake and one at the very entrance to the village was of special interest (pl. XI*b*). It was painted inside, but no one could assist us in identifying the frescoes, so we had to rely upon our own limited knowledge. Around the walls there were eight buddha-figures. Three of them were recognizable as the Buddhas of the Three Times and the remainder as the Buddhas of the Five Families, Brilliant' (*Vairocana*), 'Imperturbable' (*Akshobhya*), 'Jewel-Born'

(*Ratnasambhava*), 'Boundless Light' (*Amitābha*) and 'Infallible Success' (*Amoghasiddhi*). The only unexpected feature was Amitābha's throne, which was supported by tigers instead of by the usual peacocks. The ceiling was far more difficult, for it was divided into nine squares, each occupied by a mandala (mystic circle) of miniature divinities (pl. XII*b*). To the wondering amusement of the villagers we would lie on our backs peering up into this dark ceiling with the help of binoculars and a torch, shifting our position now this way and now that, as we strove to see one divinity after another the right way up.

The central mandala is itself divided into nine squares, of which the centre one is the true heart of the mandala, containing the 'Blazing Gem' (*nor-bu 'od-'bar*), which represents the supreme nature of p'ön, and the four supreme manifestations (pp. 47–8). The remaining eight squares of the central mandala are each divided into twenty-five squares, in each of which there was a letter of the Tibetan alphabet, which remained however beyond the scope of our strained vision. The other eight mandalas are best listed around the points of the compass:

NE. 1. The 'Precious Master' (*gu-ru rin-po-che*) (blue) with partner (red), surrounded by an entourage of twenty-four divinities and four door-keepers.

E. 2. 'Composite Conqueror', surrounded by the six chief tranquil divinities, eight attendant divinities and four door-keepers.

SE. 3. The 'Precious Master' (blue) with partner (red), surrounded by four supreme manifestations, blue, white, yellow, red, eight attendant divinities, seemingly *ḍākinī*,[a] and four door-keepers.

S. 4. Wäl-sä (white), surrounded by five garuḍas, eight attendant goddesses and four door-keepers.

---

[a] The *ḍākinī*-s are the feminine partners of tantric yogins. Sometimes they are real women, sometimes imagined forms. They are the means to the realization of mystic experience, conceived as the unity of two co-efficients ('two-in-one', tib. *zung-'jug*).

SW.   5. Central Garuḍa surrounded by eight garuḍas.

W.   6. The 'Precious Master' (blue) and partner (red) with 'All Good' (white) and partner (white) above. They are surrounded by four supreme emanations together with partners and attended by ḍākinīs and other figures, two of whom ride white horses and one a white bird, while a fourth seems to be a lama flanked by two more ḍākinīs.

NW.   7. The 'Precious Master' (blue) with partner (red), surrounded by four ḍākinīs, blue, white, yellow and red.

N.   8. Wäl-sä (blue) with 'All Good' (white) above his head, surrounded by four emanations (inner circle) and nineteen yogins (central and outer circle).

The blue figure with red partner, which appears at the centre of four of the mandalas, is identified as the 'Precious Master' (*gu-ru rin-po-che*), viz. Padmasambhava, on the authority of the Lama of Pungmo, in whose temple we later saw the same painting. In any case he is represented not as an historical being, but as a supreme 'buddha-body', for these colours are those of the 'Holder of the Vajra' (*Vajradhara*) and his partner, who symbolize supreme buddhahood for all the great yogins (see p. 77). Other problems of detailed identification remained, but we were delighted with this ceiling as one of the finest pieces of painting we had seen on our travels, and it was all the more remarkable since there is now no one in the village, who can do anything comparable. One can only assume that 150 and more years ago Tibetan culture flourished in this remote valley and that as a direct result of attacks from the south its whole spirit has been destroyed.

Pungmo

Leaving most of our belongings in the headman's house, we took two men with us to carry sufficient luggage for two or three days and set out on the short journey to Pungmo (SI: Pudāmigāon). We left Ringmo Village by the track that keeps above the right bank of the stream. At first it ascends a little, so that one can look back to the lake beyond the village and the encircling cliffs of rock that close the view. A little further on the great waterfall becomes visible plunging down below (pl. XIII). Here the track begins to zigzag in a steep descent, so that after passing the deserted houses of Palam, one finds oneself once more walking along the right bank of the river with the waterfall out of sight behind. We turned up the Pungmo Stream (SI: Dojām Kholā) and after more than two hours walking passed some chötens and reached the village. It began to rain heavily at once, so we had little choice but to settle there as best we could and postpone our visit to the monastery until the following day. There is a small temple in the village, quite uncared for, containing a large image of the 'Victorious One' (p. 50) and three smaller ones of the 'Conquerors' of the Three Times. The entrance-chöten resembled the one at Ringmo. There were nine mandalas on the ceiling, too worn away to be identifiable. There were also eight figures around the walls, but instead of confirming old identifications, these created new problems for us. On the four walls outside were depicted in little plaques the four animals of the directions according to regular Buddhist iconography, elephants (east), horses (south), peacocks (west) and garuḍas (north). The whole complex seemed to be a mixture of Buddhist and p'ön iconography, yet there is no doubt that this chöten was conceived as purely p'ön-po, so very naïve are these cheerful plagiarists. In any case there was no one in the village to enlighten us.

The night was disturbed by barking dogs and biting insects. The next morning we left early and leaving our helpers in the village, ascended a side-valley to the west. It is by this route

66

that one can reach Tibrikot over an 18,000 foot pass to the south-west (see p. 29). But we kept to the northern side of the valley and within two hours came to the monastery which is situated above a small tributary stream. We found the lama in his temple, which was certainly the finest which we had yet seen. He remembered us from the brief meeting at Dri-k'ung of three weeks before (p. 38), but I remembered him not at all, so very different was the general impression now. He was friendly, but calm and restrained. He asked how old we were and we in turn learned that he was forty-three. He told us that his grandfather, who had been acknowledged as an 'incarnation', had founded this monastery, and that it had passed to his father and now to himself; so far he had remained celibate. There were about a hundred manuscripts and he showed us some that his grandfather had copied and others that he had copied himself. This work had mostly been done at Samling, where he urged us to go. The walls of the temple were painted and we recognized the four supreme p'ön manifestations, the 'Composite Conqueror', Wäl-sä and the 'Tiger-God'. There was another divinity which we had seen in the temple at Ringmo and whose identification we could now confirm. This was the 'God of the Dart' (*phur-pa'i lha*), who is also known as 'Dragon-Prince' (*'brug-gsas*). He has three faces, blue, red and white. He is dark blue himself and clasps a partner of lighter hue. His two lower hands clasp a dart behind her back and he waves darts in his other four hands. His body is winged like that of Garuḍa. Lastly there was the 'Precious Master' (*gu-ru rin-po-che*), as he appeared in the chöten at Ringmo. His body is blue and he has six arms, of which the top two hold sun and moon, the next two a skull and a vajra and the lower two, which also clasp his red partner, hold a drum and a bell.

The lama invited us to his house, which was about fifty yards beyond, and offered us tsamba and buttered tea. Also living with him were his old mother, his two brothers and their children. We then learned that the family was from Kham in eastern Tibet. In the top storey of this house there was another temple, which the lama was having made, but the paintings were far inferior and the *terra-cotta* images, which had come from Tarap, were of no artistic merit whatsoever. These people were so friendly to us, that we regretted the shortness of our visit. The family possesses a few small terraced fields cut into the mountain-side, but their wealth comes mainly from trading and we heard that they own some fifty yaks and cross-breeds (*dzo*). The lama also receives offerings for his services, which are in demand throughout the whole area.

We left in the afternoon, collected our porters at the village and after a hasty meal set out on the return journey. By evening we reached Palam, where I resolved to stay. Having passed a quiet night by the empty houses, we ascended in the morning above the waterfall to the wonderful view of the lake above. These villagers dwell in one of the most glorious places on earth without being remotely aware of it. But how should they be? It is we who have somehow grown weary of the benefits of modern life, who can tarry in such a place with keen enjoyment. We imagine that we should be content with the simplicity of their life, scheming how we would improve this within proper limits. We would repair the temple, rebuild the mill and import tools for better craftsmanship. We would build a house by the lake, maintain yaks and sheep and improve the crops many-fold. But these were all idle dreams, for at the same time we were planning the next stage of our journey to Shey.

We spent only two more days by the lake, although the headman was urging us to wait longer. The pass had not yet been crossed that year and he insisted that it was still too early. We compromised by agreeing on lighter loads, so when we left on the morning of May 8th, it was with an odd assortment of porters. There were six men, an elderly woman, two girls of about twenty years, a small boy and six goats. Three more girls joined the party on their own account. The boy and the goats all belonged to a Tibetan, named She-rap, who happened to be staying in the village. He was a man from the plains to the far

68

north, who wandered about making a living as best he could, working in the fields of the villagers, trading in a small way or cutting prayer-stones. He now loaded his goats with twenty pounds each of our rice and wheat, all neatly packed in little saddle-bags. His son, who was eleven years old, carried his father's provisions in a small basket on his back. All our other porters were villagers of Ringmo and since nobody's load was more than 60 lb., they all set out cheerfully enough. I too was eager to know what the lake looked like at the other end and even more curious to know what kind of a monastery Shey Gomba (SI: Syā Gömpa) would prove to be. Of Dolpo as a cultural unit we had as yet no idea, for at this time even the name 'Dolpo' was unknown to us.

Vajradhara
(*see* p. 77)

III

THE LAND OF DOLPO

THE PHOKSUMDO PASS

The track climbs round the western side of the Phoksumdo Lake, keeping close under the cliffs that tower above. Where it can go no further one must trust oneself to a slender gangway of silver birch, supported on pegs driven into crevices in the rock (pl. XIV*a*). Half a mile further a stream descends from the glaciers of Kānjirobā, thus making a breach in the enclosing walls. Once across this little valley, one must climb high up above the cliffs, whence one can look back towards the southern end of the lake and the snow-mountains beyond the lower valley. The porters advanced slowly, but we who were free from heavy loads, could forget the effort of climbing by turning back to gaze upon the entrancing scene of water, forest and mountain. The track descended towards the northern end of the lake where the silver birch was just bursting into leaf. The water was milky green in colour and so disturbed by the wind, that one might imagine oneself standing by the sea at home. How completely different are the two ends of this lake, which is barely two miles long! We were now in a wide flat valley, making our way through gorse and over the murky streams which meandered here and there, abandoning the mother-bed. The porters were so slow that Pasang stayed behind to bring them on, while I continued with Takki Babu, hoping to come upon a suitable site for setting up camp. But before long we were caught in a maze of undergrowth and muddy channels; after helpless floundering we reached the river itself, a swollen, turgid, swirling mass. Retracing our steps, we lighted on a little island of firm mud, where we awaited the rest of the party, hoping that they might know of a way out of

70

this labyrinth. They arrived in due course, only to advise us that we could progress no further until the morning, when the river, now swollen with melted snow, would have subsided for a while, thus allowing us to make a crossing. We set up camp where we were, for there was no shortage of brushwood and we would just have to be content with muddy water for cooking our evening meal.

Thus we began our next day's journey by wading painfully through ice-cold water. The valley rapidly became a gorge, through which the track wound its way, adorned with blue primulas and willow catkins of various species. Then it forked and we began to climb up the course of the right-hand stream, which was now leading us due north. Progress became difficult at once and we had to make our way first to one side of the torrent and then to the other. Since we were the first to pass this year, the bridges were all broken and Takki Babu and She-rap were busily employed repairing them. This type of bridge is a simple affair, consisting of three or four light trunks of silver birch laid across from rock to rock and secured by piling heavy stones on their ends. On the trunks are laid flat stones, which provide a level if unstable foothold. We had to cross several bridges of this kind, but only one goat out of our whole party lost courage and fell into the torrent. She-rap who was standing by, seized the frightened creature by its horns, and we suffered nothing worse than twenty pounds of rice soaked prematurely. This gorge also provided an unexpected pleasure, namely some wild rhubarb. When we stopped for our morning meal, we cooked it with sugar and mixing it with condensed milk, placed it in the snow to cool. It provided a dish, which in those harsh circumstances seemed to us sheer luxury. Eventually the gorge became a smooth glacial valley and the muddy torrent disappeared beneath beds of frozen snow. Progress became easy once more and we were able to camp comfortably enough under the shelter of the cliffs at the very head of the valley. The porters had carried up some brushwood for themselves and we prepared soup on the petrol stove. We were now at a height of about 17,000 feet, 3,000 feet above the lake and almost as much again below the pass.

The next morning we ascended the last stage (pl. XIV*b*). There was little snow on the southern side, but advance was slow because of the fine slaty scree which caused loss of height at every step. The top of the pass was snow-covered and the edge beyond was a delight of frozen snow and glittering cornices. There were summits on the range that we were crossing, only slightly higher than where we stood, and we looked northwards to a land of summits mostly of 20,000–21,000 feet. The valleys had been cut out by glaciers and dug deep by the rivers, but if we were to trust our maps, we would not expect to find a village at much less than 15,000 feet and many of them would be appreciably higher. We were wondering if they would be occupied all the year round, for if this was so, we might well claim this as the highest region of permanent human occupation on the earth's surface.

Pasang cut steps at the top of the glistening slope that stretched down below us and when we were safely below this steep and brittle section we swept down in a superb glissade. The porters followed down in our steps and then allowed their loads to slide before them, checking them by the ropes. It was now Thursday, May 10th, Ascension Day, the day of crossing our first major pass and of our entry into the land which we would always remember with delight. Only the poor goats were unhappy in the snow and She-rap concerned on their account. Then we were slushing through the beginnings of another river, the headwaters of the torrent that passes below Shey and Phijor, flowing northwards to join the other streams that drain this great upland region and then westwards, where they become a main tributary of the Karnāli. We were soon following our new river downstream and looking back we saw how formidable was the pass from the northern side. It is doubtful if a loaded porter could cross this way so early in the year. We ourselves had made an early crossing, but the women had shown themselves as hardy as the men and so high were their spirits that they were just then engaged in pelting the unfortunate Hemrāj with snowballs. When we reached the first signs of scrub, we stopped to boil water and make tea; then we followed the track down to Shey.

SHEY

Shey Gomba (SI: Syā Gömpa) stands above the right bank of the river (SI: Sibu Khola) about an hour's gradual descent below the snow and at the junction with another stream which flows down from the east.[a] The contours show its height as about 16,000 feet and this would seem to be a reasonable estimate. It is quite an impressive collection of red-washed buildings ringed with prayer-walls and chötens (pl. XVIb); it was disconcerting, however, to find every door closed against us. The headman of Ringmo had warned us that we would find no one at Shey until later in the month, but we had not expected his words to be literally true. There are five houses in the immediate vicinity of the temple and three more about a quarter of a mile downstream. We wandered round the deserted buildings, marvelling at the vast quantity of prayer-stones, and eventually decided to camp by the door of the temple, where there was a balcony that would give shelter to our luggage. At last an inquisitive little boy betrayed the fact that one house was occupied, so Pasang went to investigate, accompanied by the Ringmo girls. Reassured by the sound of familiar voices, his mother opened the door, which she had barred in fear at our approach. She told us that all the active members of the community had gone to the north to bring back the yaks and sheep for the summer, so that there was no one else except the old

---

[a] Shey Gomba, 'Crystal Monastery' (*shel dgon-pa*) is named after the 'Crystal Mountain of Dolpo' (*dol-po'i shel gyi ri bo*) which rises above the pass over which we had come. The misleading Survey of India spelling 'Syā' is explained on p. 275.

lama nearby and a woman with a sore leg in one of the houses beyond. She was still a little concerned at the presence of strangers, but consented to sell us some brushwood and lend us a large water-pot. As we returned to our camp by the temple-door, Pasang noticed quantities of young nettles growing from the walls, so Takki Babu was instructed to pick them and make soup. This was the first Ka-gyü-pa monastery that I had visited, so it was by no means inappropriate that we should have as our evening meal the food on which Mila Räpa, the most famous of Ka-gyü-pa lamas, had lived while he endured the rigours of solitary meditation. But no doubt our nettle-soup was better spiced than his had ever been, and served with rice, it seemed almost a delicacy.

The next morning we paid off our porters, who returned unladen the way we had come. They had agreed to assist us as far as Shey and since they were quite unwilling to come any further, we had no choice but to let them go, although it seemed that we would be stranded. We decided in any case to stay that day at Shey, for the last three days had been parti-cularly strenuous, and who knows what might materialize if one is patient? But on this particular day nothing at all happened that we could turn to our advantage. The woman supplied us with more wood and we learned that she was the daughter of the old lama, who was all but confined to his house next to the temple. When she heard that we were planning to return to Shey later on, she said that she would prefer not to open the temple for us. We protested mildly, but in the plan that we were now beginning to formulate, Shey would remain the the centre for our supplies and we would certainly return there on more than one occasion. The woman advised us to go to Saldang, where we would find Nyi-ma Tshe-ring, the most in-fluential man in the whole of this region, who would give us all the help we needed. We had heard of him as far away as Dunyer and so this confirmed our immediate plan. We also learned that there was another lama, a man of about thirty years, who was staying in a hermitage half a mile away, but since he had not broken his vow of solitude for three years, there was no question of disturbing him on our account. The other inhabitants of these houses would be returning with their animals in about a week and we now understood that the 'north', whither they had gone, referred to the high Tibetan plateau beyond the frontier range about six days' journey away, where the animals were regularly sent for winter pasture. No man of any kind appeared during that day, so we had no choice on the morrow but to shoulder a few necessities and set out for Saldang. We carried a tent, our bedding, some clothes and enough food for four days, leaving our boxes and stocks of grain in the house of the lama's daughter. Takki Babu carried about 60 lb., Pasang about 40, and Hemrāj and I about 30 each. The woman had described the route to us, and Pasang with unerring sense followed it without hesitation. We walked up the stream to the east and then turned north up a smaller tributary, leaving the track to Tarap to continue eastwards. So far we had not seen a single tree on this side of the pass; we walked across grassy mountains and ascended by the rocky stream. The ascent to the pass (about 19,000 feet) was an easy one. We might well have been in the Cairngorms in spring, when the rounded summits are still covered in snow, and snow still fills the craggy gullies.

NAMGUNG

From the top of the pass a new land lay revealed—the typical Tibetan landscape, bare grey-brown mountains, white clouds against a lucid blue sky and no sign of tree or forest. While we rested by the summit cairn, sheltering from a freezing west wind, a woman and a little boy appeared, ascending the pass from the other side and driving two yak cross-breeds before them. She told us in response to our enquiry that they had set out from Saldang at dawn and that Nyi-ma Tshe-ring's house was certainly beyond our reach that day, but we could stay the night at Namgung Village, a place which did not appear on our maps.

The descent, always towards the north, was a long and tiring one, but at last we caught sight of Namgung Monastery, its red walls perched like an eyrie against the rocks. As we descended, the houses below the temple gradually came into view. We crossed a gorge, which as we now saw divided the village into two, and came to a halt by the first house. We called to a villager on the other side of the gulf, but he merely beckoned to us to come over to him. This was a small matter, but typified the independent nature of the people with whom we would now be dealing. They are in fact Tibetans and differ racially in no way from their fellows on the other side of the political frontier. A difference is sometimes suggested by the name *bhotia*, which is generally applied to peoples of Tibetan stock who live within the frontiers of India and Nepal, but this name is just the Indo-Nepalese term for Tibetan. At the same time these people know full well on which side of the frontier they live. Some of them can speak a little Nepāli, but we met no one capable of reading or writing it. Their own language is Tibetan—a dialect not far removed from that of central Tibet, so that conversation with them presented no difficulty to Pasang and little enough to me. They are all more or less literate in Tibetan. But just now we were concerned for our night's lodging and since the villager would not come to us, Pasang climbed across the gorge to meet him on his own ground. Meanwhile I began collecting nettles which grew by the walls of the first house, unassisted by Takki Babu, who showed little enthusiasm for this delicacy. Other villagers gathered around and once satisfied that we were harmless and friendly, they led the way to a little house and said we were welcome to use it. There was a small yard nearby, where we could erect a tent, and so we settled in and began our cooking with the brushwood and dried dung that they brought us. The house was filled with acrid smoke, but we were at least protected from the wind, if not from the small crowd of friendly and inquisitive villagers who very quickly surrounded us. The house belonged to the sacristan (*sku-gnyer*), who was living up at the monastery and so had no immediate use for it. He asked us about the route we had come and our future intentions, was delighted to hear that we were pilgrims and promised to show us around the temple in the morning. The man we had shouted at across the gorge brought us a measure of tsamba and a woman from a house nearby produced a jar of chang at our request.

The next morning we visited the temple which is built against the cliff on the far side of the gorge. It is undoubtedly old and it is significant that Namgung should have given its name to the whole district from Namdo and Saldang to Karang and Phijor (see p. 83). Like Shey it is a Ka-gyü-pa monastery of the Karma-pa sect. The order of the Ka-gyü-pas (see p. 38 fn.) was established in Tibet by *Marpa* of *Lho-brag* (1012–97), who was a great translator and collector of texts. He made several journeys to Nepal where he met the renowned yogin, Nāropa, who gave him initiation into the mystery of Hevajra, a combination of mental concentration and sacramental ritual, which claimed to produce buddhahood in the course of one human life. Nāropa and his master Tilopa are two of the eighty-four great yogins (*siddha*), in whose circles were transmitted those weird texts, the tantras, to which Tibetan religion owes so much of its symbolism. Their name for the supreme buddha-body is 'Holder of the Vajra' (*Vajradhara*), who is represented as a crowned buddha, seated cross-legged, his arms crossed before his breast and clasping in his hands the *vajra*, which symbolizes compassionate activity, and the bell, representing the pure sound of the doctrine which is perfect wisdom (p. 203). Marpa's chief disciple was the famous Tibetan yogin Mila Räpa, who is believed to have gained the supreme enlightenment of buddhahood and the concomitant miraculous powers in the course of one life.[a] His chief disciples, *Ras-chung* and *sGam-po-pa*, had many followers and subsequently the Ka-gyü-pas ('Order of the Transmitted Word') split into four sects. The Karma-pa sect, which is represented at Shey and Namgung, originated with *sGam-po-pa's* greatest disciple, who was named *Dus gsum*

[a] see W. Y. Evans Wentz, *Tibet's Great Yogi Milarepa*, O.U.P., 1928.

mkhyen-pa ('Knower of the Three Times') and nicknamed *Karma-pa* ('Man of Karma'), as were also his successors.[a] *Dus gsum mkhyen-pa* came from eastern Tibet and although he seems to have been chiefly active in the central provinces of Ü and Tsang, the next incarnation Karma pakshi, spent many years in Mongolia and China. Kublai Khan is said to have been his disciple. It is probably thanks to the Mongolian connection that his followers together with the Sa-kya-pas, whose hierarchs were also welcome visitors at the court of the Great Khan, became predominant in central Tibet. It was not until the sixteenth century that they were ousted by the new order of the Ge-luk-pas (Yellow Hats), who had now secured for themselves the support of the Mongols. These remote regions of the Himalayas, having been converted to Buddhism by the Sa-kya-pas and the Karma-pas, have remained totally unaffected by subsequent developments in Tibet itself. Rather we observe a separatist tendency to abandon Sa-kya-pa and Karma-pa traditions for the more popular Nying-ma-pa ones, which centre around Padmasambhava. Thus the main hall of Namgung Monastery seems at first to be dominated by a large *terra-cotta* image of this wonder-working lama. He appears again in bronze on the right next to an image of Śākyamuni. On the left is an image of 'Lord Spell-Power Victorious' (*Jo-bo sngags-dbang rnam-rgyal*), founder of the temple. There are some fine painted banners (*thanka*), especially of Śākyamuni, 'Boundless Life' (*Amitāyus*) and the Goddess of Wisdom (*Prajñāpāramitā*). Around the images is arranged a set of the canonical 'discourses' (*sūtra*) in thirty manuscript volumes. Above them all is a large bronze image, very beautiful indeed, of the Buddha 'Holder of the Vajra' (*Vajradhara*). There is another small temple on the next storey containing a collection of *thankas* and Tibetan printed texts. This monastery has no lama at present and is cared for by two brothers, one of whom is the sacristan,

[a] see Roerich, *The Blue Annals*, pp. 473–80, 485–7 and the important article by H. E. Richardson, 'The Karma-pa Sect. A Historical Note', *Journal of the Royal Asiatic Society*, 1958, pp. 139–164.

who had lent us his house. Several of the villagers are 'lamas' in the popular sense, viz. capable of reciting the liturgies and so playing their part in ceremonies. Also there are lamas at Namdo who are invited on special occasions. The villagers of Saldang make regular offerings of grain to this monastery.

We clambered down the steep bank and followed the track down the gorge for about 300 yards to another little temple. It is new and manifestly Nying-ma-pa with its bright paintings of 'Lotus-Born' manifested as 'Union of the Precious Ones', the tutelary divinity 'Unity of All the Blessed', Buddha Heruka and the rest.[a] We learned that it was built eleven years ago at the inspiration of the Lama of Shang and that it is now occupied by one of his disciples, a man from Mugu. We were unable to see him, as he was living in solitary meditation in an inner room, but he broke silence to speak a few words to us through the partition. The houses of Namgung are scattered over their scanty fields and number only fifteen or so. I doubt if there are more than fifty inhabitants. The height is probably about 16,000 feet.

SALDANG

In the afternoon we continued down to Saldang (SI: Sāldāng-gāon), traversing the mountains to the north of the Namgung gorge, until from the head of a long, even slope we saw flocks of sheep and the first of the houses far below us. We hastened down to ask for Nyi-ma Tshe-ring and were directed still further down and round the mountain-side. His house proved

[a] 'Union of the Precious Ones' is a special manifestion of 'Lotus-Born' (*Padmasambhava*), conceived as the unity of the ancient Buddhist trilogy of Buddha, Doctrine, Assembly. 'Unity of All the Blessed' is the 'Lotus Lord of Dance' (*Padmanarteśvara*) of Indian tradition. In origin he can be closely associated with the Hindu god Śiva, but he is accepted in Nying-ma-pa tradition as a form of 'Glancing Eye' (*Avalokiteśvara*). It is in preferences such as these that one notes differences between the different orders of Tibetan Buddhism. These divinities are described fully in *BH*, p. 228 ff.

to be the last of all, standing on a spur some 300 yards above the river and resembling from a distance as much a fort as a dwelling. We made our way round the bare ridges of the dry, eroded valley and drew near to the little oasis which represented his estate. The ground was levelled into fields, which could be irrigated from a small stream. There were a few clumps of willow-trees, some scanty grass above, and no other sign of present vegetation. A party of five or six men and women were engaged in planting barley. The entrance was guarded by a fierce mastiff with a red scruff round its neck, whose barking became a frenzied fury at our approach. One of the men signalled to us and following his direction, we climbed up onto the fields beyond the range of the animal's chain. A slightly portly man of about sixty-five years, who was supervising the work, came forward, rather grudgingly it seemed, to meet us. We explained briefly who and what we were, and learned that he was Nyi-ma Tshe-ring. Pasang referred enthusiastically to the wondrous fertility of these fields in the midst of a mountainous wilderness, but this friendly overture evoked no response. We next asked where we might camp and he pointed bluntly to an especially stony place by a chöten outside his grounds. We protested gently that it would be a rather uncomfortable place, at which he led us to a corner of one of his fields and left us there without more ado. We put up the only tent we had, feeling very conscious of our lack of most things needful for a decent camp. Takki Babu went to ask for a water-pot and returned with one that leaked. He went to ask for wood and was given a mere handful of brush. We felt quite saddened, for we had expected Nyi-ma Tshe-ring at least to lend us a room in his house until we could collect the rest of our belongings, and now we seemed to be faced with blank unfriendliness.

In retrospect this initial reception seems all the more surprising, for from now on we were to experience in this land nothing but friendliness and helpfulness. There were probably two reasons: firstly Nyi-ma Tshe-ring's own slow and stolid nature—once satisfied with us, he helped to the full; secondly

IX.

a. Monastic dance at P'ar-lä. (p. 52)
*b. **Magar villagers of Tārakot. (p. 52)***
c. gShen-lha 'od-dkar. *Fresco in the chöten*
below P'ar-lä. (pp. 48 & 54)

X.

a. Sa-trig yer-sangs. *Fresco in the chöten below P'ar-lä. (pp. 48 & 54)*

b. The Lama of Kham. (p. 63)

XI.

a. Ringmo Monastery. (p. 60)
b. Ringmo chötens. (p. 63)

XII.

a. Ringmo Lama. (p. 61)

*b. Ceiling of the entrance
chöten of Ringmo
(p. 64)*

XIII.

a. The upper valley of Ringmo with the lake just visible. (pp. 59 & 66)
b. The great water-fall, which drains the lake. The trees below are
60–70 feet tall.

XIV.

a. The route round the Phoksumdo Lake. (p. 70)
b. Ascent of the Phoksumdo Pass. (p. 72)

XV.

a. Yang-tsher Gomba. Main group of buildings. (p. 86)
b. Row of prayer-wheels, decorated with stone plaques. (p. 91)

XVI.

a. Yang-tsher Gomba. General view. (p. 86)
b. Shey Gomba, looking south towards the Phoksumdo Pass. (p. 73)

that fact that we arrived as a small party of total strangers without a single porter from a neighbouring village to vouch for our good name. Pasang and I now returned to the great man's presence and explained politely that we were expecting to pay for the wood and for any other services; we then produced the letter of commendation given us by the Nepalese Government. As no one else could read Nepāli, we had to provide an oral translation into Tibetan on our own behalf; no one seemed particularly impressed. We returned to our tent, however, with sufficient wood and another water-pot. We made tea and then Pasang went back alone determined to establish friendly relations. He entered the house and returned an hour later, saying that we were all invited to come inside and that Nyi-ma Tshe-ring was a really splendid fellow.

After our meal we passed through the courtyard and a bare lower room and ascended by the usual knotched ladder to a dark and smoky upper storey. There were six people in the room including Nyi-ma Tshe-ring, who motioned us to be seated on grubby carpets against the blackened wall. A fire burned in a brazier and extra light was supplied by chips of pine, which were lit one after another upon a low stand. Everyone was busy eating from their bowls of barley tsamba moistened with buttered tea. We were offered some chang which was clear and delicious and an intelligent conversation began about conditions in Pasang's country, in central Nepal and in the outside world, although our hosts' ideas of the world beyond India were very vague. We learned that Nyi-ma Tshe-ring's wife had died a year before and that since his son was married and maintained a separate house, this establishment was being run by his grandchildren, all four of whom were present eating their supper. I turned the conversation to local affairs and Nyi-ma Tshe-ring insisted that he was in no real sense a headman. He had come from Namdo, he said, where two of his brothers and his own son were living. He had acquired the property at Saldang by marriage, for his father-in-law had had no son of his own. There were headmen in all the villages, who had some authority, but he himself had none. By indirect inquiries, however, we learned that he was so greatly esteemed throughout the whole region, that he was accepted as the leading man and many would come to lay their problems before him and seek his advice. He seemed to have shown himself a natural leader in troubles that afflicted this country some eight or nine years ago. Bands of brigands, known locally as the 'Ha-shi-ka-wa', had come from the Tibetan plains of the north and begun to lay waste the villages, burning, slaying and plundering. He had organized the villagers for defence and beaten off these raiders. In recognition of his services the Rāna Government of Nepal had sent him a rifle and other presents. The rifle eventually reached him, but the other presents had been so diminished by the hands through which they had passed on the way, that little or nothing remained. He seemed to be equally renowned for works of peace, for he had financed the building of the new temple which we had visited that morning at Namgung, and was well acquainted with the Lama of Shang, whom he clearly held in great respect. Every year he adds to the numerous prayer-walls which line the track between Saldang and Namdo and he was just now having a large new prayer-wheel made for the old Saldang temple.

It was during this conversation that we heard the name 'Dolpo' for the first time and learned that it referred to the whole region bounded on the west by the great watershed which we had crossed above Phoksumdo and on the south by the Dhaulagiri massif (map, p. 296). To the north-west beyond Phopa it is separated by several days of difficult travel from the nearest villages of the Mugu Karnāli. To the south-east beyond Tsharka (SI: Chhàrkābhot) it is likewise separated by bare mountains from the valley of the Kāli Gandaki. To the north and the north-east it is bounded by the great Tibetan plain, which these people refer to simply as the 'north' (*byang*). It is on this side that their country is most easily accessible and it is thither that they send their cattle and sheep for seven to eight months of the year, when their own mountains are void of pasture. There they are cared for by the nomads (*'brog-pa*) who receive five pounds (2½ *bre*) of grain for each sheep and ten pounds (5 *bre*) for each head of cattle as well as a natural right to the produce of the dri-mo (*'bri-mo*—female of the yak) and the dzo-mo (female cross-breed). They have to return to the owners the hides of any animals that die. The sheep are sheared on their return to Dolpo in the summer. We learned that the villages are occupied the whole year round. The main trading exodus to Tichu-rong takes place in July and except for a few adventurous spirits who visit Pokhara and Kathmandu in the winter everyone stays at home spinning and weaving and giving more time to religion than they have to spare in the summer. We pressed our questions about Dolpo as a unit and were told that it consisted of four districts, Namgung, Panzang, Tarap and Tsharbung.[a] We told Nyi-ma Tshe-ring that the area was marked on our maps as Dānbhansār and Chharkābhot. He accepted the latter name, pronouncing it, as we had already learned, as Tsharka without the suffix -*bhot* (p. 276), but corrected the first one to Dastapla, interpreted as meaning 'ten townships'. These he said were the names that the 'Nepalese' had given to the country.[b] As I sat in the dim light peering at the map, this strange land where we now found ourselves, gradually gained in coherence. With Nyi-ma Tshe-ring's assistance we began to form plans to visit it throughout. He promised to help us to bring whatever we needed of our stores from Shey, and when these had arrived, we decided to go north to Yang-tsher Monastery (SI: Yānjar Gömpā) and then visit the eastern side through Shimen (SI: Simengāon) and Ting–khyu (SI: Tingjegāon). We could then return to Saldang by way of Koma and thence go through Karang to Phijor and Samling. From there we could easily visit Shey again and so be within

[a] Tsharbung is a composite name including Tsharka and Barbung. The district name of Barbung has been given by the surveyors to the upper Bheri. Panzang (Pānjāng) and Namgung (Nāngung) they have also applied to streams. See p. 285.

[b] The term used for Nepalese is the old Tibetan word *mon-pa*, which refers vaguely to the people of the valleys south of Tibet.

83

reach of our stores. We would pass through Tarap and Tsharka when we finally left Dolpo on our way down to the Kāli Gandaki (see p. 297). Pasang and I returned to the tent, feeling much happier after the evening's conversation, while Hemrāj and Takki Babu remained to sleep in the house.

The next morning a villager appeared very early with a horse, saying that he had been sent by Nyi-ma Tshe-ring to assist us in getting whatever we needed from Shey. Pasang and Takki Babu set out with him on this essential mission, leaving me to rest and write with Hemrāj as company. Oppressed by the stony treelessness of our surroundings, we moved the tent to the next field, where a clump of willows was in sight and the stream much nearer. Here we spent two peaceful days, receiving occasional visits from members of the household, to whom a plastic mug or soap-box, not to mention a petrol cooking-stove, was a thing of wonder and admiration. Pasang returned the following evening, bringing another tent, more food, my box of photographic equipment, notebooks and medicines. We bought some barley tsamba from Nyi-ma Tshe-ring, but we were still depending on our own supplies of wheat and rice. Butter was difficult to obtain, because it was early in the season. We received as a present two great goose-eggs, which had come from Tibet; one was eatable. In Dolpo there are no chickens and also no potatoes, although these would certainly grow. We foresaw lean times ahead of us, but learned to our great joy that wheat grew at Phijor. It was now impossible to make leavened bread properly, for brushwood and smouldering dung would not heat the tin-oven sufficiently and our supplies of oil-fuel were too limited for so lengthy a process as baking. Tsamba became the staple food for the rest of the party and flat wheat-cakes for me. Our rice was reserved as a luxury.

We decided to visit Namdo and the rest of Saldang on our return to Nyi-ma Tshe-ring's house, so on the following morning we set out for Yang-tsher. As porters we had T'ar-gyä (*Dar-rgyas*), who had just accompanied Pasang to Shey, his son and another village-boy. The horse was left behind as it had proved too young to be of much use and was already overtired from the previous day's journey. We descended into the gorge (SI: Nāngung Kholā) and followed the river downstream, keeping to the left bank. At first it was just a stony barren place, but after a while little yellow potentilla (*Potentilla bifurca*) began to appear along the track and we passed small clumps of yellow gorse-like shrub (*Caragana sp.*) and bushes covered in tiny white roses (*Rosa sericea*). A young woman, returning from Saldang to her home in Nyisäl, caught up with us. Our porters teased her for travelling so lightly, whereupon she freely consented to take our camp-beds on her shoulders. She asked nothing of us, and it was a joy to see her unaffected delight, when we later offered her a silver coin. Then we met the men of Shey shepherding their flocks home from the north. We told them that some of our belongings were left at their monastery and that we hoped to visit them soon.

When we came to the junction with the Panzang gorge (SI: Pānjāng Kholā), we crossed both rivers by the firm bridges provided and turned eastwards towards Nyisäl (SI: Nisālgāon). T'ar-gyä pointed out the great chötens of Yang-tsher on the near side of the village and I realized that this monastery is not at all where it is shown on the Survey of India maps.[a] We followed the gorge a little way and then climbed up the mountain-side direct towards the chötens. Little red rock-plants (*Androsace muscoidea* and *A. rotundifolia*) grew here and there

[a] Yang-tsher (*gYas-mtsher*), meaning 'right-side settlement', is the old local place-name surviving from before the monastery was built 600–700 years ago. Its religious name is 'Island of Enlightenment' (*byang-chub gling*). The position of SI: Yānjar Gömpā seems to be confused with that of Sh'ung-tsher (p. 93).

85

amidst the arid stones. The monastery stands on a level platform about 300 feet above the river and is enclosed behind by great walls of rock. We circumambulated the prayer-wall that surrounds the whole compound of buildings and entered through a ka-ni chöten at the eastern end. Here we were welcomed by two 'monks', who promptly put the monastery kitchen at our disposal and brought us wood and water, while I erected a tent in the courtyard. Never before had we been so quickly settled for the evening. It was still early, so I began to look around the buildings (pls. XVa, XVIa).

The main courtyard is about fifty yards long and twenty yards across at its widest. Three major temples (nos. 1, 2 and 3

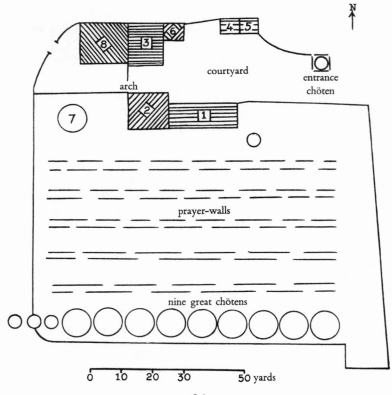

on the diagram), a little temple containing a large prayer-wheel (4), another small temple known as the 'nuns' temple' (*chos-mo'i lha-khang*) (5) and the kitchen (6) all open off from it. Between this group of buildings and the row of nine great chötens which flank the southern side, there is a stony court lined with rows of prayer-walls. Another great chöten (7) opposite the sacristan's house (8) is said to contain the relics of the founder-lama, 'Religion's Defence Glorious and Good' (*chos-skyabs dpal-bzang*).

Temple no. 1 is in the form of a large hall containing eight chötens. The walls are covered with splendid frescoes, of which the identification causes little difficulty. We walked slowly round from left to right, studying each painting carefully.

In the northern wall are:

'Glancing Eye of Great Compassion' (*Avalokiteśvara—mahākaruṇa*)

'Lotus-Born' (*Padmasambhava*)

'Holder of the Vajra' (*Vajradhara*)

'Sage of the Śākyas' (*Śākyamuni*)

'Essence of All Joy' (*kun-dga snying-po*)

'Banner of Fame' (*grags-pa rgyal-mtshan*) ⎫ Sa-kya-pa

'Exalted Protector of Living Beings' (*'gro-mgon 'phags-pa*) ⎬ lamas

'Glorious Gentle One—Lion of Speech' (*Mañjuśrī—simhanāda*)

'Glorious Gentle One' in his normal manifestation.[a]

On the eastern wall:

'Hey Vajra' (*Hevajra*)

'Imperturbable' (*Akshobhya*).

On the southern wall:

'Brilliant' (*Vairocana*)

'Great Brilliance' (*Mahāvairocana*)

---

[a] *Mañjuśrī* as the prototype of manifested wisdom holds a sword in his right hand, with which he cuts off ignorance at its roots, and a book supported on a lotus, in his left hand. The book represents the perfection of wisdom. As the manifestation 'Lion of Speech' he is discussed below (p. 110).

'Glancing Eye—Infallible Noose' (*Avalokiteśvara—Amoghapāśa*)
'Buddha Master of Medicine' (*Bhaishajyaguru*)
'Victorious Lady of the Chignon' (*Ushnīshavijayā*)
'Boundless Light' (*Amitābha*).
On the western wall:
'Boundless Life' (*Amitāyus*)
'Supreme Bliss' (*bde-mchog* = *Cakrasamvara*)

Yang-tsher Monastery is a Sa-kya-pa foundation and this is reflected in the choice of paintings that adorn these walls. There are three famous lamas of Sa-kya of the thirteenth and fourteenth centuries and buddhas and bodhisattvas (divine saviours) who were the object of special devotion. 'Glancing Eye' (*Avalokiteśvara*) is a universally popular divinity with many different forms. He is shown here in two distinct manifestations, as the 'Great Compassionate Lord', who is ever active striving to save living beings throughout all the spheres of existence, and as the 'holder of the noose' with which he binds offenders. 'Lotus-Born' (*Padmasambhava*) is present, for he is invoked by all the 'Red Hat' orders, although only the Nying-ma-pas regard him as the supreme manifestation of the ineffable buddha-essence. 'Holder of the Vajra' (*Vajradhara*) is shown surrounded by the eighty-four Great Yogins. He is the buddha specially favoured by the Ka-gyü-pas (p. 77), but is acknowledged universally throughout Tibet (p. 203). The Buddhas 'Boundless Light' and 'Boundless Life' are likewise acclaimed universally. The most significant buddha in this whole gathering is 'Great Brilliance' (*Mahāvairocana*), whom the Tibetans refer to by the brief title of 'Omniscient' (*kun-rig*). His great importance in Sa-kya-pa practice is shown by the frequency with which his mandala (mystic circle) is painted on the ceilings of the ka-ni chötens throughout this whole area. There was a tendency in Indian Buddhism from about the second century onwards to symbolize the notion of supreme buddhahood by transcendent buddha-forms, for it was conceived as something absolute and essentially ineffable, transcending any local manifestation such as Śākyamuni had been. We may regard Śākyamuni as the only historical buddha, as a man who lived and taught in the sixth to fifth centuries B.C. But in later Indian Buddhism and consequently in the Buddhism that reached Tibet his manifestation in the flesh had become a secondary consideration. Supreme buddhahood was ultimately attainable to all who chose to strive for it and hence someone such as 'Lotus-Born', who played so great a part in establishing Buddhism in Tibet, could be regarded as a buddha just as Śākyamuni had been. This transcendentalizing of the notion of buddhahood was achieved succinctly in the theory of Five Buddhas who are individually just aspects of one supreme reality. The number five corresponds with the centre and four points of the compass (thus expressing universality), as well as with other cosmological and philosophical conceptions.[a] Of these five the central one, known as 'Brilliant' (*Vairocana*), was conceived as comprehending the other four. As such he was known as 'Great Brilliance' and around him there developed several sets of meditational and ritual texts. These seem to be the earliest of the tantras. They were developed in Kashmir from perhaps the fourth century onwards and were introduced into western Tibet in the tenth and eleventh centuries. Subsequently they were adopted by Sa-kya Monastery and thus we find these paintings in the Sa-kya-pa monastery of Yang-tsher. In other Indian Buddhist schools, 'Imperturbable' (*Akshobhya*), was revered as the central buddha, for he was head of the family of the *vajra* (p. 37). From mystical association with the ideas of power and wrath he came to be identified with certain fierce manifestations of divinity, which were being accepted by some teachers. Of these manifestations Hevajra and 'Supreme Bliss' are among the most important. Hevajra in particular was adopted by the Sa-kya-pas as their tutelary divinity. Thus he

[a] Thus the cosmos consists, according to early Indian ideas, of a sacred mountain surrounded by four islands. Phenomenal existence is compounded of five elements, human personality of five constituents (*skandha*), etc., (*BH*, p. 64 ff.).

and 'Imperturbable' appear side by side on the eastern wall. But the practice of the present inmates of Yang-tsher is no longer that of the Sa-kya-pa Order, as we observed as soon as we entered temple no. 2. Here the walls have recently been redone by the local painter and the old frescoes are lost under daubs of garish colouring. The choice of paintings, giving prominence to 'Lotus-Born' and his two fierce manifestations, bears witness to the Nying-ma-pa practice, which is now spreading throughout this whole region. While we were looking around us, the painter himself came into the temple. He was a lively, intelligent man of less than thirty years, but unfortunately no artist. We congratulated him on his work none the less and I expressed light-hearted regret at the absence of Hevajra. 'People here used to hold to Hevajra', he replied, 'but when he ceased to help us, we turned to the Fierce Master (guru drag-po) instead'.

'Perhaps he ceased to help you, because you no longer believed in him.'

'We believe in him, but since he does not help us, we offer our ceremonies to the Fierce Master.'

Later I noticed that Hevajra's name was included in a general invocation, but the whole ceremony was directed to 'Lotus-Born' in his fierce manifestation.

This temple also contained some very fine bronzes, especially a set of three, which the painter referred to as the 'Three Princes'. They represent Śākyamuni with 'Lotus-in-Hand' (Padmapāṇi) on his right and 'Thunderbolt-in-Hand' (Vajrapāṇi) on his left. The symbols of vajra and lotus are missing, but the two figures can be identified by their gestures.[a]

The set of canonical volumes on mystic philosophy (prajñā-pāramitā), which is honoured as the verbal manifestation of the goddess of Perfect Wisdom, was stacked neatly in racks on one side. The volumes on 'discipline' (vinaya) were lying untidily on a wooden trestle, covered in dust and dirt. The long wooden

---

[a] These are a special trio, whence seems to be derived the idea of buddha-families (BH, pp. 62–4).

boards, which serve as covers to these volumes were all finely carved at their ends.

Temple no. 3 is in regular use for ceremonies. Following Nying-ma-pa practice 'Lotus-Born' (*Padmasambhava*) is placed to the centre with 'Glancing Eye' (*Avalokiteśvara*) on his left and 'Boundless Light' (*Amitābha*) on his right. Placed behind them almost out of sight and covered with dust we noticed other fine bronzes (*Vairocana, Vajradhara* and *Śākyamuni*). On a rack above stood ten other smaller images (*Amitābha, Amitāyus, Avalokiteśvara* and several of *Śākyamuni*). Ascending to the floor above, we realized that we had seen only a part of the collection. Here there were numerous images arranged on dusty racks, leaning back against *thankas*, which were once examples of the finest period of Tibetan painting. Most of them were cracked and worn away, but we found a very fine painting of Hevajra. There were piles of block-prints and manuscripts heaped up in the dust. We identified Mila Rāpa's 'Thousand Songs', the *Hevajra-Tantra,* the *bKa'-thang sde-lnga* and several volumes of mystic philosophy. There were more thankas rolled up, in varying stages of decay. The whole monastery tells the sad story of past glory and present ignorance and neglect. Only the painter seemed to take any creative interest in the place. Leading us to his house, he showed us several thankas that he had painted, as well as a text on classical Tibetan grammar, which he was zealously teaching himself. Earlier on I had suggested tentatively that he might perhaps make a copy for me of the mandala of 'Great Brilliance', but now doubting his ability to reproduce it well enough, I pressed the matter no further. The main wall on the southern side of the compound is not only fitted with prayer-wheels, but also decorated with a whole series of stone plaques, illustrating buddhas, bodhisattvas, lamas and monks (pl. XV*b*). Many of them were delightfully carved and painted, and we later discovered that this is an art that is by no means dead.

The 'monks', who are mostly married, live separately in twelve houses just outside the compound. Some of them own a second house in Nyisal Village. At the time we were there, the lama and other members of the community had gone to fetch their animals from the 'north', so we met very few of them. On the third day of our stay they performed the ceremony, which regularly takes place on the 10th of every Tibetan month. The main divinity was the 'Fierce Master' and the liturgy was a Nying-ma-pa one. It was rather a pathetic performance, for there were only two 'monks' available for most of the reading and meanwhile a group of women and children waited eagerly for their share of the offerings. We made a present of money for the general provision of tea (*mang-ja*), but by general consent barley-beer was distributed instead, for Tibetan tea is very scarce locally. Pasang was able to buy barley tsamba in Nyisäl, some of which we gave as a contribution to the general offerings, adding the remainder to our own stores. At the end of the ceremony we received a share of the sacrificial cakes (torma).

When we asked about local gods (*gzhi-bdag*), we were told that the god of Yang-tsher and Nyisäl was called Wa-la-gyap, of Mugu Dü-ba-gyap and of Shimen (SI: Simengāon) Kün-ga-gyap. They seem to conform to the type of the indigenous mountain-god, who having accepted Tibetan Buddhism, is allowed to remain as local protector, receiving a regular share of offerings. Over the doorway of one of the houses we noticed a 'protector' carved on a stone slab. The arms were raised in just the same gesture of those at Rohagāon (p. 57), but the figure was far better cut and was equipped with a flat hat. He is referred to as the 'King Protector from Disease' (*rgyal-po nad-pa'i srung-ma*) and when Pasang suggested that it was the Tibetan god Pehar, all present agreed. One observes how easy it is for local cults of the same kind as we had met along the Bheri to be absorbed by Tibetan Buddhist culture. But while this occurs on the northern side of the watershed, there is little sign of it on the Hindu side.

One day we went to visit Sh'ung-tsher Monastery which stands high above the left bank of the river downstream from Yang-tsher. We crossed the two bridges by the river junction and then climbed up to Lhori (SI: Lurigāon), the village of the 'Southern Mountain' (*lho-ri*); it consists of about fifteen houses, spread out over steeply terraced fields (pl. XVII*a*). We climbed another 1,000 feet or so until at last the temple of Sh'ung-tsher (*zhugs-mtsher*) appeared above us at the end of a saddle-like ridge. We found here a small community of married 'monks'. Men, women and children were sitting in the sun turning over grain as it dried in the sun. We noticed a quantity of maize and learned that it had been traded through Tibrikot (p. 29). They showed little surprise at our sudden appearance and the sacristan's wife came at once to unlock the temple and show us around. It contained a small collection of fine images and *than-kas*, but the whole place was filthy and the paintings were just rotting away. We rescued a thanka of Hevajra from behind a wooden trestle and Pasang supervised the repair of its torn edging, chiding them for their lack of care. Meanwhile I looked through their dusty collection of texts. This monastery is likewise a Sa-kya-pa foundation, but nowadays they have become Nying-ma-pa in practice. We bought some tsamba, made tea at the sacristan's hearth and then returned the way we had come. It was now early evening; at Lhori we passed a party of men and boys playing happily at archery (pl. XVII*b*).

PANZANG

Our maps showed a route from Nyisäl (SI: Nisālgāon) to Shimen (Simengāon) along the right of the Panzang river (SI: Pānjāng Kholā), but when we set about negotiating for porters, we learned that no such route existed and that the river-gorge between the two villages was quite impassable. We would have to ascend another valley towards the north-east (SI: Mai Kholā) as far as the village of Mö (*mod*).[a] From there

[a] The SI name *Mai* for the stream has been taken from the village-name Mö, which seems to have been misheard. The village is not marked on the SI maps and presumably was not visited by the surveyors.

we would cross the ridge to the south, thus bypassing the main gorge, and descend to the next main tributary (SI: Chālā Kholā) which would lead us down to Shimen. We discovered that quite a number of the Nyisäl villagers had never been to Shimen in their lives. We could obtain only two girls as porters and they would go with us no further than Mö, one easy day's journey. We walked round the monastery for the last time, for it is one of those places which seem to haunt the mind. It represents an oasis of great religious culture amidst what is perhaps the harshest scenery imaginable—bare rocks and coarse eroded soil. One thinks of the zeal and energy of those former inmates, who brought such a place into existence, practising their religion in all holiness and sincerity. These temples still continue to bear witness to a certain standard of belief and conduct, and even nowadays there appear from time to time among these villagers men who are genuinely marked out for a religious calling.

We passed below Nyisäl and down into the gorge, which was a wild and precipitous place (pl. XVIII*b*). Then we climbed round into the valley that leads up to Mö; it was more gentle, but still enclosed by bare grey-brown slopes rising steeply on both sides. At length we passed a chöten, harbinger of village-life, and soon Mö itself came into sight, a scattered group of about fifteen houses standing on both sides of the stream. We found a grassy place to erect a tent just below the village and then went at once to find the headman, since we would need to arrange porters for the morrow without delay. Our reception was again most friendly; the headman and several villagers returned to the tent with us, bringing wood and milk, for which they would accept no payment, and assuring us that all the help we needed would be forthcoming in the morning. An icy wind blew up the valley and we were cold as we had never been before. We cooked in the open in the greatest discomfort and that night, while Hemrāj and Takki Babu slept in the headman's house, Pasang and I lay shivering in the tent. There was heavy frost and not until the sun had risen above the encircling mountains did physical content return. Yet this was the approach of summer, the 11th day of the fourth Tibetan month, by Western reckoning May 21st and Whit Monday. The headman came to visit us again and said that a man and a boy had been found to come with us. In reply to our enquiries we learned that the village was occupied in winter, but that quite a number of people went across to Shimen, with which Mö has close associations. It was here that we saw for the first time the characteristic head-dress of the women, a pair of curved rectangular plates of silver or brass, laced together with leather thongs and worn on the top and back of the head (pl. XVIIIa). Here and throughout the eastern side of Dolpo they are worn every day. Towards the west, around Saldang and Phijor, they only make their appearance on festivals and holidays.

After a last exchange of friendly words we began the ascent of the mountain-side to the south. It was a long climb—over the coarse grass where grew tiny white primulas (*Primula glandulifera*), edelweiss (*Lentopodium himalayanum*) and other little rock-plants (*Androsace muscoidea, Oreosolen wattii*), and then up amidst rock and shale. The ascent of this pass (over 19,000 feet) brought us so close to a summit which rose another 600–700 feet on the eastern side, that we left our loads and climbed to the top. Looking northwards now we could see to the end of the valley beyond Mö and across to the Tibetan plain (pl. XXa). This is as close as we shall come to crossing the Himalayas and we thought back over the last two months' journey, remembering the different regions through which we had passed and the various peoples we had met. A political frontier may prevent us making the last stage of such a crossing, but at least we have seen the end and know what to expect there. Westwards we looked down to the gorge we had come along the previous day, and south and south-west we gazed over this fantastic land of Dolpo, different from any other high Himalayan land that I have seen (pl. XXIa). Mountains of 20,000 feet and more are high enough in all consequence. Yet here one lives so near to their summits, crossing close by them when one journeys from village to village, that they are neither challengingly hostile nor grandly magnificent. Ascending such passes, often no more than 2,000–3,000 feet above the village, seems no more arduous than hill-walking in Scotland. The gradual progress across Nepal through ever higher regions had already acclimatized us to living at these altitudes. The only member of our party who felt ill effects was the unfortunate Hemrāj. Remembering always the ease with which we used to cross these passes, I have come to regard the contouring on the Survey of India maps as generally reliable, so that the villages in this land would seem to lie at heights between 14,500 and 16,500 feet and in one or two cases even higher. Thus Dolpo must be the highest inhabited region in the world.[a] The villages are scattered over some 500 square miles of mountainous desert and the total population cannot exceed 2,000. From the summit where we now stood we saw no trace of human habitation, for most of the villages were concealed within the deep-set valleys. We were alone amidst a chiaroscuro of light and shade falling upon ridge after ridge of grey and brown, while the far horizon was edged by a rim of snow.

It was a long way down over scree and stones to the rocky track, down ever more steeply till we entered a gorge and the mountains above were hidden from us once more. We followed the stream along (SI: Chālā Kholā) until it led us down to SHIMEN (SI: Simengāon) in the Panzang valley. The temple, where we would make our lodging that night, was high above

---

[a] It is only fair to observe that the number of inhabitants living at high altitudes in the Andes is considerably greater than in any of these scattered Himalayan villages. For example the city of Cerro de Pasco in Peru, situated at 14,270 feet, has 25,000 inhabitants. (See Jean Brunhes, *La Géograph e Humaine*, édition abrégée, Presses Universitaires de France, Paris, 1947, p. 96.) In other high Himalayan regions besides Dolpo there are small settlements at 19,000 feet and over, but these are only occupied during the short summer months. (See S. D. Pant, *The Social Economy of the Himalayas*, London, 1935, p. 41.) The Dolpo villages are occupied the whole year round.

the left bank of the stream, and these last steps were slow and unwilling ones. We reached a small platform, where there was room for a tiny monastery, a courtyard and a number of chötens, near which we would be able to pitch a tent. We looked down upon terraced fields and well-spaced houses and here and there a little grove of willow-trees. The great cliffs still enclose the valley, but they have withdrawn for about a mile of the river's length, far enough to allow men room to settle. We counted some thirty-five houses. The sound of solemn recitation came from the temple behind us and inside we found six villagers, all clad in dark red homespun, reading the 'Perfection of Wisdom' texts (pl. XIXa). Seeing us, they very soon stopped for a break and came out to ask who we were, readily giving their consent to our camping nearby. They had just acquired a new set of thirty volumes of block-prints from Lhasa, they told us, and they were reading them all before stacking them away on the racks. This was quite a perfunctory performance, the volumes being divided amongst those present, so that they could all read together and finish the sooner. The temple itself is a small one, but quite pleasingly painted. Around the walls there are frescoes of the Karma-pa Lama, of 'Lotus-Born', Śākyamuni, 'Boundless Life', 'Glancing Eye', the 'Saviouress' (*Tārā*) in her twenty-one manifestations and the four kings who guard the quarters.

The next morning the man and the boy who had come with us from Mö, were duly paid off. We began to regret this daily change of porters, for these villagers were always persons of sturdy character and made such friendly companions, that we felt the loss every morning when the time came to say farewell. Pasang had already engaged a man of Shimen and a horse as replacements, and so, descending from the temple, we followed the path through the terraced fields, by the grey stone houses and under the hanging willow-trees. Pasang went to buy some meat from a villager who had come to our camp earlier to offer it to us, and while I waited by a little stream in the shade of the willows, I realized that Shimen was the most pleasant of Dolpo villages just because of its many trees (pl. XIX*b*).[a] Flowers grew on the bank, violets (*Viola kunawarensis*), anemones (*Anemone obtusiloba*), little purple trumpet-flowers (*Lancea tibetica*), the Tibetan incarvillea (*Incarvillea younghusbandii*) and little stock-like clusters of bloom (*Solms-laubachia fragrans*). The track passes the last of the houses, then a row of prayer-walls; soon all cultivation is left behind and one is climbing along the steep walls of the gorge. We met a caravan of about twenty yaks, carrying loads of salt and wool and pressed ourselves back against the rocks, so that the timid animals should pass. About three miles above Shimen one crosses a large tributary stream which flows down from the north. High up above it is the little village of Mä (SI: Mäjhgāon), consisting of just six houses.[b] It is an offshoot of Shimen. On the far bank of the stream and surmounting the crags of the gorge we saw the ruins of what was once quite a large monastery. After another three miles we passed through a ruined and deserted village. Beyond this the gorge began to open out and a great herd of antelopes appeared on the rocky slopes above. These were the first we had seen; they wander at will over the mountains of Dolpo, for no one molests them. Soon we come upon the ruins of more houses and a large group of chötens of various shapes and sizes. There is no doubt that this valley was once well populated, but now no one lives between Shimen and Ting-khyu, a distance of some ten map-miles.

As one approaches TING-KHYU (SI: Tingjegāon), the valley becomes an open basin about half a mile across. Two valleys unite here, one leading south-by-east to the Tibetan plain and the other southwards towards the great watershed, beyond which

[a] Shimen may mean 'place of many trees' (*shing-mang*), but I was unable to confirm this. The spellings used locally are *shing-sman* and *shing-man*, neither of which makes good sense.

[b] Tibetan *mad*, pronounced like English *met* with no final -*t*. The SI has recorded this name for the stream (Met Khola). Mäjhgāon seems to have no justification as a local name.

are Tarap and Tsharka. The south-eastern valley is a wide glacier-cut trough, watered by a gentle stream and carpeted with short grass[a] (pl. XX*b*). The height here is about 16,500 feet and there is not a single tree. The thirty houses or so that go to make up the village are strung along the foot of the northern slope. We passed beyond them and set up camp near the old fort which reminded us how close we were to the present political frontier. The headman's house was nearby and we went to pay him a visit, as always in search of food. Hearing our call from the outside gate, a boy came down to let us in and withstrain the fury of the great mastiff whose chain permitted him just to reach the door. We ascended by a knotched trunk and entered a room on the first storey, where the family was seated round the kitchen-hearth. We were offered tea, which the others accepted while I politely refused. It is not dislike of the buttered brew which restrains me, but a resolution to eat and drink nothing which has not been prepared by Pasang or Takki Babu, for even slight illness can have dangerous consequences when the only hospital is four weeks distant on the far side of massive mountain ranges. Occasionally I broke this resolution, when it would have been ill-mannered to persist in refusal, but it was probably a wise precaution. Pasang, Hemrāj and Takki Babu all have stronger constitutions. Much as I came to admire the people of Dolpo for their integrity and well balanced humour, it must be confessed that they are as unclean in their habits, as simple Tibetans everywhere are reputed to be. Biting insects never attacked us in their houses, however; perhaps this is to be attributed to the high elevation of their land. Thus we were able to sit comfortably in the dark of the kitchen, distressed by nothing worse than the smoke from the fire. The headman and his wife were there and also his son and daughter-in-law; they were eating tsamba with their buttered tea. (I recall now that we never saw anyone eating anything else, but they certainly prepare meat-broth on occasions and also make flat cakes of bread with buckwheat.) We

[a] Ting(*gting*) means a 'deep place'; khyu ('*kbyu*) means 'run' or 'flow'.

answered questions about ourselves, and the headman's wife told us of Oleg Polunin. No one knew his name any more than they will know mine, but her brief description left no doubt that it was he. They had all been most impressed by the zeal with which he collected plants and had concluded logically enough that he must be a kind of medicine-doctor. I left them in this belief, for it justified his activities well enough, and it is useless trying to explain the pursuit of pure knowledge to people who are essentially practical. They accepted us as pilgrims, for a pilgrimage brings religious merit and as such is very practical indeed.

Their whole life, it seems, is oriented towards Tibet, for they rely upon the grassy uplands beyond the political frontier for their winter grazing. The main Tibetan centres of civilization are still far away, but it is to these that they go on pilgrimage and occasionally in search of religious knowledge. Very few of them had been to the Nepal Valley and no one among those we met had been to India. This land seemed so remote to them, that it was useless to explain that we had come from even further. We returned to our tent and prepared an unusually good meal, for there was fresh yak-meat to be chopped up and curried.

Among our spectators was a youth, whose face was covered in appalling sores, and I asked him if he wanted medicament. His face lit up with hope at once. When he had washed his filthy features, I cleaned off the foul scabs and applied Cetavex ointment and a lint dressing wherever practical. Then he begged me to finish the task and lying on the bank revealed his thighs which were covered with the same vile sores. The fortitude with which these people endure such disease, is truly amazing. He was by no means the only one affected in this way. We made him wash his whole body and cleaned the sores as well as could be. He came just before we left two mornings later and received a second application of ointment. Later we heard that he was cured completely.

There are two temples on the mountain-side above Ting-khyu, one old, deserted and in ruins, the other new. The old one still contains some frescoes in the same style as temple no. 1 at Yang-tsher and likewise must have been a Sa-kya-pa foundation. The new temple is known as Drölung, 'Place of Salvation' (*sgrol-lung dgon-pa*). The old lama who lived there, received us in a most friendly manner (pl. XXII*a*). He was looked after by his niece and her husband, the local painter, who seemed far better skilled in his art than the painter at Yang-tsher. There was also a real monk, one of the very few in Dolpo. We sat in the sun in the little upper courtyard, chewing at the little lumps of dried cheese which they offered us, and looking through some of their books. The temple itself was manifestly Nying-ma-pa with its paintings of 'All Good', 'Unity of All the Blessed', 'Lotus-Born', 'Glancing Eye', 'Boundless Light', Śākyamuni, Supreme Heruka and 'Adamantine Being' (*Vajra-sattva*). On the altar were numerous little buddha-images. Grotesque masks were hanging from the painted wooden pillars; cymbals, drums and trumpets lay as though ready for use. The whole place was clearly well cared for. We paid for some butter-lamps to be burned and took our leave. It was early afternoon when we descended to our camp and the sun shone warm and L.ight. Not far from the tent was a shallow gentle stream. In the morning it had been icy cold but now it was almost luke-warm. We could bathe again at last. Not since we left Tibrikot six weeks before had we been able to brave the cold of mountain-waters, and not until we reached the Buri Gandaki four months later, would we experience this joy again.

In the evening we walked over to look at the fort, a plain stone building of solid walls, rendered still stronger by the angle at which they were built. On the way we passed a party of a dozen villagers engaged in cutting and inscribing the stones of a new prayer-wall. The villagers themselves were financing this whole row of walls as an act of general merit. It seems a very practical scheme for a village-council and men could scarcely appear happier at their work (pl. XXI*b*).

Since we would pass through Tarap and Tsharka later on,

we retraced our steps the following day to Shimen and set up our tent by the temple. It was the 15th (full moon) of the 4th Tibetan month, and so having completed the reading of their thirty new volumes, the villagers were performing a general ceremony. The central divinity invoked was the 'All Unity of Absolute Essence' (*yang-snying kun-'dus*) who is an impersonalized manifestation of the Buddha 'Boundless Life'. The main object of the long invocations and prayers was the acquisition of long life and general prosperity. We were given a very liberal share of the offerings and the chang was quite as good as Nyi-ma Tshe-ring's. A further diversion was provided by an all but total eclipse of the moon. The celebrants took it in turn to circumambulate the temple, blowing conch-shells and trumpets, that Rāhula (*gza-lha*), the demon of the sky, might be induced to let loose his prey. Within the temple no one seemed unduly perturbed at the danger that threatened the moon, and the distribution of offerings and the final blessing followed their usual course.

From Shimen a track lead steeply out of the valley westwards; thence across the mountains above Koma (SI: Komāgāon) and finally by a choice of route to Namdo and Saldang. We had to return to Nyi-ma Tshe-ring's house, where we had left some of our supplies, for now our stocks of food were running very short. It was possible to obtain tsamba regularly, and as we left Shimen the second time, we bought a lump of sun-dried sheep, but I cannot live long without wheat-flour in such needy circumstances, and rice and sugar would be welcome. The man and woman who accompanied us, came no further than the next village, for such is the practice; so we had to wait above Koma, while replacements were found. At length two lusty laughing maidens presented themselves and we continued with enlivened spirits, so infectious was their mirth. But we had been much delayed and it seemed a very long way indeed across that great upland plateau. It was already evening when we reached the edge and looked down into the valley below us. There was still a long steep descent to the river and since there is no bridge below Saldang, we had to wade the cold surging water in the gathering dusk and pick our way up to Nyi-ma Tshe-ring's house in darkness. In spite of all this the good humour of the two girls persisted to the end. As we put up the tents the moon began to rise only slightly less than full for it was the 16th night. We cooked and ate our meal contentedly; it is always something like a home-coming to return to an old camp-site. The girls spent the night in the house and came to us in the morning for their wages, still joking and laughing.

NAMDO

That day we left Takki Babu in camp and set out to visit the temples beyond Namdo. We passed by the lower houses of Saldang, keeping well above the river until the track descended to a little rocky gorge, down which flows the stream from Namgung Village. We ascended the other side and traversing the steep river-bank soon came to Namdo, a small village of about fifteen houses. About a mile beyond on the summit of a little rocky eminence is Säl Gomba (*gsal dgon-pa*). We called out at the gate and were shown by a woman through the yard and up a knotched ladder to a little temple on the first floor. The walls were unpainted but hung with several pleasing thankas. 'Lotus-Born' occupied the central position over the altar, which was set with the regular offering-bowls and little butter-lamps. It was clear that this monastery was a recent Nying-ma-pa foundation and that it was well cared for. The lama entered, a man of forty years or so; we had already heard that he was an 'incarnation' (see p. 137). He invited us to be seated and asked whence we came. We told him how we had travelled across Nepal and were now visiting the villages and temples of Dolpo. He commended the undertaking as a meritorious way of passing one's time and asked what he could do for us.

'We have come to visit your temple, Rin-po-che, and to offer

some butter-lamps.[a] You take great care of everything. Have
you lived here many years?'

'I have been here six years. There was a monastery here long
ago but it had fallen into disrepair. Nyi-ma Tshe-ring asked
me to come and live here and has given money to enable me to
do the little I have done.'

'Where then is your own home, Rin-po-che?'

'I was born in Lhori Village.'

'Are you acquainted with the Precious Lama of Shang?'

'It was he who consecrated me and I spent several years with
him at Phopa, where he used to stay.'

'We have not yet met him, but have heard much of him.'

'He is a very great lama and has done much for the doctrine
throughout all these lands. Now he is staying in Lo (Mustang).'

The lama was reticent in his replies and it would have been
rude to persist with a series of questions. The woman, who
proved to be his sister, came into the room with a pot of hot
buttered tea, which he pressed us to have.

'Rin-po-che, how should the name of your monastery be spelt?'

'It is Säl Monastery, spelt GSAL' (a word meaning 'clear').

'I see. There is the same word in Saldang (gsal-mdangs meaning
"clear lustre") and in Nyisäl (nyi-gsal meaning "sun-clarity").'

He had not thought of this before and was clearly impressed
with this little show of knowledge, which was simply intended
as an opening gambit. The place-names in Dolpo are all good
Tibetan, but many of them are so distorted on the Survey of
India maps, that it is all but impossible to work out their
proper pronunciation from that source alone. The villagers pronounce the names properly of course, but very rarely know how
to spell them correctly. My hope of gaining help from this
lama was not disappointed and we were able to check through
all the local names. This inevitably revealed my knowledge of
the classical language and the lama could ill conceal his surprise,
for there are few laymen in these regions who have any precise
knowledge of it.

[a] *Rin-po-che*, 'Precious One' is a title accorded to incarnate lamas.

'Are there many monks in India?' he asked.

'There are few monks in India, but my country is beyond India far across the ocean,' I replied and looked to Pasang for amplification.

He told of the journey across a sea so vast that no land is seen for days, of the great ship that carried hundreds, even thousands of passengers, and of aeroplanes that make the journey of 5,000 miles in a single day. In Nepal, England is known, if known at all, as Bilait, a name which was popularized among British troops in the form of 'Blighty'. But here the name Bilait is unknown. So too is the name *Inji-lungpa*, 'Land of the Inji', which is the name usually given to our country by educated Tibetans. Throughout all these Tibetan regions of western Nepal there are just two terms for foreigner. One is *rong-pa*, meaning 'valley-man', used generally of the races who live in the lower valleys, but also of a traveller such as myself who comes from that direction. The other is 'gya-mi' (*rgya-mi*), meaning 'man of the expanse' and applied in central Tibet and in the classical language specifically to the Chinese. Here however it is used of any foreigner who comes from afar. Thus Indians, Europeans, Chinese and Japanese (see p. 245) are all indiscriminately referred to as 'gya-mi'. Chinese may be specified by calling them 'gya-mi kung-teng'. 'Kung-teng' is of course a corruption of Kuo-min-tang, but is still used nowadays although the Chinese who are just across the frontier are Communist soldiers. The most precise term that could be applied to me was 'gya-mi rong-pa' implying a foreigner who had come from a great distance from the direction of the southern valleys. How could I begin to describe my own country? It was a task best left to Pasang, for he had once been almost as vague in his ideas when he first went aboard at Bombay.

He told of the crops and the livestock, of the well-carpeted houses, of the populous towns, of the mountains that were something like Dolpo. He told of the temples (churches) and monasteries, never specifying that they were Christian, for this would merely have added further complications to an already bewildering conversation. These people know only of 'the religion', which is Tibetan Buddhism, its close relative p'ön and of the irreligion of the lower valleys through Nepal to India. They would speak with sorrow of the 'valley-men who have no religion'. We were accepted as 'pilgrims' from a distant country where 'the true religion' was practised and there the matter was allowed to rest. Having offered three butter-lamps, we thanked our host and departed.

Further upstream and high above the river bank stands Sham-tr'ak (*shel-brag*) Monastery. We climbed up to it and in response to our call a little girl opened the door and led us to the upper floor where a man and a woman were grinding a great quantity of tsamba and straining off pots of chang. They told us that they were preparing for the first anniversary of their lama's death, which would take place on the morrow. Our arrival was accepted as nothing unusual, and having offered us tsamba and tea, they continued with their preparations. The man was a Tibetan proper, who had been living there for many years, helping to look after the monastery. The woman was the lama's wife. She had been married before, she told us, and had a grown-up son of her own, who had just returned from the north with the animals. By the lama she had had two children, this little girl and also a boy. We asked her who would be lama next and she explained that her son played the part in cere-monies and was acting as lama, but that the little boy would eventually become the next lama, if he showed enthusiasm for religion. We answered their questions about ourselves and then asked to see the temple. It contained little other than a few images and thankas and there was nothing to be learned from it, so we took leave of them and returned towards Saldang. On travels such as these one does not expect to find erudite lamas and splendid temples wherever one goes. So far as the study of a culture is concerned, their absence can be as significant as their presence. One travels to see what is there and if there is nothing at all, which is rare indeed, one goes on one's way to the next place of call. All the time one is quietly observing and gradually learning.

The track from Namdo to Saldang is flanked with innumerable prayer-walls. Not content with mere walls, these people have built great squares filled solid with inscribed stones. The OṂ MAṆIPADME HŪṂ HRĪḤ formula (p. 39 fn.) is the most common, but extracts have also been made from confessional texts (*ltungs-gshags*) and philosophical literature, and again and again one reads the refuge-taking formulas (*skyams-'gro*) and praises and salutations to the buddhas. If one pondered all these as one went, this brief walk would in itself become a veritable pilgrimage. On the outskirts of Saldang is an entrance chöten, the ceiling of which is painted with the mandala of 'Great Brilliance' (p. 88). We suspected that the temple nearby was a Sa-kya-pa one and it proved to be so. The walls are covered with ancient frescoes, of which the central one behind the table of offerings is the 'Glorious Gentle One, Lion of Speech' (*Simhanāda-mañjuśrī*). Mañjuśrī is popularly regarded as the princely lord of wisdom, but his real significance is to be sought in earlier traditions, which treat him as the first divine teacher of Buddhist doctrine, who is able to speak in Śākyamuni's stead. He thus became the supreme prototype of the *tathāgata*-family ('family of the buddhas'), while 'Glancing Eye' (*Avalokiteśvara*) became prototype of the *lotus*-family ('family of the gods') and 'Thunderbolt-in-Hand' (*Vajrapāṇi*) of the *vajra*-family ('family of powerful beings') (p. 35). When buddha-names appeared at the head of these families, Mañjuśrī became linked with the buddha, 'Brilliant' (*Vairocana*), who is head of the *tathāgata*-family. In the development of Buddhist tradition they may both be regarded as representing a transcendent ideal of Śākyamuni. The name 'Glorious Gentle One' (*Mañjuśrī*) or more properly 'Gentle Voice' (*Mañjughosha*) was originally a title, although it may have once referred to an historical teacher. He is first named in Buddhist scriptures as a divine aspirant to buddhahood (*bodhisattva*). The name 'Brilliant', (*Vairocana*) refers to the transcendent aspect of buddhahood. These two remain closely related in *Mahāyāna* traditions and the patterns of meditation and liturgy that were woven around them were of similar design and were elaborated within the same schools. In fact these elaborations represent the early tantric period centred in Kashmir, whence they passed to China and Japan and rather later to western Tibet. They are free from reference to the orgiastic rites, with which the later tantras are so weirdly affected. It is not without significance that the great Tibetan religious reformer, the founder-lama of the 'Yellow Hats' (*dge-lugs-pa*), was acknowledged by his followers as an incarnation of Mañjuśrī. But reformers must ever be concerned to represent the old ways as unfavourably as possible. The older sects of Tibetan Buddhism could have counted a fair proportion of sincere practisers of the doctrine and among them there were many who were devotees of the Buddha 'Brilliant' and the Bodhisattva of 'Gentle Voice'. It is clear that they were once honoured in these Sa-kya-pa temples of Dolpo.

On Mañjuśrī's right are Śākyamuni and Maitreya, the future Buddha. On his left is the great saviour 'Glancing Eye'. Along each of the side walls are depicted the Five Buddhas, heads of the Five Families. Thus Mañjuśrī was conceived at the centre of a most august assembly. Nowadays his fresco is hidden by an enormous image of 'Lotus-Born', which has been placed above the altar. It was impossible to photograph it; he is represented here by an image at Karang (pl. XXIII*b*).

We returned to our camp, content with the day's exertions but also very tired, so we spent the next day resting and writing up notes. We had visited all of central and eastern Dolpo. There remained now Phijor and Shey in the west and Tarap and Tsharka in the south.

KARANG

On Monday, May 28th, we bade farewell to Nyi-ma Tshe-ring, who saw us off with bowls of chang, and climbed up to Karang (SI: Karāng), accompanied by four Saldang lads, who carried our belongings. Karang, a village of less than twenty houses, nestles in a gentle upland valley beside a stream which drains eastwards into the main gorge (SI: Nāngung Kholā) about three miles north of Saldang. Westwards the valley leads up towards the 20,000 foot range, beyond which lie the scattered communities of Phijor, Samling, Trä and Shey. We found a delightful camp-site on a little grassy place beside a spring, where cairns were piled up in honour of the local water-spirit (*klu*). Grain which had been offered to him lay at the bottom of a limpid pool.

Karang Monastery is situated at the lower end of the village and is approached by a group of chötens, one of which shows the mandala of 'Great Brilliance' on its ceiling. Supposing that this would be a Sa-kya-pa foundation, we hoped to find other paintings of age and beauty. Nor were we disappointed, for a small side-temple (used as a store-room by the present incumbent to his greater shame) has frescoes covering its walls, illustrating the life of 'Lotus-Born' (*Padmasambhava*) in little scenes. We had seen nothing else of this kind in the whole of Dolpo, but it is suffering, alas, the effects of age and neglect. In the main temple, a room about eighteen feet square, a man was at work submerging other fine old paintings beneath his daubs of bright red, blue and yellow. His painting was the worst that I have ever seen, yet the villagers were sincerely intent on improving the interior decorations. One learns not to be surprised at the total lack of appreciation of the masters of old. In one corner the original paintings of the 'Holder of the Vajra' and 'Lotus-Born' remained, but they too would be gone by the following day. Above the offering-tables there were two large bronze images, seated figures some five feet high, representing

Maitreya and Mañjuśrī Lion of Speech. It was very satisfactory to see them together, for this form of Mañjuśrī might be easily confused with Maitreya. Maitreya has both hands raised in the gesture of preaching, his regular pose. Mañjuśrī has his left hand resting on his lap and his right hand raised in the explanatory gesture (pl. XXIII).

On the mountain-side to the north about 500 feet above Karang are two more small monasteries. The upper one, Pälding (*dpal-lding*), was once Sa-kya-pa, but has now been repainted in Nying-ma-pa style. It possesses what were once fine thankas and also a few images. It is surrounded by a few houses belonging to the small married community. The lower one, Yab-Yum Gomba, is recent and also Nying-ma-pa. It is owned by a single lama.

During our brief stay in Karang the headman showed great friendliness, supplying us with dried meat and a pack of butter and making no demur at our request for porterage. We claimed porterage as a right, for we would have been totally stranded without it, but we were aware that it must often be a nuisance to the villagers and were surprised at the readiness with which they accompanied us.

SAMLING

We left Karang together with two men and a horse and slowly ascended the valley westwards. Our companions warned us mirthfully of the fearful pass above us, as we advanced slowly and steadily to its crest. It rises to about 20,000 feet, but the climb was scarcely more arduous than the ascent of Ben Nevis, for Karang itself already lies at 16,000 feet. The coarse grass of the upper valley gradually disappears and one progresses across a sloping wilderness of rocks into a world of black cliffs, scree and snow. I left the others behind and climbed obliquely up a smooth snow slope which led straight to a lonely eminence just above the pass. Westwards the view is closed by the snow-summits of the Sisne Himāl. Immediately south of the pass, whence it might be easily ascended, rises the peak marked 21,125 feet on the Survey of India ¼" map. This is Muk-po Rong (*smug-po'i rong*), the 'Purple Mountain', which dominates Phijor and Samling and is the abode of a mountain-god.[a] To the east one looks back over Dolpo. I joined the others below on the pass and found Hemrāj suffering from severe headache. No one else was affected; rather we counted this as one of our most enjoyable days (pl. XXII*b*). Skirting the 'Purple Mountain' closely, we descended to a grassy ridge and followed this towards the setting sun, until Phijor became visible below us on the right. At this point we began to follow another track down to the left towards the Shey River (SI: Sibu Khola).[b] The little temples and houses of Samling Monastery lay before us, scattered over a grassy alp which hung above the gorge (pl. XXIV*a*).

Our approach was heralded by the furious barking of a dog. Pasang had hastened ahead while I followed slowly and reflectively, for this was the destination we had longed to reach. When I arrived, he was already in occupation of one of the houses and engaged in conversation with the Lama and a monk. 'Would this house do for us?' 'Would we like to visit the temple at once?' We had to answer the usual questions about ourselves; our porters had doubtless explained already that we travelled with Nyi-ma Tshe-ring's blessing. Sometimes through tiredness I would grow impatient, and so am thankful indeed that on this occasion I remained courteous to the end, for Samling was to prove the main object of our travels and this old Lama our truest friend (pl. XXIV*b*). At last they left us and we were able to relax and make our arrangements for the night.

We had already ascended to the first floor of the house and found ourselves in a small open courtyard about twenty-five

[a] The Tibetan word *rong*, which is often translatable as 'valley' seems more properly to have the meaning of 'chasm'. It is commonly used in mountain-names in Dolpo.

[b] The SI name Sibu is derived from She-phu (*shel-phu*), referring to the 'head of the valley' (*phu*) above Shey (*shel*). It is an invented name unknown locally.

feet long by fifteen feet wide. Two small rooms opened off on one side and since one of these had a hole in the roof and was intended as a kitchen, Takki Babu set about preparing tea. The lama's boy, whose name we learned was Yung-drung, brought some sticks, dried yak-dung and a bronze water-pot filled with rather murky water. The other room was intended for the master of the house and we later learned that the Lama himself had lived here before he built his present dwelling. Since then it had become a form of guest-house where the young lama of P'ar-lä regularly stayed whenever he made a visit. Both rooms however were very dark, for there was no window and the only light came through the door-way. They were also very dirty. From one end of the courtyard one could climb through a hole into the roof of the main temple and with the light of our torch we looked down through a large square hole in the centre of the ceiling upon a jumble of dusty images and books and thankas. On the opposite side of our courtyard there was a covered latrine of regular Tibetan style. From the courtyard one could ascend by a knotched ladder onto the flat mud-roof of the 'kitchen' and 'living-room' and here I resolved to pitch a tent, for the darkness of the house was depressing. Thus Hemrāj and Takki Babu settled in the 'living-room', while Pasang and I used the tent.

Night was now falling and we were very tired. Hemrāj, affected by the altitude, was still suffering from headache and biliousness. We gave him Codeine tablets, to which he always reacted favourably, and then turned our attention to the rice and Knorr soup that Takki Babu had prepared. Later Hemrāj was well enough to drink some hot chocolate and then fell sound asleep. It was strange that he should always be the one affected, for he has lived his whole life between 4,000–5,000 feet above sea-level, far higher indeed than I have. He seemed to typify the innate dislike of the cultured city-dweller for the life of wild mountains, all the antipathy that the man of Pātan or Kathmandu tends to feel towards the people of the hills. Poor Hemrāj! In spite of his seeming desire to accompany us, he was now unhappy. We had done our best to tell him what to expect, but he was clearly totally unprepared for the actual conditions of our journey. So far he had scarcely complained at all and had caused no trouble, but he was now wondering how to extract himself from his present plight. This we were to learn a few days later.

The next morning we descended from our courtyard by a knotched ladder to the dark ground-floor. The floor here was bare hard-pressed earth and the place might serve as stable or store-room. Now it was quite empty. From this room another door, usually kept locked, led straight into the temple, to which this 'guest-house' formed an annexe. Our first duty was to visit the Lama, whose house was next to our own. It was far larger, but constructed in just the same manner. The ground-floor was very dark, but one could make out stacks of wood and unwanted pots which were stored there. One ascended by a knotched tree trunk to a square courtyard. One side of this was covered and here the Lama was seated on a raised carpeted plat-form. The boy Yung-drung spread some antelope skins on the ground for us. We offered a white scarf and a small present of silver rupees and then took our seats. He asked us again about our journey and the land we had come from. He had travelled in Tibet, but never to India or 'Nepal' and he knew nothing of lands beyond the seas apart from the 'four islands' of Buddhist cosmology. When we told him that to reach my country we must go by sea for sixteen days, he clearly conceived of Britain as one of these islands. We marked out a map in the hard earth floor and explained as best we could. Yung-drung brought buttered tea for us and called across to Takki Babu to bring our cups. Everything was covered with dust and Yung-drung him-self was especially dirty. The Lama himself was not over-clean and his eyes were inflamed and watering. He rubbed them on the grubby sleeve of his gown and asked if we had any medicine. Pasang went to get some boracic powder, cotton-wool and Gol-den Eye Ointment, while I visited the kitchen to find a pot in which to warm a little water. A fire was smouldering on the hearth in the middle of the room with the earthen tea-pot resting on an iron stand. In the dark and dust and smoke the people of Dolpo drink tea and talk, eat and sleep. The windows are just small square holes which can be easily blocked to keep out the raw winter air; often there is no window at all. We only saw this country in summer, when the men are out on the mountains and the women sit weaving in the sun. In winter they must spend far more time around their smoky fires and it is little wonder that their eyes should be affected. We washed a metal ladle, warmed some water in it, for this was a task Yung-drung could not be trusted to do, and made a solution with boracic powder. Meanwhile the Lama was busy counting his beads; we paused until he had finished. 'I think your medicine will be successful' he said, and we realized that he had been forecasting the measure of our skill. We bathed his eyes, applied the ointment and gave him cotton-wool to wipe them with, begging him to use his sleeve no more. Pasang delivered a short and polite homily on the benefits of cleanliness and threatened jokingly to bath Yung-drung.

The Lama then lead us into another room across the courtyard, which proved to be his private chapel. He had a large collection of books and we asked specifically for the 'Tantra of Tibet' (*bod-yul rgyud*), which the Pungmo lama had once shown to us, and the records of Samling Monastery. He took them down for us to see. They were manuscripts written with headless Tibetan letters and numerous verbal abbreviations. There was no doubt that they would be difficult to read. Many of the other texts were rituals, but we noticed other titles of interest, 'The Great Perfection'—Great Sphere of the Uttermost (*rdzogs-pa chen-po yang-rtse klong-chen*), 'Treatise on the Basic Traditions of the Great Perfection' (*rdzogs-pa chen-po zhung-snyan-rgyud kyi nyams-rgyud*), 'Collected Teachings of the Spell-Holders' (*rig-'dzin 'dus-pa'i man-ngag*), and hoped that he would be willing to lend his books when he knew us better. There were several small bronze images, all really Buddhist, but the lama gave them p'ön names, referring to Śākyamuni as Shen-rap and

Amitāyus as 'Shen-God White Light'. I commented on this and he agreed at once that they are the same (see p. 62).

Then Yung-drung, who had washed his face in the meantime (pl. XXV*b*), brought the keys and we all went over to visit the main temple, entering by way of the ground floor of our house. We found ourselves in a room some forty feet square, extremely dark, for the only illumination came from a covered opening in the ceiling. Pasang brought a torch and we looked around. The ceiling was supported by four carved wooden pillars and there were traces of frescoes on one of the back walls, but otherwise the building itself was as plain as any ordinary dwelling-house. Around the side and back walls there hung some very fine *thankas*, among which we recognized the regular p'on divinities, Shen-rap, 'The Pure 10,000 times 100,000', Sa-trik and others. Above the altar-table stood a large roughly made cupboard where one would normally expect to see the central divinity. It contained a sacrificial cake (torma) as a form of reserved offering. There were several images, Shen-rap and the Conquerors of the Three Times, set in rough frames on the right-hand side. On the left there was a large collection of very dusty volumes, all wrapped in cloths and strapped up between heavy boards in the usual Tibetan manner. Since the frames were inadequate for their number, they were just piled one upon another. Here was a large collection of p'ön literature such as I was unlikely to find again, but it would clearly be a formidable task to look through it. Meanwhile the Lama was ready to lead us away and lock up once more, so we stumbled out and ascended by the knotched trunk to our home.

From our courtyard we could climb through and look down into the temple we had just visited and I was wondering if we could devise means of descending by that way and bringing up one volume at a time for investigation. But Pasang would not agree and suggested a far better scheme, namely that we should ask for the books to be read ceremonially. The reading of books is often performed out of desire for merit, to counteract evil or to give power to one's entreaties. The words are sacred and thus potent in their own right, whether understood by those reading or not. This was clearly a splendid idea, for the books would have to be taken down, dusted and opened, and meanwhile we would be able to see them, assisted by willing helpers. We approached the lama with our request forthwith and he readily consented to arrange for the ceremony in four days time, which would be the 25th of the Tibetan month and an auspicious day.

For the present a more urgent problem awaited solution. Our main supplies were still stored at Shey, and the provisions that Pasang had fetched from there seventeen days ago while I waited at Saldang, were now almost exhausted. Shey Monastery stands about fourteen miles from Samling further up the river, but the river-route is only practicable in winter when the gorge is frozen. In summer one has to follow another route high up across the mountains—a long and hard day's journey. Pasang would have to go, but this time I would not let him take Takki Babu, so we had to find another helper. Such a one could only be found at Phijor, two hours' climb across the hills towards the NE, or at the little village of Trä, an hour's walk upstream to the south. The river cannot be seen from Samling, for the ground falls steeply down to a precipitous gorge. Thus we decided to investigate our immediate surroundings by way of visiting Trä. Later on there would be occasion to go further afield to Phijor. The track led round the hillside climbing very slightly and at one point the river could be seen in its deep gorge towards the south.

Trä like Samling has taken root upon a small alp high above the river and both places are sheltered by steep mountainsides behind. At Trä there is a stream which can be used for irrigation, so a small village of about twelve houses has developed. At Samling there is no stream, just a little turgid pool fed by a small spring, sufficient for a monastery supported from outside, but useless for growing crops. Trä is closed to the south by great rock-cliffs and there is no habitable site higher up the river until one reaches Shey. We came to the nearest house and asked where the headman lived. The young wheat was beginning to sprout and the buckwheat was due for planting. There was a small temple by the stream containing a large revolving prayer-wheel. It was Nying-ma-pa and not p'ön. As we approached the headman's house, we noticed a great black mastiff unchained by the door. Pasang went at once to the attack with the ice-axe; the animal retreated with snarls and bared fangs and thereafter kept at a safe distance barking furiously the whole while. No half measures will do for these animals. At a show of fury they retreat, but at the least show of irresolution they will be on top of one. We were now free to bang at the door, and after calls from above it was opened; we fumbled into the dark interior and felt our way up a knotched trunk into the bright sun-light of the upper courtyard. Here we found the headman and another villager in conversation. This ceased at once as soon as they saw the strange attire of their visitors, but they motioned us to sit and the headman's wife brought a pot of tea from the brazier and expected us to pro- duce our cups. We had none with us and so refused politely and set about explaining once more just who we were and what we wanted. When the headman was satisfied in these matters, he expressed willingness to help us and called out from his roof for someone named Gyel-tsen. 'He is a poor fellow', he said, 'with no land of his own and will be glad to earn a few rupees.' We learned later on that Gyel-tsen like all the other landless fellows in Dolpo, had come in search of work from the Tibetan side of the frontier. They might in rare cases marry into a Dolpo village, but otherwise they were always regarded as outsiders. They were usually in need of work and money and we observed a tendency for the more prosperous villagers to exploit them. Within a few minutes Gyel-tsen presented himself, seemingly cheerful enough. He promised to come the next morning to Samling, ready to set out for Shey, and (just to be sure) asked for his money in advance. Having transacted our business, we took our leave. The dog awaited us, but continued its barking from a safe distance, following us in this manner to the out- skirts of the village.

At Samling we found a large number of cattle, yaks, dri (female of the yak) and dzo (yak cross-breed), with women and children in charge of them. All these animals had been brought back from the north, where they had spent the winter, and were now grazing in the vicinity of the monastery, where there were no crops for them to damage. We were now just beginning to learn something of the community among which we had arrived. Everyone was very curious about us of course, and women and children were constantly ascending our ladder to see what went on in the 'guest-house'. Phijor, Samling and Trä form one social unit, the wealthier villagers owning houses in all three places. The Lama's family was certainly one of the richest and his nephew was seemingly the most influential villager of Phijor. The twelve houses at Samling had presumably all been built at a time when at least one member of the family was a full-time practiser of religion, but now apart from the Lama there were only two celibate monks in permanent residence. The others were part-time practisers, assembling for the performance of ceremonies at any time when they were available, and remaining in residence for longer periods during the winter months, when their fields and their animals no longer demanded attention. In the summer labour was divided, the men attending to the fields and the women and children to the animals. They were still rather suspicious about us, but friendly enough, and we obtained some excellent milk, butter and cream-cheese, so long as the animals were staying near the monastery. A week later they all moved up to the regular grazing grounds on the way to Shey.

Pasang left the following morning with Gyel-tsen, while I stayed with Takki Babu and the ailing Hemrāj. I visited the Lama and attended to his eyes. He said there was already a great improvement and this encouraged me to make bold to ask to visit his chapel again. Once inside I drew his attention to the history of the monastery (*gdung-rabs*) and asked him if I might borrow it. He agreed readily and so I carried it away to my tent and spent the rest of the day making some sense of it. The numerous abbreviations, unfamiliar letters and names made reading very slow, but the references in the first chapter to the early kings of Tibet aroused my immediate interest and so kept my mind to the task. Throughout the day the place was entirely tranquil. We put up a tent just beyond the monastery-wall and there I stayed except at meal-times when it was convenient to come up to the courtyard of our house. The following evening Pasang returned with the provisions, rice, packets of dried soup, tins of tomato purée, biscuits and chocolate, coffee, tea and a precious tin of jam.

The following day was the 25th, which we had arranged for the reading of the books. I visited the Lama again to attend to his eyes and found his nephew and several other villagers from Phijor all sitting drinking tea. Supported by Pasang, I did my best to answer all the questions asked and was much complimented on my ability to read Tibetan. The Lama now knew that I could not only read, but also understand the sense of the words, and he never ceased to be amazed that one who had never undergone instruction in p'ön teachings, should seemingly understand them intuitively. In fact our methods of learning are so different from theirs, that it could not seem but miraculous. They learn by rote, by constantly reciting certain texts, and when they have learned the words, some will go further and enquire of the meaning, but very few indeed can ever dissociate the meanings from the phrases they have learned and construe them with different words. We learn the sense of the words and the significance of the connecting particles. Thus we can make sense of any text within the limits of our vocabulary. These p'ön texts caused me many problems because of words and phrases of which I did not yet know the implication, but the greater part was quite comprehensible. I soon discovered that the Lama was most knowledgeable and when I asked him about these textual difficulties, he could measure to what extent I already understood. There is no doubt that Pasang's friendliness and tact and my wondrous (for so it seemed to them) comprehension of their doctrines made us appear the most welcome of guests. The Lama took to calling me a p'ön 'incarnation' (*bon sprul-sku*), but his eyes always twinkled on these occasions and he had already expressed his opinion of other 'incarnations' in the neighbourhood. We sat for an hour or so until all those expected had arrived and then at last it was decided to begin the reading. Meanwhile Takki Babu had borrowed a cauldron from Yung-drung and was engaged in brewing a sufficient quantity of well buttered tea. Pasang set about preparing rice-pudding as a very special delicacy, making it with milk and butter, raisins and sugar. Rice alone is a luxury in Dolpo, sugar even more so, while raisins are quite unknown.

The performance began with a general invocation (*gsol-'debs*) and then the books were brought down from the shelves. We started with the 'Mother' (*yum*) in sixteen massive volumes. The pages with their gilt and silver letters on a black ground measured about 2' 6" long by 6" wide. There were three hundred or more pages in each volume, all wrapped in cloths and bound between carved half-inch boards. There was dust everywhere. This work is properly known as the 'Great Sphere' (*khams chen*) and corresponds to 'Perfection of Wisdom' section of the Tibetan Buddhist Canon, which is also nick-named 'Mother'. I have referred elsewhere to the fundamentally feminine nature of Wisdom. In Mahāyāna teaching it is the universal womb whence all arises and the universal void where all disappears. This basic Buddhist notion has tended to coincide with the Shamanistic notion of space which is part of the indigenous religion of the Tibetans. Thus both in Buddhist and p'ön-po monasteries the 'Mother' holds pride of place and it would be a poor temple indeed which did not possess at least this set of books. It must not be thought that the villagers or even most of the monks are anxious to read them in the sense that Westerners read. Revered as the formal expression of absolute wisdom, they are read as a rite to give immediacy to wisdom's innate power. Certainly the reading on this occasion was a perfunctory affair. Everyone present opened one of the volumes, flicked the dust out of the pages and began to read sonorously. Gradually the rhythm quickened, the pages were turned faster until the reader was reading no longer, but merely repeating ĀḤ OṂ HŪṂ—OṂ MATRI MUYE SALE 'DU. Then three pages were turned together, then ten and so on. In such a manner a volume could be read in fifteen minutes. Nevertheless my purpose was served, for I was free to move from one reader to another, to look through the pages which they had finished reading, and to note the general contents. The 'Mother' revealed itself as a complete imitation of its Buddhist equivalent. It began: 'In the language of Sh'ang-sh'ung —— —' instead of 'In the language of India —— —', instead of 'buddhas' we read of 'guides' (dran-pa) and instead of 'bodhisattvas' (byang-chub-sems-dpa) we read of 'eternity-beings' (gYung-drung sems-dpa), but all else was the same: the essential voidness of the fivefold personality, of body, feelings, perceptions, impulses and consciousness; the voidness of the six great perfections, liberality, virtuous conduct, forbearance, energy, mental concentration and wisdom; the essential voidness of all moral and philosophical conceptions. Thus in spite of its vast bulk I was no less willing than the readers to consider this work 'read' in half an hour or so. The volumes were rewrapped and restacked and we at least had the satisfaction to know they were free of dust. Attention was now turned to the 'Hundred-Thousander' in eight volumes. The full title of this work is 'The All-Pervading Essence of True P'ön in a Hundred Thousand (verses)' (bon-nyid snying-po bdal ba'i bum) and it was soon apparent that this was nothing more than an imitation of the 'Perfection of Wisdom' Sūtra in 100,000 verses (Śatasahasrikaprajñāpāramitā). This work was soon disposed of and returned to its place. After this we read 'Many Discourses' (mdo-mangs) in one large volume. This contains several short texts in praise of the main p'ön divinities, Sa-trik, 'The Pure 10,000 times 100,000', Shen-rap and 'Shen-God White Light'. I noted another short work entitled 'Sūtra of the Eightfold P'ön', which merely imitated the regular Buddhist teachings of the eightfold path. Another, entitled

'Sūtra of the Means and the Way' gave instruction in the six Buddhist perfections. Another, entitled 'Sūtra concerning the Removal of the Grief of King Kyi-sha', told the story of how this king lost his only son and was overwhelmed with grief. Shen-rap heard of this and came to the capital, where he was acclaimed by the populace. He visited the king and instructed him in the doctrine of univeral impermanence. The whole theme and especially the phrase 'all compounded things are impermanent' ('*dus-byas thams-cad mi-rtag-ste*) represents a complete appropriation of Buddhist teachings. We went rapidly through other volumes of sūtras and then passed on to the tantras, which were not so easily analysed because their contents were far more heterogeneous. One important text was called 'The Tantra of the Magic Dart' (*phur-pa'i rgyud*) and consisted of three separate works, all concerned with the same cycles of divinities. The central divinity is 'Sky-Gape' (*mkha-'gying-kha*), who is also known as 'God of the Dart' (*phur-pa'i lha*) and variously identified with Garuḍa (*mkha-lding*) and the 'Dragon-Prince' ('*brug-gsas*). The divinities of the four quarters are 'Falcon-Prince', 'Fire-Prince', 'Summit-Prince' and 'Lightning-Prince'.[a] Although one of these texts is entitled 'The Tantra of the Self-Release of the Impediments, which cuts off the Five Poisons from the root' (*nyon-mongs rang-grol dug-lnga rtsad-gcod kyi rgyud*—all Buddhist terminology), yet the names of the divinities reveal their indigenous Tibetan character. Other titles and proper names were not so easily interpreted and it was clear that these tantras deserved closer study. For the present we could merely note the titles for future reference.

In the meantime tea was served and then the bowls of rice-pudding. The Lama merely tasted his and left the remainder, but I erred in thinking that he might not like it. When the reading was at last finished, he told Yung-drung to carry the bowl to his house. I thought then, still wrongly, that he intended Yung-drung to eat the contents. The day's performance had fully served its purpose, for I now had a general idea of the contents

[a] In every case here 'Prince' translates *tib. gsas*. See p. 49 fn.

of the collection and knew which books were worth looking at again. The works of chief interest were those in the lama's own chapel and the tantras in the main temple and I decided to look at them one by one. By now it was early evening and we withdrew to our house for a meal. We were not left alone however, for everyone wanted to see our domestic arrangements for himself.

Early the next morning one of the villagers from Karang, who had served us as porter five days before, appeared again. He had come with his wife to have the after-death ceremony read for his father who had just died. We asked him why he had troubled to come all this way again, when there were lamas in Karang. He replied that the Lama of Saldang was far more expert in these matters. This reasoning of his was quite logical, for the efficacy of any Tibetan ceremony depends primarily on the mental disposition of those taking part. Contrary to popular belief, there can be no arbitrary magical effect. The spells are effective only in so far as the celebrant is skilled in them. Hence a lama of reputation will be always in demand. We went to attend the ceremony which was to be held in the Lama's own chapel. He was assisted by the two monks. A long painted scroll illustrating the six spheres of existence was spread out on the floor and a name-card was prepared for the consciousness of the deceased. The ceremony progressed in just the same manner as the corresponding Buddhist rite such as we had witnessed at Jiwong, except that the chief divinity addressed was 'Shen-God White Light' instead of the Buddhist saviour Avalokiteśvara.[a] Yet in the course of this ceremony I learned to think of these p'ön-pos as more than just imitators of the Buddhists, for their profound sincerity made them practisers in their own right.

The Lama revolved his prayer-wheel as he chanted, revolving it in the p'ön manner, anti-clockwise. The idea of doing this had always seemed to me deliberately perverse, yet here was a man

[a] For the rNying-ma-pa rite of guiding the consciousness after death see BH, pp. 262 ff.

doing it while intent on prayer and as though it were the natural thing to do. This form of p'ön would prove of special interest in any comparative study of religions, for it represents a kind of Buddhism which has been completely divorced from its historical setting. It has been argued by some that the historical existence of a 'founder', viz. Śākyamuni, is quite irrelevant to the development of Buddhism, in so far as this religion is an expression of a 'universal metaphysical tradition' and so transcends the limitations of any one teacher or any one period. This notion of absolute truth ever concerned to express itself in forms adapted to different hearers is certainly a very neat one, but it seems to be an invention of Western thinkers who themselves stand apart from any particular tradition.[a] Throughout the whole history of Indian Buddhism Śākyamuni held the central position and continued to do so in the early days of Buddhism in Tibet. Later he came to be regarded generally as just one of many buddha-forms, but this was not primarily because of any loss of historical perspective, but because so many other buddhas and would-be buddhas (bodhisattvas) were believed to have appeared upon the scene. The different orders of Tibetan Buddhism have remained aware of their historical development. But in the case of p'ön it might be argued that here is a religion which is conscious of no development. It has appropriated the philosophical and moral ideas of the Buddhists and adopted their practices by simply claiming that they are the true p'ön, as revealed by a Teacher Shen-rap, to whom however no historical substance can be given. That it should have been felt necessary to invent such a person, serves to confirm the central importance of the historical Śākyamuni for the type of Buddhism which was spreading in Tibet during the eighth and ninth centuries. The founder of 'white p'ön' (p. 43 fn.), 'Life-Empowering Knowledge-Holder' (tshe-dbang rig-'dzin), the supposed brother of 'Lotus-Born' (Padmasambhava), lived presumably in the eighth century. I have observed elsewhere (BH,

[a] The best illustration of this theory is Aldous Huxley's *The Perennial Philosophy*, Chatto & Windus, London, 1946.

p. 140) that Tibet was then surrounded by countries which had been Buddhist for centuries and it seems most unlikely that nothing should have been known of Indian doctrines before that time. Moreover the 'Old Sect' (Nying-ma-pa), who claim to be the faithful followers of 'Lotus-Born', introduced whole cycles of texts, which were later judged to be spurious, viz. not properly Buddhist in origin. These texts, like the whole p'ön canon, of which we had seen so much the day before, were supposed to have been translated from the language of Sh'ang-sh'ung, the land west of Mt. Kailas. Although the Sh'ang-sh'ung titles, which are quoted in the texts, would seem to be completely fictitious, it is none the less very likely that Indian doctrines and actual texts reached central Tibet from Kashmir via Sh'ang-sh'ung. It was possibly in this area that certain Indian ideas first mingled with Tibetan ones and it should not be difficult to distinguish some of them. Thus it is significant that the p'ön-pos have connected the line of the early Tibetan kings with the Pāṇḍavas, the famous 'brahmanical' dynasty of the *Mahābhāratā* (*BH*, p. 291). The mythical bird *khyung* would scarcely be so important in their mythology, were it not for the Indian *garuḍa*. The supreme being of both the 'Old Sect' and the p'ön-pos is represented iconographically as a naked Jain ascetic; his name 'All Good' (*kun-tu bzang-po*) is manifestly Indian Buddhist (*samantabhadra*), for it is one of the titles of the Supreme Buddha Vairocana. The p'ön-pos specify their supreme being as the divine father of *Tshe-dbang rig-'dzin* and there seems no need to doubt the Tibetan nature of this father-god 'Sky-Guide' (*gnam-mkha dran-pa*). The characteristics of the chief p'ön divinities are space and light; thus when they are given form, the creatures of the upper air become the first symbols, the mythical bird *khyung*, identified with the Indian *garuḍa*, the vulture and the dragon. The idea of a founder can have no place in original p'ön-po notions, for the earthly representatives of divine knowledge were presumably the shamans and perhaps at a later stage of development the line of ruling kings, who are supposed to have descended from the sky. The Teacher Shenrap seems to be a complete invention, modelled on Śākyamuni. The next important divinity, 'Shen-God White Light' (*gshen-lha-'od-dkar*) belongs to the old p'ön tradition, but his original character is lost by association with the Buddhist divinities, 'Glancing Eye', 'Boundless Light' and 'Boundless Life'. The conventional image of 'Boundless Life', a seated buddha with hands placed together on the lap in the gesture of meditation and supporting a 'vase of life' (*tshe-bum*), is commonly identified by p'ön-pos as 'Shen-God White Light'. Another interesting divinity is the 'Foremost King of Phantom Forms' (*gong-mdzad 'phrul gyi rgyal-po*). He is identified with 'Glancing Eye' (*Avalokiteśvara*), but in origin he can only represent the divine nature of the early Tibetan kings (p. 47 fn.). This kind of p'ön consists of a combination of early Tibetan myth, miscellaneous Indian ideas and Buddhist morality and philosophy. The history of its development may prove traceable, but it continues to be practised with total disregard for historical considerations. All that it contains of religious worth is manifestly of Buddhist origin and yet it stoutly affirms its essential independence. I doubt if any religion could be 'debunked' so easily, yet its practice has every appearance of validity and I certainly learned not to regard these p'ön-pos just as foolish imitators of the Buddhists. It seemed in fact that their religious practice excelled that of all the other monasteries of Dolpo.

The ceremony was over by midday and I asked if I might borrow 'The Tantra of the Magic Dart' and 'Many Discourses' from the main temple. The Lama sent Yung-drung over with the key, and from that day on it was taken for granted that I should borrow what I pleased. Thus Pasang's scheme had certainly proved the right one in every way. I used to carry the books to my tent, look through them there, and then take them to the Lama to ask questions. It was an excellent arrangement. His eyes had now quite recovered but he never ceased to rejoice in the recovery, saying almost every day: 'See how well my eyes are!' We gave him a small mirror as a present, so that he could see them clearly for himself. Thereafter we had many patients with inflamed eyes from Phijor, but never so successful a cure.

The next day we invited the Lama and his two monks to a meal. The roof of our house seemed the best place to serve the food, so we removed our small green tent, borrowed small tables and carpets from the Lama's house and the scene was set. Pasang and Takki Babu prepared a meal of boiled rice, curried vegetables and spiced cheese together with a plentiful supply of buttered tea. The only fresh vegetables available in Dolpo were turnips, but we had not yet exhausted our stock of dried ones. Peek Frean's biscuits were served as a final delicacy. Once again our guests left part of their food, but on this occasion the Lama asked if he might have three biscuits as a general offering (tshogs). Thus the destination of the rice-pudding and all other tit-bits was revealed. Whatever was delicious, must be put aside for the chosen divinity and afterwards placed in the little cupboard together with the reserved sacrificial cake (torma). Pasang, Hemrāj and I ate together with our guests. There was little conversation, but it was pleasant to be seated tranquilly on a roof-top in the warmth of the midday sun. We looked across to the snow-free rocks of the 'Copper Mountain' (zangs-kyi rong), whose god is remembered in all the monastery ceremonies, for he is the local god (gzhi bdag) of Samling (pl. XXIVa). We talked of winter when its summit would be covered with snow and the river below would be frozen. In that season all villagers who are 'members' of Samling, have to spend three months there as full-time practisers of religion or pay a fine for their absence. In the village the main occupations would be spinning and weaving. Food would consist of what had been stored in the summer, grain in the form of tsamba, dried meat, butter and tea. The yaks and the sheep would all be away on the plains to the north and only a few dzo (cross-breeds) would be kept on the ground-floor of the houses. They would provide a little milk in return for the hay that was stored for them. When snow falls it is unwise and often impossible to travel, but it may not lie for long and then the route through Tarap and Tsharka and down to Kāgbeni is traversable. The two monks said they would be going to the Nepal Valley on pilgrimage that year, and we suggested that they should plan to reach Kathmandu in the tenth Tibetan month (November) when we would still be there, but they insisted that it would not be cool enough for them until the twelfth month. As we should be gone by then, we promised to leave copies of our photographs with the Mongolian lama of Bodhnāth, from whom they could collect them. We imagined ourselves staying in Dolpo the whole year round. Our day-to-day life seemed to be timeless; my watch had now been broken for several weeks and we used to guide the conduct of daily affairs by the sun. Pasang's watch, a present from Smiths Ltd., functioned well, but he had forgotten to wind it and thereafter it was only by the sun that it could be reset. The dog now accepted us as members of the monastery and so had ceased his fierce barking. The cat no longer kept a safe distance, but would sit boldly in our courtyard confidently awaiting pats of butter. In the whole seven months of travel it was only at Samling that we felt as though we belonged to the place. Trains and ships and aeroplanes became part of another order of existence; in explaining to the Lama what they were like, one seemed rather to belong to his world than to theirs.

When the meal was finished, we directed the conversation towards our latest need. I had been looking carefully at the 'Tantra of Tibet' and the 'Samling Records' and had decided that I wanted copies. We knew that the two monks spent their time copying manuscripts, and so we asked them if they would undertake this work for us. They protested that they were working on a copy of the 'Mother', which must be finished by the time they left for Kathmandu in the winter; it would be impossible to spend a month working for us. The Lama urged them on our behalf and at last they agreed to copy the 'Samling Records' and two selected chapters of the other work.

These two monks, Tshül-trhim and Hla-kyä, had really become very friendly to us. Each lived in his own house, a smaller

XVII.

a. Lhori Village. (p. 93)
b. Lhori villagers practising archery. (p. 93)

XVIII.

a. Woman of Mö, wearing the typical Dolpo head-dress. (p. 95)
b. The gorge above Nyisäl, looking downstream. (p. 94)

XIX.

a. Reading texts in Shimen Gomba. (p. 97)
b. Shimen. (p. 98)

XX.

a. View from the Mö Pass, northwards to Tibet. (p. 95) The pass between the mountains in the centre of the photograph leads straight down to the Tibetan uplands, where the men of Dolpo take their animals for grazing in winter. (pp. 82–3)

b. View SE beyond Ting-khyu, towards the Tibetan frontier, which is in fact the sky-line. Ting-khyu Village is in shadow immediately below. The tall fort is visible nearer to the river. (p. 99)

XXI.

a. View from the Mö Pass southwards over Dolpo. (pp. 95–6). Pasang, myself and Takki Babu in the foreground.
b. Ting-khyu villagers, inscribing stones for a prayer-wall. (p. 101)

XXII.

a. *The Lama of Ting-khyu.* (p. 101)
b. *Two men of Karang, sharing a pipe as they rest on the Karang Pass.* (p. 111)

XXIII.

a. Maitreya in Karang Gomba. (p. 110)
b. Mañjuśrī, Lion of Speech, in Karang Gomba. (pp. 108 & 110)

XXIV.

a. Samling Gomba and the 'Copper Mountain' (about 19,000 feet) beyond the gorge of the Shey River. (pp. 111 and 127)
b. The Lama of Samling. The flowers all around are Stellera chamaejasme, *which bloom in profusion over the mountains of Dolpo.*

version of the lama's, with a small open courtyard, a chapel and a kitchen on the first floor. They sat copying most of the day, working either in the sunny courtyard or else inside the chapel. Sometimes they would visit me in my tent and then I could ask them about difficulties in the script. My typewriter delighted them greatly and they would look wonderingly through the few European-style books I had with me.

Two days later, now June 7th, we climbed over the mountains to PHIJOR (SI: Phijorgāon). Light showers of rain were beginning to sweep across Dolpo and the grassy slopes were blossoming forth in a variety of flowers. Among these predominated the red-white clusters of star-like flowers (*Stellera chamaejasme*), which we had first noted above Rohagāon (p. 56), white anemones (*Anemone rupicola*) and purplish incarvilleas (*Incarvillea grandiflora*). The landscape was, as always, completely treeless. The village of Phijor, consisting of about fifty houses, has grown up around a small stream which descends from the direction of the 'Purple Mountain' (*smug-po'i rong*) and flows into the Shey River some two miles below Samling. The track from Samling leads up behind the monastery and over the ridge which forms the watershed of the two streams. We reached there in two hours and established ourselves by a little p'ön-po temple at the southern end of the village. One tent was sufficient, for we were able to make use of the temple-kitchen. The temple inside had been recently repainted and contained nothing of note. There is no lama; it is maintained by a few families who count themselves its members and on set days, the 10th, 15th or 22nd of the Tibetan month, certain of the men will gather to intone the liturgies. At the northern end of the village there is a little Sa-kya-pa temple, which we visited the following morning. It contains a complete set of the Tibetan Buddhist Canon and a fine gilt image of Maitreya. Repainting was in progress. We visited the headman to arrange a porter for the return journey that evening, and then called on the lama's nephew, who agreed to help us in replenishing our supplies of wheat.

LANG MONASTERY (*glang dgon-pa*), which we now went on to visit, stands at the head of a narrow gorge that cuts eastwards into the heart of the mountains about a mile below Phijor. It is a solitary place of bare and desolate rocks (pl. XXV*a*). A woman appeared in response to our shouts, promptly disappeared and then returned with the lama, who willingly showed us around the temples. One of them contained a collection of images and thankas comparable with those we had seen at Yang-tsher Monastery, but happily far better cared for. There was another temple which had been repainted recently, and finally the chapel of the lama which contained a large number of books. We took the opportunity of asking to see the liturgies of 'Great Brilliance'. The two chief Sa-kya-pa monasteries in Dolpo were once Yang-tsher and Lang, yet at Yang-tsher we had not been able to find trace of these texts, for they have been replaced there by Nying-ma-pa rituals. Faith in the Supreme Buddha 'Great Brilliance' (*Mahāvairocana*) has been replaced by faith in the buddha-magician 'Lotus-Born' (*Padmasambhava*); the Indian Buddhist tutelary divinity Hevajra has been rejected in favour of the indigenous 'Tiger-God' (*stag-lha*), who is acknowledged both by Nying-ma-pas and p'ön-pos. It is significant that the newly painted temple at Lang contains only Nying-ma-pa divinities. But this lama was not ignorant of the earlier traditions, and willingly produced the relevant texts for us to look through. This as last enabled us to set about identifying the figures in the mandalas, which are painted in the old Sa-kya-pa chötens. Meanwhile Takki Babu had been preparing a meal in a kitchen, which the woman had put at his disposal, and while we ate, we were able to learn something about our hosts. The lama was married, but this woman was not his wife as we had supposed. She was just a woman of religious disposition who lived at the monastery as general caretaker. The lama was brother to the headman of Trä, with whom we were already acquainted. As well as his house at the monastery, he owned a family-house in Phijor, where his wife and old mother were living. He begged us to call on our way back and give his mother ointment for her eyes. Later he decided to accompany us, as he had some business of his own to attend to. By no means unlettered, he none the less gave the impression of a man of the world rather than of a man of religion, and we compared him unfavourably with other lamas of Dolpo. But his was an hereditary position and there seemed to be no one to support him in the religious life. Here in Dolpo the old Sa-kya-pa practice is dead and now that its followers have turned to Nying-ma-pa ritual, the p'ön-pos who practise something so similar, seem to outdo them in their enthusiasm and their popularity.

In the afternoon we returned to Phijor accompanied by the lama, and having anointed his mother's eyes, went on to the headman's house to ask for the man he had promised. A young fellow was duly awaiting us; like Gyel-tsen of Trä, he proved to be a landless Tibetan who had come to Dolpo in search of work and money. His name was Shi-shok (*srid-srog*), 'World-Life' and his features were sad and of a feminine delicacy. We learned later that he had a young wife and a little boy and it was with difficulty that he earned enough for his family, who lived in a hired house in Phijor. Pasang now transferred his things to the house of Nam-gyel Wang-dü, the Lama's nephew, where he would stay until the wheat-flour was ready.

I returned to Samling across the mountain with Hemrāj, Takki Babu and our new helper Shi-shok. Samling seemed to have become our home; it was with gladness that we looked down on it once more from the top of the pass and then hastened down to pay our respects to the Lama before settling in our own house and preparing an evening meal. As dusk was falling I erected the yellow tent in a better position than before just out-side the ring of the prayer-walls and among a host of our star-like flowers (*Stellera chamaejasme*). It was now the last day of the fourth Tibetan month and in the total absence of the moon the sky was a spangled canopy of brilliant stars, suspended above the great black silhouette of the 'Copper Mountain'. One seemed to be totally alone.

That day and the next passed happily, for there were still books to be looked through and the Lama was always available to answer questions. Pasang arrived in the evening with Takki Babu and Shi-shok, who had returned to meet him, carrying a great bag of flour apiece. Then Pasang came to the tent with me and took two books out of his rucksack, 'The Tantra of Tibet' and 'The Treatise on the Basic Traditions of the Great Perfection' (see p. 114). Nam-gyel Wang-dü had sent them with the approval of his uncle, and since they possessed other copies we could have these as our own. They were the two p'ön-po books which we wanted above all others; there would be no need now for the monks to copy out just two precious chapters, for we possessed them all. But we were asked not to mention it locally, for although the Lama was merely concerned to help us, tongues would soon be wagging in the village, saying that he was selling religious things for profit. Thus Pasang agreed discreetly on their monetary value and I offered this sum as a general present to the monastery. The next day we offered a further present of money in recognition of the hospitality we were receiving. The Lama responded immediately by making me a present of another manuscript, a little text on meditation entitled 'Instructions of the Great Spirit Sky-Guide' (*bla chen dran pa nam mkha'i man ngag*) and by promising to seek out other texts of use to us. This was a most happy state of affairs and I set to work on our new acquisitions, so that some extracts at least could be read with the Lama's assistance.

We could have lived contentedly at Samling until the autumn; for a while I considered staying on here and foregoing much of the travel that still lay ahead. Our food supplies were organized satisfactorily. There was all the wheat-flour we wanted and occasionally a piece of mutton could be obtained from the village. The cattle were now being pastured up on the mountains about two hours' climb away, and Pasang would go and fetch butter and cheese. The butter was hairy and grubby, but he washed and salted it and turned it into appetizing pats which went well with our crusty bread. For midday and the evening we had rice or wheat-cakes accompanied by soup made from packets and reinforced with Marmite, or there might be meat-patties (for the mutton we received was better for being minced and well seasoned) or cheese cooked and flavoured with onions and spices. It is interesting to recall how delicious everything seemed, especially the clear Darjeeling tea and Peek Freans' biscuits which Takki Babu brought to my tent every afternoon. In a place so remote as Samling this was truly great luxury. The rest of the party used to brew a great pot in the Tibetan style, well buttered and salted and even Hemrāj had developed a liking for it, preferring it to my milkless variety.

But all this time Hemrāj had been unhappy; now fearful lest our stay in Samling should be much prolonged, he began to make known his discontent. Slight contention developed and the peace was broken. He had withstood the rigours of the last four months quite well and I was agreeable to his returning to Kathmandu forthwith, but how to arrange this was a serious problem. I was not to be persuaded to hasten away and the only alternative was to split the party. For me to lose Pasang would be like losing both my hands; yet Hemrāj and Takki Babu were not a sufficiently strong combination alone. Neither of them spoke Tibetan and they were totally inexpert in dealing with these Tibetan villagers, even those who spoke a little Nepāli. The only solution was to find a reliable man of some local standing to travel with them, but our enquiries led nowhere. We were planning to visit Shey in a few days time and so hoped we might find someone there. To send Takki Babu in advance would serve my purposes quite well, for there would be a mail-bag awaiting me down at Pokhara and he would be able to bring this up to meet us; it would mean parting with him for about a month. Pleased to serve in any way asked of him, he readily agreed to the plan. In the meantime there was nothing to be done but continue our life as before until the time came to set out for Shey.

FESTIVAL AT SHEY

The occasion of this expedition was the great yearly festival celebrated in the 5th Tibetan month from the 10th to the 15th (full moon). This event seems to represent the Spring Festival of Dolpo. There is no life in the land throughout the winter months. Then in May the villagers travel down to the northern plain to bring back their yaks, dzos and sheep for the summer pasture. By the end of May they are at work in their fields and by mid-June full life is under way. This will regularly be the 5th Tibetan month, and the best time for a festival in any month are those most auspicious days which culminate with the full moon.

We set out early on the 8th, intending to reach Shey in one day. The route ascends behind Samling and then crosses the western flanks of the 'Purple Mountain', where women and children of Phijor and Trä were watching over the cattle. There is a small group of rough stone huts which are abandoned during the winter and then rendered habitable again for the summer. Cattle-watching is work for women and children, for the men are now at work in the fields. We rested here a while and made cocoa with the fresh milk they gave us. The track continued high above and well in from the river; the precipitous gorge could be seen now and again far down on the right. One passes over slopes now gay with many flowers (see p. 149) and clambers carefully across bare and broken hill-sides. The whole route lies between 16,000 and 18,000 feet but again one might be somewhere in the heart of the Cairngorms, for the relative heights of mountains and valleys are much the same. As we continued, the sky became overcast and a cold wind blew upon us. Amidst gathering storm-clouds we descended to a subsidiary stream and had barely crossed to the far side when hail began to fall. There was nowhere to take shelter and it fell forthwith with such violence that all we could do was to crouch together covering ourselves with capes. Thus we remained becoming increasingly cold and wet until the fury of the storm began to abate and it was possible to walk against it. We could not hope to reach Shey that day, so we made our way towards a group of herdsmen's tents which Pasang had seen from above. I had not seen them and he had not referred to them before, but now he led the way towards them with complete assurance. The occupants of the first tent made us welcome; slipping in under the flap we settled around the fire, willingly enduring the smoky atmosphere in return for a little warmth. We boiled water, Takki Babu made tea and all seemed well once more. Our two porters, Gyel-tsen and Shi-shok, arrived. They had been some way behind us and more fortunate in finding cover. The storm had now abated and we erected a tent between those of the herdsmen. Several of them knew us, for they were people of Saldang and this was one of their regular summer pastures. We cooked a meal with the help of the dry twigs and dung they gave us, and then slept as peaceably as ever. The next morning was fine; we climbed over the mountain and descended to Shey.

The main door of the temple was open and we could walk straight in. A group of men and youths all dressed in dark red home-spun were moulding tormas (sacrificial cakes). They showed no surprise at our appearance, for everyone in Dolpo knew about us by now. It was the first time that I had seen the inside of this temple, for when we had arrived here five weeks before from across the Phoksumdo Pass, there had been no one to open the doors to us. The frescoes were comparatively recent, perhaps fifty years old or so, but well drawn and of pleasing colours. This monastery is nominally Karma Ka-gyü-pa (see pp. 77-8) and there is a great painting of the Karma-pa Lama on the rear wall, but all the other paintings suggested the prevalence of Nying-ma-pa practice and this was to be confirmed by the ceremonies that we were about to witness. There were a number of fine bronze images; especially noteworthy was one of the 'Holder of the Vajra' (*Vajradhara*), supreme buddha of the Ka-gyü-pas.

Shey Monastery stands just above a river-junction and by the bank of the eastern tributary there is a small grassy plain, where we decided to establish a camp. While we were busy erecting the tents, the first party of pilgrims arrived along the track from Saldang. Like us they were coming to spend the days of the festival at Shey; they came mostly on foot, leading loaded yaks and ponies. Up till now we had met the Dolpo villagers while they were at work and we had grown used to the coarse woollen cloth of natural colour in which they were normally clad. But now the men were wearing new clothes of dark hues with shawls of bright colours slung round their shoulders, while the women were dressed in the gayest of patterned garments (frontispiece), all made from their own wool on their own looms. Men and women alike wear an under-garment of lighter wool and wide trousers drawn in with tapes below the knees. Next comes a short shirt or blouse of silk or cotton, imported material and almost luxury-wear, and on top of this the main gown, sleeveless for women and long-sleeved for men. Married women wear a striped apron of many colours in the regular Tibetan manner. Thus they made a very gay company indeed. The saddle-bags of the pack-animals are of coarse homespun [woven in pleasing striped patterns. People gradually arrived from all parts of Dolpo and the monastery-buildings were soon overflowing with visitors. Many of our acquaintances from Phijor had arrived, for no distinction was felt between p'ön-po and Buddhist.

By the afternoon the tormas, butter-lamps and general offerings had been arranged on the great wooden stand (tiered mandala) in the centre of the temple and the reading of the liturgy began. At the head of the row of 'monks' was seated a very old man. We learned that he was the acting head of the community and merited the title of 'lama' on account of his long years of religious life. He seldom leaves his house by the temple. Next to him was seated a boy-lama eight years old. He was the son of the lama of Ting-khyu and had been recognized as the reincarnation of the brother of the previous head-lama of Shey. Some people seemed to doubt the legitimacy of this incarnation for it was an entirely new one. The head-lama of Shey is a regular reincarnation of the founder-lama Ten-dzin Rä-pa (*bstan-'dzin ras-pa*). The present incumbent is about thirty years old. It was impossible to meet him for he had been in solitary meditation in the little hermitage near Shey for the last three years and in spite of rumours that he would be present at this festival, he still did not appear. As for the founder-lama Ten-dzin Rä-pa, so far we knew nothing of him, but hearing that the printing-blocks of his biography were actually herein Shey Monastery, we assumed it would be an easy matter to obtain a copy of the text. Next to the boy-lama was seated his preceptor, the monk of Ting-khyu (p. 101). Also present was the acting-lama of Sham-tr'ak (p. 106). The remaining eight or nine celebrants were all men of Shey, married householders and reputedly men of religion. Small as the land of Dolpo is, it contains examples of every kind of religious life. There are five incarnate lamas, of whom the best authenticated is the Lama of Shey. The others, such as the lama of Säl Monastery above Namdo or the lama of Yab-Yum Monastery above Karang or the boy-lama at Shey, are merely reputed to be incarnations (*sprul-sku*) and the term is used in a popular sense, as though any one who showed unusual aptitude for religion must be an incarnation of some deceased lama and it were only a matter of deciding who it must be. But no authoritative tests are carried out and these identifications remain nothing more than general opinion. Then there are the hereditary lamas. Some of these are the owners of their temples like the lama of Sham-tr'ak or of Lang Monastery, who, as married men, transmit their functional and property rights to their sons. Such a one comes to merit the term 'lama' ('superior') by the size of his religious estate. Our Lama of Samling really belongs to this category in that he is a member of a comparatively wealthy family with property in Phijor and Trä as well as at Samling. Yet he chose to devote himself single-mindedly to the religious life and so remained celibate, becoming lama by religious merit as well as by inheritance. The aged lama of Shey and presumably the lama of Yang-tsher, whom we never met, are similarly placed. Then there are the monks proper, few in number, who will all probably be acknowledged as lamas when they become a little more venerable. Their families have property rights in the monastery where they are living, be it Samling, Yang-tsher or Ting-khyu. There are no proper monks at Shey just because no one there has chosen to be one. Then there are the lay-practisers owning houses in the monasteries and taking part in the ceremonies when it is convenient for them to do so. Their forefathers built houses there in the past when some members of the family were full-time monks, and now their successors continue to acknowledge their religious responsibilities. These varied circumstances account for the motley collection of celebrants who were now taking part in the festival.

The liturgy in use was 'The Lama's Perfecter of Thought, Remover of All Impediments' (*bla-ma'i thugs-sgrub bar-chad kun sel*). The 'Lama' in this case is 'Lotus-Born', invoked primarily in the manifestation of 'Fierce Master' (*gu-ru drag-po*); the intention of the ritual is clear from the title, the impediments being in the first place all hostile spirits and demons and secondly all mental obstructions to the proper performance of the religious life. The intoning of this liturgy, repeated 108 times, continued throughout that evening and the whole of the following day. We passed the time sometimes seated in the temple at the lower end of the row of performers, and sometimes down at our tents cooking and eating and entertaining the many visitors who were continually coming to see what we were doing (pl. XXVIIIb). Wherever one went, there were happy laughing faces. It was rumoured that there would be monastic dances ('*cham*) in the evening, and later when it was suggested that they might not be held this year, we made our own offering to the monastery, accompanying it with the request that the dances should take place. This request was not to be refused. By this time night had fallen; since it was planned to hold them inside the temple, everyone crowded inside and sat cross-legged around the walls several rows deep. Pasang brought our Aladdin lamp and suspended it from the roof. Its vulgar glare contested with the gentle yellow light of the hundreds of butter-lamps, but at least we would see the dancers. There were just three of them, representing the 'Fierce Master' (*gu-ru drag-po*), the 'Lion-Headed' Ḍākinī (*senge gdong-ma*) and the 'Fierce Blue Master' (*gu-ru drag-mthing*). They whirled and twirled in far too small a space and perhaps partly for this reason I was conscious of a feeling of active participation which I have never experienced before in such a gathering. These grotesque divinities seemed to be really rejoicing at the sight of all the piled-up offerings and the rapt expressions of the onlookers seemed to urge them to acceptance.

There now followed another ceremony in order to dispose of the eight classes of harmful divinities. For this thread-crosses were used, representing space in general and the sphere of activity of these divinities in particular; they are enticed inside as it were, by the heaps of offerings that are piled around. The wood and thread structure, in which they are now caught like birds in a cage, is then carried outside the monastery and destroyed. The text employed was entitled 'The Purifier of the Depths of Foul Dregs, extracted (from secret fundamental texts) and arranged as the Ceremony of the Thread-Cross of the Proud Ones of the Eight Classes'.[a] It is filled with the usual repetitions and the last page or two will give an adequate idea of this type of ritual.

'Now you hosts of Proud Ones in the spheres of existence, let us hope that you will cheerfully take your departure! Since there is no place for you to stay here, we beg you to leave together with your whole following. The way to the Thread-Cross has been shown. Shown as what? Shown as the realm where the spirits of the directions and intermediate directions and the zenith and nadir all gather together. There is no need to tell them. The sun and moon, the lunar mansions and the stars, the 'lords of the soil', spirits below ground (*klu*), spirits

[a] *sde brgyad khengs mdos khol phyungs bltas chog tu bkod pa rtsub 'gyur rnyogs ma gting dwangs* (*Rin-chen gten-mdzod*, vol. *phi*).

above ground (*gnyen*), all of them find joy in the Thread-Cross and yearn after it. They delight in the substitute offerings and revel in the riches. Therefore let the hosts of gods and demons of the spheres of existence accept as suitable possessions these limitless riches of the Thread-Cross Substitute which has been set up as representing the spheres of existence.

'In order to pacify the harm-doing of arrogant perversity, arouse pure thought of great tranquillity!

'In order to prosper long life and good fortune, produce increase of strength and physical power!

'In order to gain power over the threefold world, let fly the lasso of the wind of red light!

'In order to cut off at its roots all hostile opposition, emit the wrathful power of fierce apparition!

'For the spontaneous operation of these four rites, come now together at the Substitute Thread-Cross.[a] SHA-RA-RA!

'Now they have come! SI-LI-LI!

'Hearken to the word of truth of the Precious Ones!

'Keep to the bond of all the gods of the three bases![b]

'Take the awards bestowed by the Thread-Cross!

'Be pleased by the substitute and let a smiling countenance appear!

'Consider the infallible law of cause and effect! Do not congregate here; go harmlessly elsewhere, willing us good! But if you do not hearken and do us harm, in the form of 'Lotus Garland of Skulls' (*padma thod phreng rtsal*), the wrathful form that quells the spheres of existence, we will encompass heaven and earth and intermediate space and cleaving your hearts, we shall extract your life-force.'[c]

The thread-cross and the substitute offerings were then taken outside the temple and hurled away.

[a] The four rites are those of Pacifying, Gaining Prosperity, Empowering and Destroying (*BH*, pp. 257–60).

[b] The three bases (*rtsa gsum*) are Body, Speech and Mind.

[c] *op. cit.*, folio 19. For a general account of thread-cross ceremonies see Nebesky-Wojkowitz, *Oracles and Demons*, pp. 369 ff.

After this we descended to our tents and the rest of the gathering retired to their night-shelter in and around the monastery. They must have slept as close as sardines. The whole of the next day was spent consecrating and finally distributing the general offerings (*tshogs*), and the merry-making greatly increased. While the celebrants were intoning their invocations inside the temple, the lay-folk were dancing in rings in the court-yard outside (pl. XXVIII*a*). I stood for a while in the door-way between these two ways of life, religious and secular; however different in time and tune was their singing, one was conscious of a single culture, of a single united interest.

There was still one ceremony to be performed and for this everyone was now waiting, uncertain whether it would be held this day or the next. This was the rite of 'Life-Consecration' (*tshe-dbang*), which has been compared rather superficially with the Christian Eucharist.[a] I had never been present at this cere-mony and was now most anxious to see it. Towards evening the old lama of Shey announced that 'Life-Consecration' would be given the next morning, news that was received with general satisfaction, for there had been rumours that it might not be performed this year. It was in fact certain to be, but such was the mood of expectancy, that inevitably contrary doubts were being expressed.

The following morning everyone gathered in the temple. The ceremony began in the usual way with the invoking and praising of the chief divinity and his entourage. This divinity was still 'Lotus-Born', who was now envisaged as identical with the Buddha 'Boundless Life' (*Amitāyus*). Having described 'Lotus-Born' in the usual way with his glorious robes and cornered cap, holding a *vajra* in his right hand near the heart and a skull-cup with vase of life in his left and the magic wand supported against his left arm, the liturgy goes on to describe the 'Knowledge-Being Boundless Life' as the corresponding 'Body of Enjoyment' (*sambhogakāya*), red in colour, seated cross-legged upon a lunar disk in the sphere of the blazing self-light of

[a] see Waddell, *Lamaism*, pp. 444 ff.

141

THE LAND OF DOLPO

knowledge, which is imagined as manifesting itself above the three prongs of Lotus-Born's magic wand (*khaṭvānga*).

'O Lord Protector Boundless Life!
Bestow thy consecration on these worthy sons,
That life and knowledge may be widely manifest.'

The chief offering on the altar is a skull-cup filled with spirit, consecrated as the 'Thought of Enlightenment' (*bodhicitta*), the regenerative fluid which is conceived as pervading the whole of existence.

'Infusing as the Great Bliss, it mingles in the single flavour of the flow of the Thought of Enlightenment of the Father and Mother (*Amitāyus* and his partner *Pāṇḍuravāsinī*). It falls from the unseen heavens and whirls around in the skull-cup. You taste it in your throat and the whole body is pervaded with bliss. Let the threefold world vanish in clear light, and the arteries, breath and vital fluid be perfected as absolute knowledge!'[a]

The consecrated spirit is then sprinkled about. After the consecration of the 'Thought of Enlightenment' the officiants enact by means of the appropriate gesture (*mudrā*) and spell (*mantra*) the consecration of the 'Knowledge of Wisdom' (*prajñājñānābhiṣeka*). Next comes the consecration of the 'Sphere of Knowledge' (*jñānadhātvabhiṣeka*), which is bestowed by the sacred crystal.

'By means of this self-created mirror of the "Adamantine Being" (*Vajrasattva*), spontaneously pure from the very beginning and of translucent form, upon you O worthy sons may consecration be bestowed. and may celestial knowledge, the manifestation of the "two-in-one" (*zung-'jug*), be finally realized!'

These conventional consecrations have little interest for the

[a] Concerning the real significance of this process see my edition of the *Hevajra-Tantra*, Oxford University Press, 1959, especially vol. I, pp. 35-7.

villagers, who are awaiting the distribution of the life-giving spirit and pills. There is no doubt that they conceive of this ceremony as bestowing upon them long life and health in the physical sense, and the difficult technical terms describing the progress towards enlightenment are all but meaningless to them. Indeed the 'Life-Consecration', which now follows, seems to be of a different nature from the earlier consecrations and certainly approximates to the common interpretation. Its intention seems to be the nourishing of the 'supernal life' (*bla-tshe*) in living beings. This supernal life may well bring health and happiness in this world, but it is something distinct from the normal life-force. Thus it can be lost through evil-doing or even as a result of sudden fear without the man dying physically. There is no Buddhist Sanskrit equivalent known to me and it seems certain that it is a genuine p'ön-po idea. [a]

'O you whose supernal life has wandered, strayed or disappeared! The pure essence of the four elements of earth and water, fire and air, the happiness and splendour of living things who dwell in the threefold expanse of the threefold world, the whole essence derived from the compassionate grace of the ocean of buddhas of past, present and future, all this is compounded as nectar in the form of light rays of various colours. It seeps through the pores of your bodies and vanishes into the the centre of the heart, which is identical with the syllable HRĪH, the pure force of Wisdom itself; thus the well-being of your supernal life will be restored and you will gain the perfection of deathlessness. [b] Passing into the living items (*tshe rdzas*)

---

[a] see also Nebesky-Wojkowitz, *Oracles and Demons*, pp. 481–3.

[b] HRĪH is the syllable placed at the centre of the mystic circle (*maṇḍala*) of Avalokiteśvara. This circle consists of six segments, symbolizing the six spheres of existence, which are associated with the six syllables of his spell: OM MA ṆI PAD ME HŪṂ (p. 39 fn.). The centre of the circle is divine wisdom itself, whence phenomenal existence appears to evolve, and whither the aspirant to buddhahood must ultimately return. Thus it is identified with the heart of perfected man.

that lie before us, they become the great adamantine essence. Even thus must we concentrate our thought!'

The officiants then wave a wand to which streamers of various colours are attached, over the 'living items', namely the sacrificial vase, which is filled with water, the skull-cup, which is filled with spirit, and the dish containing the little pellets of cooked flour (tsamba). On this particular morning the old lama of Shey was presiding over the sacrificial vase, the boy-lama over the skull-cup and his monk-preceptor over the dish of pellets. Beginning with the officiants themselves, next the other celebrants and afterwards the whole congregation who formed a row and came before the lamas one by one, all received this 'communion'.

Consecration of the Sacrificial Vase

'From this life-abode (tshe-'brang), this sacred palace of the five lights of wisdom, where dwell the immortal Lotus-Born and all the masters of his succession, from this sacrificial vase the flow of nectar streams and percolates the summit of your head. May your inner body be filled and may you receive the life-consecration of the unchanging adamantine body!'

The officiant places the vase on the head of the man bowed before him. He then pours a drop of water from it into the man's palm, which he rubs on the top of his head. The officiant pronounces a spell in Sanskrit:

'KĀYA-ADHISHTĀNA ABHISHIÑCA OM (= Body-Empowerment Consecrate!).'

Consecration of the Life-Spirit

'Having tasted in your throat this life-spirit (tshe-chang), which is the very essence of all things stationary and moving, compounded into a nectar possessing the nature of the Thought of Enlightenment, having tasted this, may you receive the life-consecration of the unobstructed adamantine word!'

144

By means of a little ladle the officiant pours a small quantity of the spirit into the man's hand and he drinks it.

'VĀG-ADHISHTĀNA ABHISHIÑCA ĀḤ (= Speech-Empowerment Consecrate!).'

Consecration of the Life-Pellet

'Eat this life-pellet (tshe-ril) consisting of the pure essence of the root of being manifested as living seed (thig-le). Eat it and may you receive the life-consecration of the unchanging adamantine mind!'

The officiant then gives the man who has now moved up in front of him one of the pellets, which he eats.

'CITTA-ADHISHTĀNA ABHISHIÑCA HŪṂ (= Mind-Empowerment Consecrate!).'

'May the pure life-essence sink into the centre of your heart, the indestructible vital syllable HRĪḤ! May you be bound with the web of the five lights of adamantine knowledge! May your whole body be clad with the adamantine armour of the seven doctrines, so that you may be sealed with the adamantine seal of permanence and stability which is ever free from the destitution and destruction of birth and death!' [a]

Men, women and children, all came forward to receive this consecration. Some received extra pills for members of their families who were not present, and when everyone had filed past, there were still pills and ladle-fulls of spirit to spare. Some came up a second time until all was finished. This tended to produce a scramble, which for the first time slightly marred a ceremony which had been performed with the utmost decorum.

---

[a] These extracts will be found on folios 10b and 12a–13a of 'The Ritual of Consecration together with Life-Consecration, known as the Flow of Immortal Knowledge' (dbang gi cho ga tshe dbang dang bcas pa 'chi med ye shes chu rgyun ces bya ba—Rin-chen gter-mdzod, vol. cha).

The final blessing (*bkra-shis*) was intoned and thus ended the whole great performance.

Many of the visitors began to leave, but since it was already afternoon, we who come from the direction of Phijor had no choice but to wait till the following morning. After interminable discussion of our plans with others, Pasang had at last found a man of Shey who was willing to accompany Hemrāj and Takki Babu as far as Tukchä. He said he would be prepared to leave in six days' time. Rather than return to Samling for so short a period, Hemrāj elected to stay on alone at Shey. By the time we had settled him in one of the houses and equipped him with pots and provisions, everyone else had left, the visitors on their way home and the residents to attend to their cattle and flocks. Shey appeared as deserted as when we had first arrived there six weeks before. Our party consisted of myself and Pasang with Takki Babu, Gyel-tsen and Shi-shok carrying the tents and clothing and utensils. Since they were lightly laden, we soon caught up the party that was returning to Phijor and continued to travel with them for a while; I was glad of the occasion to admire their clothes once more (frontispiece). Then we sped down to the stream where the hail-storm had afflicted us a few days before, and climbed more slowly over the mountains beyond, until we reached the grazing-ground on the flank of the 'Purple Mountain'. Here we rested, bought milk and gave medicine to those who asked it. Then we continued still high above the river until we saw the buildings of Samling below us. We hastened down to greet the Lama and give him news of the gathering at Shey.

LAST DAYS

Thereafter I passed three peaceful days, staying mainly in my tent and checking through the manuscripts which the Lama and his nephew had sought out for us during our absence. They also assisted us greatly by not only accepting Indian currency notes for these purchases, but also by exchanging high currency notes for as much Nepalese coin as we were likely to require. They would be able to use the notes when they next went trading south.

We were now under pressure to arrange our departure, for Nyi-ma Tshe-ring would soon be leaving for his regular summer expedition to Phoksumdo and this would be a sign for others to go trading too. After such an exodus of men and animals, we could not hope for assistance for several weeks at least. Moreover we were already well behind our own schedule and loath as I still was to leave, I authorized Pasang to arrange for yaks. In any case Takki Babu's departure was imminent, for he had to set out for Pokhara with Hemrāj; Pasang too would have to go as far as Shey to see them safely off with their travelling companion. We debated whether Pasang should return to Samling for a few more days, but in the event matters were decided for us, for the only day on which yaks were available was June 25th. Since we had promised Hemrāj that Takki Babu would reach Shey on the 24th ready to set out from there on the 25th, I would have to stay on at Samling alone for just one day. This suited me well enough, for it would be possible to finish photographing certain manuscripts and make printed cloth copies of the monastery prayer-flags.

The last day at Samling was a pleasant one. Yung-drung fetched water for me and blew up the ashes of the fire when it was time for food. I photographed texts by the tent and later made the prints we wanted in the Lama's house. Since there was no other cotton cloth available, I tore up a sheet sleeping-bag and with the assistance of the monks transformed it into prayer-flags. The wooden printing-blocks were available in the monastery and for ink we used a mixture of fuel-black and glue.

When I went down to my tent from the house in the evening, a herd of antelopes, wandering over a knoll nearby, started at my approach. This was the nearest I had ever come to them. In the evenings they used regularly to come to the pool just below the monastery, which is the only water-supply, always waiting until no one was near. First the bucks would come and then more timidly the mothers with their young. Samling almost attained to the ideal condition of the monastery where animals and men are friends. This was the only night on which I slept totally separated from my companions. How peaceful is Dolpo, not only its mountains but also the lives of the men who live there! There are no policemen and no soldiers; neither is there robbery, violence or murder. We have been here too short a time, for much as we have learned, there is still much more that these people could teach us. I was leaving now against my will, but earlier plans and present circumstances seemed to allow me no other choice.

The following morning a man of Phijor, named Dorje, arrived belatedly with his two yaks. The two monks and the lama's nephew helped with the packing and loading, but they were more of an embarrassment than a help, for they continually extracted things in order to ask what they were. I became bewildered and rather impatient and regretted the absence of Pasang and Takki Babu. I went to exchange white scarves of farewell with the Lama, and returned to find them using a coloured blanket, which I had recently bought, as a hold-all for our bags of flour and tsamba. They were just in the process of tying it across the back of one of the yaks. Protests were of no avail, for these cloths are used for just such a purpose, and it seemed to my willing assistants that I was now needlessly delaying an already belated departure. How could one explain the special value that this simple hand-woven cloth would have for me in England? One yak twice threw off its load, but at last we were on our way, Dorje leading one yak and I the other. We had just reached the chöten on the ridge above the monastery, when we saw Takki Babu approaching. Alarm at the breakdown of our plans mingled with the joy of seeing him. The man of Shey, who had undertaken to accompany them as far as Tukchä, had broken the contract, and since it was impracticable for them to leave unaccompanied, Takki Babu had at once resolved to return to Samling in case I needed him. He had left well before dawn and it was now past noon. His first act was to rescue the blanket, replacing it by a cotton wrap of his own. (It was indeed just that I should have given him a similar woollen blanket, which Pasang had bought the very day that I bought mine. While I was upbraiding Pasang for his choice of colours, Takki Babu, who did not understand Tibetan, had hastened forward to express his admiration. Thus to his surprise he had found himself being presented with it.) Life in high mountains would go hard without him. He took the lead-rope from me and I was left to pursue my thoughts free from all immediate anxieties. We stopped by the herdsmen's tents, prepared some tea and then continued rapidly on our way. The hail-storm which had befallen us on my last visit to Shey, had apparently been a prelude to Dolpo's summer rains, for since then the weather had tended to be overcast and showery. By comparison with the valleys on the southern side of the main range, the rain here was very slight, but even so it exceeded my expectations, and the days were now often wet and cold—again all too much like British mountains. But there was one great compensation, for throughout June flowers of all kinds had blossomed forth. Of the shrub variety there were tiny rhododendrons, some with red flowers (*Rhododendron lepidotum*), others with white (*R. anthopogon*), and potentilla of brightest yellow (*Potentilla arbuscula*). There were little white primulas (*Primula involucrata*), geraniums and anemones (*Anemone obtusiloba*). There were asters (*Aster flaccida*), yellow erysimum (*Erysimum melicentae*) like dwarf wall-flowers, and golden cremanthodium (*Cremanthodium arnicoides*) like little sun-flowers. There were blue *Microula sikkimensis*, tufts of white *Dracocephalum heterophyllum* and of purple *Nepeta pharica*, weird louseworts and curly corydalis. There were little white anaphalis and other tiny rock-plants, stone-crop, saxifrage and draba. On sections of broken hill-side wild rhubarb had taken root. We had picked and cooked some on our last visit to Shey, hoping to repeat the experience of the Phoksumdo journey (p. 71), but the stalks had been tough and uneatable. From a high corner of the route just before and beginning the long steep descent towards Shey, one can look back over the cliffs and the green ridges that lead up towards the 'Purple Mountain', back to a small green alp with the trace of red buildings upon it. This was our last view of Samling.

Pasang was comfortably established under the veranda by the temple-door, and we agreed that it would be more pleasant to stay thus sheltered in the open than in the restricted space of one of the houses. There was good news of transport. T'ar-gyä, our old helper from Saldang, had reappeared with five yaks and Pasang had contracted with him to carry our belongings to Tarap, starting the day after next. Thus our whole party would travel together at least as far as Tsharka, where we would have to try and find other means of sending Hemrāj and Takki Babu ahead. I was no longer concerned about Hemrāj, for he would reach Pokhara and thence Kathmandu soon enough, but rather about our mail, which would be waiting a long time in the Pokhara hospital to the probable anxiety of the lady-doctors. If we could arrange for Takki Babu to travel there direct and then return to meet us, we would be able to visit without undue haste the places of interest which lay on the route.

In the meantime apart from washing clothes, resorting and repacking, we had one more urgent task on hand. This was to obtain a copy of the biography and written works of the founder-lama of Shey Monastery, Ten-dzin Rä-pa (*bstan-'dzin ras-pa*). Since the wooden printing-blocks reposed here in the monastery, this might have seemed an easy task, and if there had been available sufficient paper and ink to print the full 206 pages, we would certainly have considered printing ourselves a copy. But in the absence of the necessary material, all we could hope to do was to find someone willing to part with his text. To our great surprise, however, we discovered that copies were very rare, for it seemed that no one had troubled to make more since the first few were taken off when the blocks were cut. We had seen the Samling Lama's copy; we knew that the old lama of Shey had one, but we resolved not to worry him. We found another one at Shey with several missing pages and the owner willingly parted with it for ten rupees. At last we heard of another and begged the owner to let us photograph the pages missing from our text. By now it was evening and the rain fell heavily while we sat under our veranda. The villager brought his copy and we told him the pages we required, at which he turned to one of them and began a droning recital. Then interrupting himself, he pronounced: 'Not only do I read, but I also understand the sense'. 'Yes', we replied, 'but please lend us your book.' He refused and just continued his recital, infuriating and tantalizing. But we noticed that his copy contained two sections at the end, an extra forty-six pages which were totally missing in ours. I was now determined to complete our copy. Collecting together all the Nepalese paper we could find in our boxes, we estimated there was enough to print the odd missing pages. For the last forty-six we would have to rely upon finding a copy in Tarap and photographing that.

The next morning while Pasang completed the packing and supervised the loading of the yaks, I set to work getting the printing-blocks in order and selecting the ones we would need. Tibetan books are printed from wood-cuts, a separate block being prepared for each page. As may be imagined, the carving of such blocks is a highly skilled craft. Once made, they can last for centuries, if treated with proper care. With the willing assistance of the temple-keeper, I now drew forth piles of blocks from under the image-racks, reached down yet more from above the roof-beams and began to sort them into chapters, only to find that there were still many missing. We questioned other members of the community and hunted despairingly, until at last we found a large box, filled with the remaining pieces. It was quite impossible to find at random the few we wanted. They all had to be piled up by chapters in page-order. It was a long and filthy job. Pasang, having finished the packing, arrived with all the available paper and our bottle of blue-black ink. For work such as this one needs thick black Tibetan ink, a mixture of soot and glue, but there was none to be had. We brushed the ink over the incised letters of each block in turn

and stretching the paper over it, pressed it down evenly with a
cloth. For this we needed a roller of the wood and felt variety
commonly used in Tibetan monasteries, but there did not seem
to be one at Shey. Thus we continued, selecting block after
block to the limit of our paper. The inmates of the monastery
gathered around, for they had never seen their blocks used before.

Since we could easily catch them up, we instructed the rest of
the party to start out and continued single-mindedly with our
task. But within half an hour Hemrāj was back with the news
that the yaks had thrown two of our boxes down the mountain-
side and that one had burst open. We left our printing and
hastened to the scene of the disaster. The box containing the
typewriter, flash-lamp, films and medical supplies had remained
intact. The other had just been repacked with our recently
acquired Tibetan books, and all their loose pages now lay
scattered amidst the stones and scrub. Fortunately there was
neither wind nor rain to add to these troubles. Pasang returned
to the printing, while I gathered up the pages and set about the
lengthy task of sorting out the books again and getting the pages
in order. Afterwards Pasang repaired the box and eventually
very belatedly we set out. T'ar-gyä had been chafing at the delay
and I had retaliated by blaming him quite unjustly for the
behaviour of the yak, refusing to leave until everything was
checked for breakages and restored to order; meanwhile Pasang
had infuriated me by taking T'ar-gyä's side. But within
minutes of our departure all was harmony once more, for in
such circumstances one cannot lose the right perspective for
long.

We continued eastwards up the gentle grassy valley, across the
stream that leads towards the pass above Namgung and on to
the next river junction, where from afar we could see a large
white tent on a stretch of grass. As we approached, we recognized the men who stood around it and the great black mastiff
with the red scruff round his neck. Inside the tent was Nyi-ma
Tshe-ring himself, sitting on a carpet and sipping buttered tea.

Beside him was a little temporary shrine with three small images in caskets, seven offering-bowls, flowers and incense. He was on his way to Pungmo for the regular summer trade and we noticed that the tent was stacked with bundles of wool. He was accompanied by one of his grandchildren, several retainers, a villager of Saldang who was much devoted to religion and the young lama from Namgung, who had consented to speak to us from behind a partition when we visited his temple (p. 79). Since the next part of our journey would coincide with theirs, we decided to camp nearby and travel together on the following day. Later in the evening we showed our copy of Ten-dzin Rä-pa's works, lamenting the missing chapters. The young lama then said that he possessed a complete copy and would gladly give it to us, but the book was in his house at Saldang. Pasang offered at once to make a round-about journey via Saldang, for by travelling fast he would be able to reach Tarap very soon after the rest of our party. A youth was detailed to accompany him and all happened as arranged.

The rest of us travelled the next day in the company of Nyi-ma Tshe-ring's party and their scores of yaks. It was a very long day indeed. We ascended the valley eastwards to its head and crossed the pass (19,500 feet) which brought us above the head-waters of the Namdo-Saldang river (SI: Nāngung Kholā). Here we turned southwards and traversed the mountain-side for about eight miles. Prickly mauve poppies (*Meconopsis horridula*) bloomed in the bracken and there were asters (*Aster flaccida*) and an occasional delphinium (*Delphinium caeruleum*). Then we ascended another pass (20,000 feet) on the great watershed that separates the upper waters of the Bheri from those of the Karnāli, and descended to the beginnings of a stream, which would lead Nyi-ma Tshe-ring to Murwa Village below the Phoksumdo Lake. We continued four or five miles down this valley and all camped together in a grassy treeless place. In the morning we said farewell to Nyi-ma Tshe-ring for the last time (pl. XXX*a*) and ascended towards another pass due east. The prickly poppy appeared again along the track, the little white cuckoo-flower (*Cardamine pratensis*), little yellow potentilla, edelweiss and sandwort (*Arenaria polytricoides*) and tiny flowers of wild parsley. This pass, too, comes close to 20,000 feet, but the ascent seemed an easy one and we descended happily over the snow and scree and stones down to the stream on the other side.

TARAP

Soon we found ourselves in a grassy valley, decked with flowers, which led us by a pleasant track down towards Tarap. It was early afternoon when we reached the upper village of Tok-khyu.[a] Rain began to fall heavily and so we sought shelter in the head-man's house. His wife put the roof at our disposal with the separate upper room that opened off it, and so having dragged our boxes up two flights of knotched ladders, we made ourselves at home. She brought us wood and a water-pot and offered me an enormous goose-egg which I accepted with pleasure. Strange it is that one should take for granted the hospitality of these villagers, who for the mere asking will readily offer whatever room they have. I set about making a steamed pudding as a special delicacy in celebration of my birthday, for the remnants of our dried fruit and the goose-egg suggested nothing better. Pasang duly arrived with our second copy of Ten-dzin Rä-pa's works, lamenting that some of the pages were badly stained by damp and eaten by worms. Thus I would have to find yet another

[a] Tok (*tog*) means 'upmost' and khyu ('*khyu*) means 'run' or 'flow'. Compare Ting-khyu, p. 99 fn. This village is marked as *Atāli* on the SI maps, a name for which I could find no local justification at all. One should also observe that there is no one village of Tarap, for this name refers to the whole complex of villages and monasteries, which I shall now be describing. The place marked as *Tarāpgāon* by the SI is properly known as Do (*mdo*), meaning 'lower end' of the valley. The mistake is an easy one, for travellers approaching from the south by way of Sandul (SI: Chhandul) would understand quite rightly that they had reached Tarap and would refer the name without more ado to the first village they saw. Ekai Kawaguchi made the same mistake on a larger scale when he reached Tsharka (in his spelling Tsaka) for he thought Dolpo (Thorpo) was just the name of this village (*Three Years in Tibet*, p. 73).

copy in order to check through the last two sections, which were not duplicated in our possession.

The next morning we walked down to visit the lama of the 'All-Good Isle of the Doctrine' (*kun-bzang chos-gling*), a monastery half way between Tok-khyu and the lower village of Do. We had heard that this lama was not only the master-painter in Tarap, but was also esteemed for his learning and would certainly have the book we wanted. On the way we visited the Ch'amba Temple (*byams-pa lha-khang*), a new building dedicated to Maitreya (Ch'amba) just below Tok-khyu on the right bank of the stream. Two valleys join at this point, the one from the north-east which we had followed, the other from the north and the direction of Ting-khyu. It continued to rain slightly, but this gentle valley did not loose its charm. Geologically one might describe it as a wide glacial trough, but now the upper slopes are grass-covered and the flat bottom is cultivated for barley and buckwheat. It is practically treeless, for the height is still about 16,000 feet. The lama, a man of fifty years or so, received us in a most friendly manner and led us up to a large untidy room on the first storey. After answering questions about ourselves, we asked about his painting and he showed us three *thankas* by his own hand, which were passably good and evoked sincere words of praise. None of the younger generation seem able to attain to the same standard. He possessed not only a block-print of Ten-dzin Rä-pa's works, but also a manuscript, and he placed both before me forthwith. As time was short, I began at once to complete the illegible parts on my copy, but he begged me not to try to do it so hurriedly, but to take away his copies and do it at my leisure. Opening off his living room was a small chapel, containing the sixty-three volumes of the 'Precious Treasury' (*rin-chen gter-mdzod*), an important collection of extra-canonical Nying-ma-pa works. In the centre was an image of 'Lotus-Born' and the walls were hung with several fine *thankas* of recent Tibetan origin. The lama expressed amazement at the distance we had travelled and begged us to stay with him longer. His wife appeared with a pot of buttered tea, a jar of chang and a dish of tsamba. We gladly accepted his hospitality, but had little time to spare. Since T'ar-gyä had left us, we needed other means of porterage. No one in Tok-khyu had been able to help us in this matter, so Pasang went on to Do, a further two miles down the valley, to make inquiries there. As we would have to pass through Do later on, I returned to Tok-khyu to finish work on my block-print and write up notes.

It rained almost continuously and I caught cold for the first time. Above Tok-khyu there are two more small Nying-ma-pa temples, one named Sharring, which we had passed on the route the day before, and the other Tr'ak-lung, which can be seen up a little side-valley. Hemrāj visited both and found nothing of interest.

More delightful than anything were the flowers, which grew in wonderful profusion by the bank of the river. There were little shrubs of yellow potentilla, tall yellow primulas (*Primula sikkimensis*), others delicately white (*P. involucrata*), and others formed in little sprays of pink (*P. tibetica*). There were little geraniums and varieties of vetch, sleek anemones (*Anemone rivularis*), golden cremanthodium (*Cremanthodium decaisnei*), daisy-like erigeron (*Erigeron multiradiatus*) and slender little buttercups (*Ranunculus affinis*). There were yellow medicago (*Medicago edgeworthii*), pinkish morina (*Morina nepalensis*) and the blue microula (*Microula sikkimensis*), tufts of *Drococephalum heterophyllum* and of *Lagotis glauca*, yellow stone-crop and *Draba oreades*. Over the higher banks grew long strands of clematis (*Clematis orientalis*) and delicate yellow blooms of *Dicranostigma lactucoides* like the horned poppies of British seashores.

It was still raining the following day. Pasang had found three women in Do who were willing to be our porters, and four men from Tok-khyu agreed to come after much persuading, so all was arranged for an early departure on the morrow. Work on the block-print was finished and we returned the lama's books on the way past his temple in the morning. In half an hour we reached Do and passed through the two entrance-chötens, a p'ön-po one, which had been recently painted, and a Nying-ma-pa one, which was totally neglected. Above the village there is a small monastery, once Sakya-pa, now Nying-ma-pa. An unusual feature is a side-chapel, built in the form of a chöten and containing a smaller chöten inside it. The general effect is pleasing and the wall-paintings are good. From this monastery one looks straight down the main valley, which turns south-westwards at this point (pl. XXIX), leading on to Sandul, two days journey distant. Our track ascended another valley to the north-east, which would lead us again to the Bheri-Karnāli watershed.

About half a mile up this valley on the left bank of the stream is the p'ön monastery of Sh'ip-chhok (*Zhib-phyogs*). It consists of a temple and a group of houses, occupied by a community of fifteen members, who if not already married are free to do so. Thus in organization it resembles the monastery at Ringmo, but gives the impression of a far more vigorous life. The temple has been painted recently and well. Along the walls we recognized on the right side the Teacher Shen-rap, 'Shen-God White Light', 'The Pure 10,000 times 100,000', and Sa-trik, on the left the God of the Dart (p. 67), *Ganacakra* and the Sky-Guide, flanked by 'Life-Empowering Knowledge-Holder' (*tshe-dbang rig-'dzin*) and 'Lotus-Born' (*Padmasambhava*).[a] Three images were enthroned over the table of offerings, the Teacher Shen-rap in the centre with the Victorious One on his left and Sa-trik on right, holding a 'vase of life' raised in her right hand and a mirror in her left. These images and the smaller ones to the sides are set within intricately painted frames. Five 'monks', who were in residence, gathered around to ask questions, making no difficulty about the taking of photographs. They were delighted to hear that we had been staying at Samling, for they knew the old Lama well.

I crossed the river to the other bank, where there is another small group of houses and a little Nying-ma-pa temple. This place is known as Do-ro and is the last settlement in Tarap towards the east. Thereafter one finds oneself in a steep and

[a] For all these divinities see pp. 47 ff.

narrow valley. By now it was already well after noon and so quite impossible to cross the pass that day, but our porters assured us that there was a cave higher up the gorge. It began to rain steadily and we looked forward to its shelter for the night. But the 'cave' was nothing better than a sloping face of rock with a wall of stones built against it, affording sufficient shelter perhaps for two or three hardy travellers, but totally inadequate for our party of eleven and our eight loads of luggage. There was nowhere nearby where tents could be erected. We climbed higher in the hope of finding some such place and were not entirely disappointed, although the site was stony and unprotected. But our spirits were cheered by the presence of two legs of mutton, which Pasang had been offered by a happy chance as he passed through Do-ro. We had not eaten meat of any kind for many days.

TSHARKA

We left the next morning before dawn and I was sure that we would reach Tsharka (SI: Chharkābhotgāon) despite the doubts of our porters. It was still a long steep climb to the head of the valley, about 19,000 feet, where we rested on a little carpet of grass studded with flowering purple cones (*Phlomis rotata*). Above us rose the last 2,000 feet of rock and scree, and with such a prospect before them, our porters consented to start again only after an exceptionally long halt. Thus it was already well past midday when we were all resting together beyond the snow on the other side. We descended to a stream, where scrub appeared again, and cooked a meal. We were now near the head of the Panzang river, looking northwards down the valley in the direction of Ting-khyu. Our route lay southwards to the head of the valley, once more across the Bheri-Karnāli watershed and down to Tsharka on the other side. We ascended the valley, which was gentle and grassy, and reached the summit of an easy pass (19,500 feet), whence we looked down towards the upper gorge of the Bheri (SI: Barbung Kholā), the old friend of our travels. By now it was evening; I was determined to reach Tsharka, so Pasang and I hastened down the track in advance of the rest of the party. But as dusk began to fall and the porters were still far behind, it became all too certain that they would be benighted. Pasang therefore went on in advance to seek out the headman and find a place to stay, while I returned to accompany them. They came at last and night soon befell us. I led the row of men and women, indicating the way with a torch. The track seemed endless. Although it was the only one and it was really impossible that we should be lost, it was difficult to eliminate feelings of alarm and self-recrimination, as I guided these overburdened men and women in total darkness through ravines and across streams. I had told them to call out if they could not keep up, and how great was my alarm, when checking back along the line, I discovered that a young man was missing. Telling the others to wait, but fearing they would not, for such is their independence of spirit, I retraced my steps until I found him sitting groaning by the track. He said he could come no further and would rather die. I took part of his load and urged him all I could, insisting on the folly of spending the night on the mountain. I thought how much more effective Pasang's words would have been, and lamented my own inadequacy. But at last he rose and followed me with steps far surer than my own. When we reached the place where I had left the others, they had disappeared as I had expected, and so the two of us continued anxiously alone. At last a chöten loomed up just before us, sign of Tsharka's proximity, and beyond it we found the others resting. We continued down a widened track and then below us we saw the reassuring gleam of Pasang's torch and the wild nightmare was at an end.

Tsharka is quite different from all the other villages of Dolpo, for it stands like a fort (which undoubtedly it once was) just above the right bank of the river (pl. XXXIa). By day one sees clearly enough that nothing of a fortress remains, but that night as we entered the village, my impressions were perhaps suited to the days of old. The rows of stone-walls that form the en-trance seemed like defensive bulwarks and the massive stone buildings, sloping inwards to give them strength, disappeared above us in the darkness. We moved between these walls, guided now by Pasang, who might have been sent out to lead us on some secret mission. We filed in through a low doorway, making our way between the goats which slept inside, and as-cended two flights of knotched ladders into a low room, where the fire-light played upon the smoke-blackened roof-beams and our own anxious faces. Life in Tibetan lands is often reminiscent of mediaeval Europe, but never have I seemed to live it as on that first night in Tsharka. I was shown a storey higher, out onto the roof and into the little chapel that was built there. The owner of the house was both headman and lama of the local p'ön-po monastery. He exchanged a few friendly words and after food and drink we settled down to sleep.

The next morning we looked from our high roof over the other houses of Tsharka, which number about twenty-five, and across the river to an isolated p'ön-po monastery. Later we waded the fast-flowing current, securing one another with the climbing rope. There was nothing of great interest in the main temple, but a smaller one, which is in sad repair, its frescoes defaced by damp and dirt, is unique, for the left wall is painted with Buddhist (Nying-ma-pa) divinities and the right wall with p'ön-po ones. The lama comes across every day to light a butter-lamp and recite invocations; other villagers take part in occasional ceremonies. Once yearly in winter, he told us, they use the smaller temple for a combined Buddhist p'ön-po festival. Leading into the village on the western side there are prayer-walls of both kinds and I noticed how all who went that way passed the Buddhist one on their right and the p'ön-po on their left (p. 43).

Perhaps because of the first strange night, Tsharka never lost its charm for me, although it was the filthiest village I have ever lived in. We were able to dispatch Hemrāj and Takki Babu the very next day, for there was a monk in Tsharka who was on his way to Tukchä and was glad to have their company. Pasang and I delayed a day while porters were arranged and left on Saturday, July 7th, with our chattels loaded on the backs of eight local youths.

The first day's journey led up the valley of the Bheri (Barbung Kholā) and the carefree spirit of our companions was displayed in the happy abandon with which they waded five icy streams. We camped while some scrub was still available for our fires and the next day continued the gradual ascent to the pass, which stretches ahead as a grassy plain two miles or so in length (pl. XXX*b*). It is less than 18,000 feet and on both sides rise mountains 3,000–4,000 feet higher, the same height as our friendly summits of Dolpo, which we were now beginning to leave behind and above us. The same flowers still grew by the way, dwarf cones of purple *Phlomis rotata*, little golden-eyed asters (*Aster flaccida*) and yellow potentilla (*Potentilla argyrophylla*), purplish heads of *Lagotis glauca*, curly corydalis and weird louseworts (*Pedicularis, sp.*) vetch and stonecrop, saxifrage and draba. From the pass there is a choice of routes, one which climbs 1,000 feet higher on the northern side and descends safely to Gün-sa (p. 163) and the other which descends direct through the gorge of the Keha Lungpa to Sangdak. The Tsharka youths explained that the upper route was intended for pack-animals, and so we followed them contentedly down into the narrowing gorge. In fact, as we later learned, this route has been abandoned as dangerous by wiser villagers, since sections of the overhanging cliffs have collapsed upon it. We also learned later that Hemrāj and Takki Babu had entered this gorge and then retreated to the alternative route. One may certainly describe it as an interesting descent. Where the way is completely blocked, one must wade through the swift-flowing torrent, now this way, now that, waist-deep in icy water (pl. XXXI*b*). Elsewhere one makes one's way delicately across precipitous scree-slopes, threatened by rocks that hang out from the crags above. With a rope available there is no danger except from those hanging rocks, but our porters would not be delayed, and indeed had they consented to use it, we would not have reached the only possible night-shelter before dark. My own feelings of exhileration were stifled by concern for the loads, for no one in his senses would wantonly commit the precious work of months, notes, films and manuscripts, to such risks. But having embarked upon it, there could be no turning back and those Tsharka youths proved themselves the right men for the occasion. Their movement was a perfect combination of speed and balance and they were completely nonchalant all the time, chattering and laughing as gaily as when we left Tsharka. When we finally came to rest for the night beneath a shelter of over-hanging rock, we no longer felt inclined to blame them for the reckless rending of one of our tents, of which they had been guilty the night before.

The following morning we continued the descent of the gorge for a while, until we emerged onto the southern side of the mountain, whence we could look back to the heights above the pass. Then we descended by a safer track to the village of P'a-ling, also known as Sangdak (SI: Sangdāh).

IV

THE KĀLI GANDAKI AND
THE LAND OF LO

The Upper Valley

Our Tsharka youths refused to go beyond P'a-ling. Here
they had friends and relatives, but a further day's journey
to Kāgbeni would have taken them beyond the safe limits of
their known world. On the outskirts of the village we noticed
an empty stone hut with a threshing ground beside it, the one
admirably suited for our luggage and the other for our tent.
The youths placed our boxes inside and made off to the village
to seek out their acquaintances; while I erected the tent,
Pasang went in their wake to see what food could be found. He
returned with some hens' eggs and potatoes, luxuries that we
had not seen for months, as well as a bundle of firewood. When
our meal was finished and our camp in order, we went to visit
the headman to seek solution of our next immediate problems.
We had run out of coinage and the boys had to be paid; to our
relief he accepted our Indian currency notes and gave us Nepalese
coins at a reasonable rate of exchange. He also promised to provide three yaks for the next day; they would arrive late, however,
since they were still up in the mountains. The people spoke a
form of Tibetan very close to that of Tsharka and were friendly
enough. The village stands on the right bank of the Keha
Lungpa and consists of about twenty-five houses. It is also
known as Sangdak (SI: Sangdāh), meaning 'Pure and Clean',
but this is properly the name of an abandoned village, which
can be seen on the far bank. Also on that side but higher up are
their winter-quarters, of which the proper name is Gok, but
the term Gün-sa, which just means 'winter-place' is also used.

Here begins the alternative route over the pass to Dolpo, by which we might more wisely have come. We learned that the P'a-ling villagers trade in a small way between Tukchä and Mustang, for they complained that they had lost a number of their animals as a result of recent frontier troubles. They are professedly Buddhists like all Tibetans, but have no village-temple and no lama; it was the only Tibetan village thus deprived which we found on all our travels. They dispose of their dead by burning, for wood is sufficiently plentiful, and later on the after-death ceremony may be performed by a lama of Tsharka or Tarap. This seems strange when one recalls that Kāgbeni is comparatively near, and can only indicate that the social ties of these people are stronger on the Dolpo side.

The following morning we packed our belongings and waited impatiently till noon. At last the three yaks and their keeper appeared. The animals' front legs were tied and the four boxes and two bundles of tents and clothes were strapped onto their backs. As soon as their legs were released, they threw everything off, so we had to start all over again, this time with greater success. By each leading an animal we managed to get away from the village and up the mountain-side, but as soon as they were freed, the leading yak hurtled down the slope, throwing and dragging its boxes. The other two turned in confusion and within one devastating minute all our chattels were strewn across the rocks, while the animals stood frightened and panting. We carried down the loads, re-erected the tents on the nearest piece of flat ground, and inspected the damage. One metal trunk was too badly smashed for further use, but the Aláddin lamp packed inside it had somehow survived. The typewriter and the electronic flash were broken. Laments were useless. We repacked as best we could with one box less and Pasang went to inform the headman that we wanted to see no more of his yaks and that seven porters were needed for the next day.

The following morning we made a fresh start, and, ascending to the saddle above P'a-ling, commenced the long traverse down the mountain-sides towards Kāgbeni. For most of the day cloud obscured the distant views, but towards evening as we descended from the last pass separating us from the basin of the Kāli Gandaki, we were able to see far north towards the strange land of Lo (Mustang) with its flat barren brown hills, deeply cut and eroded, a chaotic and fantastic landscape in complete contrast to the cold majestic summits to the south. Our porters progressed so slowly that it was impossible to reach Kāgbeni that evening, so we spent the night in a spacious cave and continued the descent early the next morning. Far away across the valley we could see Muktināth, where in due course we should be going; mounting up towards the south were the great snow-clad peaks of Annapūrna. Then Kāgbeni and its little oasis of fields became visible down below on the opposite bank and we descended rapidly with the excitement and expectancy of travellers approaching a new land. We had talked so often of Kāgbeni during the last ten days, for it seemed to promise the end of our most arduous travelling and open the way to other regions and other peoples.

The slowness of our porters gave us time to make a slight detour and climb up to TING-RI Monastery (SI: Tirigāon), which towers fortress-like above the right bank of the river about a mile north of Kāgbeni (pl. XXXIIb). The monastery is a complete ruin except for the main temple, which has been restored. A nun climbed up after us to unlock the door and we learned from her that the place is maintained by a small band of six nuns, although for some ceremonies they summon monks from Kāgbeni. The great number of ruined buildings indicate that Ting-ri was once a large monastery. Some stone plaques with miniature paintings of monks, very pleasingly drawn and coloured, are fixed in wooden frames in the entrance-porch. These are the only traces of age in the temple.

We came out into the sun again and looked down upon the Kāli Gandaki and across to Kāgbeni on the opposite bank (pl. XXXIIa). The four days' journey from Tsharka had indeed brought us to another land. We had descended about 8,000 feet from the Sangdak pass. Trees have made their appearance once more, but apart from these groves of green around the villages, all else is bare brown-greyish rock and sand. Gone are the flower-covered mountains of Dolpo, for the monsoon-showers that fall there, cannot reach the upper valley of the Kāli Gandaki. In Dolpo one seems to be living on the mountains and there is nothing awesome about their summits, but here we found ourselves in great clefts amidst the mountains with snow-clad monsters towering above us.

The nun then informed us that the Lama of Shang, of whom we had heard so much, was staying in Kāgbeni and that he was expected in Ting-ri that morning. We made our way down to the Kāgbeni bridge and seeing the Lama and his party approaching from the other side, waited for them to cross first. This remarkable man is now about sixty-five years old; after years of meditation he has turned his energies to reviving Buddhism in all these Tibetan-Nepalese borderlands. Our routes in fact proved to coincide with his, for we heard of him everywhere from Tichu-rong (p. 37) to Nar. It was significant that we should meet by the bridge at Kāgbeni, for this marks as it were the very centre of all his travels and ours. To the east goes the track to Muktināth and on to Nye-shang and Nar; to the south goes another down to Tukchä (SI: Tukuchā) and beyond to the faint limits of the Tibetan Buddhist world; to the west goes the track to Dolpo whence we had come and to the north there is another to Lo (Mustang) and Tibet. But now we stood watching a rather frail old man being led across a bridge. He stopped his party by the track where we were waiting and exchanged a few kindly words with us. He said he would soon be visiting Nye-shang and we replied that we looked forward to meeting him there. As we took our leave, he whispered to one of his monk-attendants, who promptly dug in his purse and presented myself and Pasang with one rupee each. The Lama said: 'Buy yourselves some chang.' This unexpected gift took me by surprise and I hesitated between acceptance and polite refusal. It was now my turn to whisper to Pasang: 'Should we accept this?' He returned the rupees begging the Lama to devote them to a more worthy cause. Afterwards I regretted our decision, for it is a rare thing to be treated in all seriousness as an ordinary Tibetan. But we were to be given a second chance later on.

On the other side of the bridge there was a crowd of people who had come to see the Lama on his way. Pasang asking if there was a house we might use, and one of them offered to lead the way. We crossed a second bridge over the stream that descends from Muktināth and entered the town by its great stone arch. We have since approached KĀGBENI from all directions, but I shall always remember it as we first saw it—as welcome as some Abruzzi village might be after the mists and rains of Scotland. The blue sky, tumbledown buildings, whitewashed walls, happy children playing in the courtyards, little load-laden donkeys, women weaving in the shade, the rocks and bare brown earth beyond and the great snow-peaks surmounting the scene, all this contributed to the illusion. We had somehow expected much of Kāgbeni and it did not disappoint us, yet it must be acknowledged that a traveller approaching from the T'hākāli villages to the south, would not have been affected as we were. The houses stand close together, but since each is built around a courtyard, there was far more space and light than we were accustomed to. Our host's kitchen, in which we were immediately interested (for we had not eaten that day) was pleasantly clean by the standards which we had learned to expect, for we had not yet seen a T'hākāli kitchen. Pasang's first comment was: 'We are already back in Kathmandu.' The son of the household hastened to buy eggs and potatoes for us and his father provided a jar of excellent arak (local spirit), so while I erected a tent in the courtyard, Pasang set to work cooking.

Kāgbeni with its fifty or so houses is perhaps best described as a citadel. It is built on the river's edge and effectively blocks the valley. The local Tibetan name is in fact just Kāk (bKag) which is a word meaning 'block'. There was once a king but his palace is falling down and his dethroned descendants are too poor to repair it. One of his main sources of wealth must have been the dues levied on the grain coming up from the south and the salt and wool going down from the north. The monastery is a fort-like structure that has suffered from the effects of war. Only the main temple remains amidst ruined walls. There are two or three monks, perhaps celibate only because they have not yet decided to marry. The lama however, seems to be completely devoted to his religion, giving his attention both to Kāk Monastery and to the small temple at Tangbe three hours' journey upstream. The temple has been redecorated inside in the typical Sa-kya-pa style with frescoes of the Five Buddhas, 'Great Brilliance' and four-armed 'Glancing Eye' on the left wall, 'Victorious Lady' (*Vijayā*), 'Boundless Life', two-armed 'Glancing Eye' and three Sa-kya-pa lamas on the right. The main image is a fine bronze Śākyamuni. We climbed to the upper storey and leaned contentedly out of an upper window to gaze on the sunlit scene. In Dolpo there had been no windows out of which to lean, just small square holes, allowing entrance to a minimum of light and a minimum of cold, the latter being the more important consideration. Now the overwhelming impression of light and colour induced a kind of festive mood. I felt rather like a boy when school-term is over and holidays are about to begin.

Just over the gateway there is another small temple containing an impressive *terra-cotta* image of Maitreya the future buddha, some six feet high. The walls are painted with the six buddhas of the spheres of existence and under each one there is an invocation to save from rebirth in his particular sphere.[a] We walked round the prayer-wall that runs the length of an open court near the river and visited a little new temple containing a large new

---

[a] These six buddhas are envisaged as forms of Avalokiteśvara 'Universal Saviour' ('*gro-ba kun-sgrol*), who appears in these different forms in the six spheres of existence, those of the gods, the titans, the human world, the animal world, the sphere of tormented spirits and the hells. *BH*, p. 271.

prayer-wheel. Thus in a very short time we had seen all that Kāgbeni had to offer us. It was now Thursday, July 12th, and we had agreed to meet Takki Babu in Tukchä on the following Tuesday. Since Tukchä can be reached from Kāgbeni in one day, I decided to go a little further upstream and visit a monastery on the far bank, which Professor Tucci had mentioned but not visited.[a] The next morning we found a jolly fellow wearing a wide-brimmed green hat with a feather in it, who was willing to carry a light load of bedding and clothes for us, and we all set out along the left bank of the river.

Three hours walking up the barren valley brought us below the village of TANGBE. Like Kāgbeni it is built above the deeply eroded river-bed with its fields spreading out by the river to the north—half a mile of greenery in a whole landscape of dull yellow and grey-brown. We climbed up the steep slope and were delighted with the neatness of the houses and the chötens, which are all painted with red and white wash. At the southern end of the village are the ruins of an old fort, once an indispensible part of local defences along the upper Kāli Gandaki. We tried to find the keeper of the temple, but this proved unusually difficult, for the villagers we approached could not understand our Tibetan and just stood laughing at us. Pasang tried Nepāli, the first time now for many weeks, with better success, but the by-standers still mirthfully repeated our sort of Tibetan, as though human beings had never been heard to enunciate the like before. But in fact it is the people of Tangbe and not we ourselves who are so odd, for they speak a distinct dialect of their own, closely akin it seems to the language of Nye-shang. We had cause for surprise, for the dialect of Dolpo is uniform except for some variations at Tsharka. We had noticed further slight differences at P'a-ling and again at Kāgbeni, but here was another language, probably as different as French is from Italian. Eventually someone consented to open the temple for us. It was clean and well cared for. There was

[a] Tucci, *Tra Giungle e Pagode*, p. 77.

even a flower-box filled with marigolds outside. Inside, the walls were pleasingly painted with the Thousand Buddhas and the 35 Buddhas of Confession. We made a small offering and continued on our way.

By now it was past noon and a great gale was blowing up the valley, carrying clouds of dust along. This is a daily occurence, making afternoon travel often very unpleasant indeed. From a corner of the track perched high above the gorge we could see Gomba K'ang on its barren sloping promontory on the far bank. Ahead of us lay the village of Tshuk (SI: Chhukgāon) with its green fields terraced down towards the river.

TSHUK consists of three compact groups of houses: Tr'a-kar 'White-Rock', clearly the dominating one for it possesses the ruins of a fort, Tse-kye, 'Point-Growth', nearer the river, and Kyang-ma, 'Solitary', on the far side of a tributary stream to the north. Our porter led us into the middle of Tr'a-kar, knocked at the door of a house and shouted. He then went inside and presumably having explained who we were, returned in a few minutes to ask us to follow. We ascended the usual knotched trunk, under which a barking dog was chained just out of reach of our legs, and passed from a small landing into the living room. The householder made us welcome and his wife put hassocks in position and asked us to be seated. While she mixed some chang for us, we did our best to explain who we were. The younger son, a lad of twenty-two, then appeared, and was promptly despatched to find us eggs; rice, tsamba and potatoes were all readily available in the house. These people were friends of our merry porter and it was agreed that we should all stay for the night. It may be more peaceful to use one's own tent, but one misses much if one does not accept such friendly hospitality. As in Dolpo our 'porters' were just villagers who could be persuaded to assist us; they come rather as guides and companions than as servants. Here our relationship was even more friendly and they would eat with us as a matter of course.

Pasang was now scheming ahead. From Tukchä he would

have to go on to Pokhara and so would need a companion. When the son returned with the eggs, he asked him if he had ever been to Pokhara. The lad had been many times. Would he join our party? Yes, but for how much? His food and seventy rupees a month. He gladly agreed and said he would start by taking us across the river on the morrow to see Gomba K'ang. His name was Karchung, we learned, and he and his whole family were the best of people. His young sister and the wife of his elder brother came to see us and thereafter various friends and neighbours. We slept on our camp beds on the open roof, round the edges of which stacks of wood were neatly arranged for the winter. The morning sun shone on the towering red cliffs beyond the river and behind us rose the gaunt ruins of the old fort. Pasang brought tea and we planned the day with Karchung's assistance.

We first visited the two temples at Tshoknam, a small settlement of a few houses less than a mile up the valley due east from Tshuk (SI: Narsing Kholā). Both temples were in a lamentable condition. The upper one was being used as a store-room; fine frescoes, already defaced, were buried behind stacks of straw. On the way back Karchung led us into a little cave-temple, which proved to be one of the most impressive places in the whole region. It is named the 'Temple of Medicinal Juice' (*sman-rtsi lha-khang*) and the central image is known as Ch'amba (Maitreya) by the villagers (pl. XXXIXa). He is accompanied by the chief buddhas: against the right wall are images of 'Boundless Light', 'Imperturbable' and 'Infallible Success' and against the left wall 'Jewel-Born', 'Great Brilliance' and again 'Infallible Success'. These images are well conceived and quite undamaged, although they must be many generations old. Our other chief joy that morning came from the little apricots which were hanging ripe in Tshoknam and of which we ate our fill, for we had not tasted fresh fruit since the beginning of our travels.

Still assisted by Karchung we next forded the swift current of the Kālī Gandaki in order to reach GOMBA K'ANG. Karchung strode boldly through the surging torrent, always sure of his footing, although the water came above his waist. He then held one end of our nylon rope while some village-boys held the other. Pasang went first and was swept off his feet in mid-stream, receiving a thorough ducking, although fortunately keeping hold of the rope. Noting his mistakes, I followed with better success. There is a way round by a bridge further upstream, but then one would have to make a circuit of the great red cliffs opposite and it would be a full day's journey one way. As it was, we scrambled up the bank just below the cliffs and walked across onto the promontory. The monastery is ringed behind with another cliff-wall, eroded fantastically like giant organ-pipes. We passed through a courtyard into a large porch, painted with the Wheel of Existence and the four kings who guard the directions. Karchung, followed by Pasang, went to the upper storey in search of the solitary monk who was living there, but I was too impatient to wait and pushed back the doors of the main temple. It proved to be one of the largest Tibetan temples I have seen, being approximately sixty feet square. The central image is an enormous Maitreya, whose head and shoulders reach up into the storey above, where they have a separate chapel of their own. There is a circumambulatory passage around this image, which adds further to the size of the temple. The walls are covered with fine old frescoes representing the same divinities as we had seen in the old Sa-kya-pa monasteries of Dolpo, viz. the Five Buddhas, 'Great Brilliance' Śākyamuni, Buddha Master of Medicine, 'Holder of the Vajra', 'Lotus-Born', 'Glancing Eye', Maitreya, Hevajra and 'Supreme Bliss'. Most of the paintings on the right wall are already rendered unidentifiable by damp and dirt. A small expanse of wall screening the main entrance on the inside is decorated with the goddesses of the offerings and is a delightful piece of miniature painting. The grandeur of this temple, still impressive in spite of its present dilapidated condition, its remoteness, to which the swift-flowing river adds yet another barrier, reminded me of that still more ancient monastery of Tabo in Spiti. They are both places which haunt the imagination and to which one feels an urge to return. It is known locally just as Gomba K'ang, 'Promontory Monastery', but its proper name is *Kun-bzang chos-gling*, 'All-Good Island of the Doctrine'. Once the centre of a large community, it is now watched over by a solitary monk, a Tibetan from Drepung, who finds it a congenial place for his meditation. We found him in a room on the upper storey, occupied in sewing cloth uppers to his boots. Having invited us to share his buttered tea, he willingly showed us round the rest of the monastery. We saw the upper temple which is built around the head and shoulders of the great Maitreya and visited another room filled with a dusty collection of small images and ritual vessels. He walked with us round the main temple, but showed little knowledge of iconography. He was a kindly man, however, and the only one who still took any interest in this great work of the past.

We bade him farewell and recrossed the river, in which quite unaccountably Pasang received a second ducking, and then returned to Karchung's house, where we prepared a meal and our departure. We were now concerned to reach Tukchä as soon as possible, where Takki Babu was due to arrive with the bag of mail. It would be our first news from the outside world since we had left Nepālganj in mid-March, now four months ago.

We reached Kāgbeni late that evening and stayed with the villager who had befriended us before. His was a sad family, for the mother had recently died and a little girl of twelve was caring for an ailing baby. She had two brothers, one a little younger than herself and another old enough to be of help to his father. They owned a number of donkeys, who used to come and stare inquisitively inside the tent as soon as it was erected in the yard. The father offered these animals to us as beasts of burden, so it was agreed that we should leave most of our belongings locked in his house and take what was needed for a fortnight. We would have to return to Kāgbeni in order to go north again and thereafter to go east.

173

Thus the next morning Pasang and I set out assisted by Karchung and our host's elder son, who drove three little donkeys before him. The valley-wind rose before we had travelled far, and driving dust and sand tormented our little caravan so long as the track led close along the river-bed. Just before it begins to climb away up the left bank, one comes upon a tiny rock-shrine containing an impress in the rock of what appears to be Lotus-Born's special cornered hat. The impress is painted so as to complete the illusion and one is led to reflect once more on the quite extraordinary ubiquity of this wonder-working master of religion, who is supposed to have passed along almost every route that connects India with Tibet.

T'HĀK

Higher up the mountain-side we were less troubled by the wind. Little junipers and olives began to appear and soon DZONGSAM became visible round the turn in the valley.[a] We hastened down and through the village-street to the 'inn', of which Karjung had told us. This was the first T'hākāli house we had entered and I gazed astounded. We found ourselves in a bright kitchen, spotlessly clean. At the far side of the room was a stove and hearth of clay neatly coated with a dull red wash. Upon the stove stood pots of polished brass and other pots and dishes were placed on shelves against the wall. It was astounding because everything seemed arranged for show; one was reminded of similar arrays in some old English hotels. The hostess spoke regular Tibetan, expressed delight at seeing us and brought little

[a] Dzongsam is the local name, spelt misleadingly Jomosom by the Survey of India. It means 'New Fort' and is known as Dzong-sarba by Tibetan speakers. The local Tibetan name of the region we are now entering is T'hāk. The Nepalese form of the name is Thākkhola, formed simply by the addition of the Nepāli word -khola, 'valley'. The local name for a man of T'hāk is T'hāk-pa. The accepted Nepalese form of this word is Thākāli, presumably formed in analogy with Gurkhāli, etc. Concerning my use of T'h see p. 278.

cups of arak. She had entertained Westerners and Sherpas before, mainly mountaineers on their way to Annapūrna or Dhaulagiri. We bought eggs and flour, made spiced pancakes and drank more of the excellent arak. Rather belatedly we set out once more, crossed the bridge and continued down to the customs' post, where we were still further delayed. It was clear that we should not reach Tukchä that day and so contented ourselves by fixing Marpha as our goal. There are two small temples in Dzongsam and another at the village of Th'in on the left bank; we proposed to visit these together with the great monastery of Ku-tsap-ter-nga on our way up the valley. Our first thoughts now concerned Takki Babu, our mail and Pasang's imminent journey to Pokhara. The wind had dropped and we travelled pleasantly along the easiest section of track which we had met in all our travels.

We reached Marpha (SI: Mārphā), a large T'hākāli village, in about two hours and looked for somewhere to stay. We found an 'inn' with a kitchen just like the one at Dzongsam; the hostess gave us a room of our own, where we could set up the camp-beds and spread our rugs. We were just in the process of settling in, when Takki Babu appeared. He had reached Tukchä that day, and learning that we had not yet arrived there, had come up to meet us on the way. He had brought the mail together with a selection of weekly papers kindly sent by the Pokhara hospital and I settled down to a most unusual evening, replying to letters and sorting films, so that they would be ready for Pasang to take with the least delay. The next morning we made a brief visit to the monastery, the description of which is better left for our return journey, and then made our way down towards Tukchä. A little way out of Marpha we noticed a large monastery in a grove of trees on the far bank (Tsherok; SI: Chhairogāon) and resolved to visit it in due course.

We reached TUKCHÄ (SI: Tukuchā) in about two hours and coming to the open grass space at the northern end of the bazaar, wondered whether we might camp there. Even as we hesitated pondering the matter, a crowd began to collect, so we sought the seclusion of a nearby house. While tea was being made, the young lama of the monastery across the way, the 'New Monastery' (Gomba Samba), came to see us and asked if we would like to stay with him. He was able to offer us a wide curtained balcony and a kitchen of our own. Since Pasang and Karchung would be leaving for Pokhara very soon, this was space enough, so we gladly accepted his offer. As is usual in these houses all the rooms opened off an interior balcony, the ground floor being used as store and stable. Some chickens also lived in the lower regions, but they were continually trespassing in the upper part of the house; their goal was our stock of various grain in the kitchen. Besides the rooms occupied by us there was the lama's room, his kitchen and living-room and a small chapel. He had a young wife, who spoke no Tibetan; she used to provide us with eggs, flour and vegetables and go shares with meat. She also had a stock of arak available, but we discovered a shopkeeper who stocked a spirit of far superior quality. The young lama was friendly, had met Europeans before and prided himself on his medical knowledge. He had certainly accumulated a large selection of drugs, both Tibetan and European. In short he attempted to give satisfaction to all comers and seemingly made an adequate living. He was even able to sell me a tooth-brush, when the handle snapped off my last one. We noticed at once that he wore Nepāli clothes and soon realized that he had totally abandoned his religion. He excused himself with the remark: 'How can I act as lama if no one believes in me.' This question and a great refuse-heap in his monastery of what were once well printed books and laboriously copied manuscripts are perhaps the two most pathetic things that I remember of Tukchä. But this anticipates our tale, since for the present we were grateful indeed for the comparatively secluded shelter that his house afforded us.

The whole of the next day was spent writing letters, packing up all the films so far exposed on our travels and drawing up lists of purchases. The following morning Pasang and Karchung

XXV.

a. Lang Gomba. (p. 130)
b. Yung-drung washing, but only to humour Pasang. (p. 115)

XXVI.

gShen-rab, *a temple-banner* (thanka) *at Samling.* (*p. 47*)

XXVII.

gShen-lha 'od-dkar, *a temple-banner at Samling.* (*p. 48*)

XXVIII.

a. Villagers dancing outside Shey Gomba. (p. 141)
b. Villagers come to visit our camp at Shey. (p. 138)

XXIX.

View of Do, Tarap, from the upper gomba looking west. (p. 157)

XXX.

a. Nyi-ma Tshe-ring on a journey. The tent, of normal Tibetan type, is filled with bundles of wool. A precious store of scarce fire-wood lies outside. (p. 153)
b. Our porters, eight youths from Tsharka, crossing the Sangdak Pass. (p. 161)

XXXI.

a. Tsharka, view from the east. (p. 159)
b. Crossing the torrent in the Keha Lungpa gorge. (p. 161)

XXXII.

a. Kāgbeni. (p. 165)
b. View from Kāgbeni up the Kāli Gandaki with Tingri on the far bank. (p. 165)

set out for Pokhara, leaving Takki Babu, who certainly deserved a rest from walking, to attend to my wants. For two days we were thoroughly occupied with repairing tents and camp-beds, washing clothes and cooking food. I discovered a great bed of watercress by the river, which the local people believe to be poisonous, but which was a welcome addition to our diet. Meanwhile we exchanged visits with the leading official of Tukchä, Suba Shankarman Sher Chand and other members of this important family.

Tukchä is the main township of the whole T'hākāli region, for it is both an administrative and a trading centre. The office of *suba* (district magistrate) is the special prerogative of senior members of the Sher Chand family and these together with members of the other three family branches, Tulā Chand, Gau Chand and Bhaṭa Chand, also monopolize the trade. It seems that the beginnings of their wealth and influence date from Gurkha times and are probably connected with the downfall of the kings of Kāk (Kāgbeni). These people speak a special Tibetan dialect, known generally as T'hākāli, which prevails as far north as Tshuk. The older generation and the more worthy representatives of the present one also speak Tibetan and it was in this language that I used to converse with Suba Shankarman. Everyone is quite fluent in Nepāli and one or two members of the younger generation have been educated at Indian Universities and so speak English. They have also acquired 'progressive' ideas, which have taken a virulent 'anti-traditional' form. Thus they have no use for the Tibetan Buddhism which represents the whole culture of their forbears and even despise Tibetan itself as a language for dolts. People often find my interest in Tibetan things incomprehensible, but never elsewhere have I sensed hostile incomprehension. Nevertheless personally they were very friendly and Professor Tucci who had been here before me, was well remembered. Many others who are free from 'advanced' ideas of this kind, share the same contempt for Buddhism as a result of their social contact with Kathmandu. They prefer to call themselves Hindu, but to them Hinduism means no more than the acceptance of caste laws and prejudices and it is significant that while the Buddhist temples fall into disrepair, not one Hindu temple has yet been built. Perhaps it is respectable to call oneself Hindu, and a sign of enlightened education to despise all religion. The older folk are bewildered, for no one in Tukchä has the necessary knowledge to argue the validity of the old religious tradition and they see the whole basis of life crumbling away. Our lama-host was himself the product of this unhappy environment. 'Is it true', he once asked me, 'that there are six spheres of possible rebirth?' I found myself speaking in defence of Buddhist doctrine, explaining the relativity of all forms of existence and the basic truth of phenomenal impermanence.

The oldest temple in Tukchä is situated at the southern end of the township and is known as the Rānī Gomba, the 'Queen's Monastery'. This is a secondary name, the origin of which seems to be forgotten, for the real one, as we learned from an inscribed bell outside, is 'Religion's Isle of Blessing' (bkra-shis chos gling). The whole place is in a lamentable condition. The cupola is in the process of collapsing. A house has been built against the northern side, thus blocking one of the entrances. Many of the frescoes inside, especially those on the right wall, are defaced. The images receive the minimum attention which is their due, for every morning a woman unlocks the doors, fills the offering-bowls with fresh water and lights a butter-lamp. She belongs to the old generation and lives in a little room that opens off the porch. One can only gain access to the temple when she is there to unlock the door. The frescoes that remain are excellent: on the left wall we see Śākyamuni and the sixteen arhats with the 'Holder of the Vajra' (Vajradhara) at the far end; on the right wall are portrayed the complete set of the 'Tranquil and Fierce' divinities.[a] On the back wall are the five fierce Herukas, all six-armed and with partners. Over the door is the 'defender' Ma-ning with Rāhula to his right. In the porchway of the blocked entrance one sees the four

a Concerning these see p. 232.

178

kings of the quarters and a large Wheel of Existence. Over the doorway are the 'Protectors of the Three Families' (p. 35). The main image over the table of offerings is that of 'Lotus-Born', but this temple was originally a Ka-gyü-pa foundation, as is indicated by the prominence given to the 'Holder of the Vajra' and by an upper row of miniature paintings above the arhats on the left wall, for here a Ka-gyü-pa lama is seen together with various divinities (*Amitāyus, Vajrasattva, Vijayā* and *Avalokiteśvara*). In the porch on the eastern side, by which one now gains access to the temple, are more paintings of the four kings and the three 'Family Protectors'. The courtyard on this side, once used for ritual dances, is now filled with an overgrown mass of flowers—roses, gladioli, dahlias and marigolds, which spread some cheer around this forlorn little site.

In the centre of the township there is another small temple known as the Mahākālī Gomba after the small image of this goddess which is placed under the main images. In fact, however, the temple was never dedicated to her, but to the three Buddhas of past, present and future, whose images occupy the chief positions above her. But in these 'hinduizing' days Mahākālī is treated as the presiding divinity and concealed by curtains from the eyes of the profane, lest harm should befall them at the mere sight of her. We braved her awesome presence, explaining to the anxious temple-keeper that this was a Buddhist and not a Hindu temple and that anyone who could appear cheerfully in the presence of the Buddhas of the Three Times, need not fear a demoness like Mahākālī. Since this temple is always locked and the keeper lives far away, it is rather difficult to gain access to it. Still it is well preserved and the frescoes are quite undamaged. We noticed the Karma-pa Lama, 'Supreme Bliss' and 'Lotus-Born' in his various manifestations. At the four corners are four fierce guardians of the portals, holding noose, hook, fetter and bell. In the cupola are 'All Good' and the five supreme Buddhas with their partners on one side of the square, 'Holder of the Vajra' and four yogins on another and 'Boundless Light' with 'Glancing Eye',

'Saviouress' and two lamas on the third side. A small window occupies the fourth. This temple too is surrounded by flowers.

There are small chapels containing the Tibetan Buddhist canon (Kanjur) and its commentaries (Tenjur) attached to two of the Sher Chand residences, but no member of the family takes any serious interest in them. The Tenjur chapel contains frescoes of the twenty-one aspects of the 'Saviouress' (*Tārā*) around the wall. We saw three other chapels in private houses. In one of them the Kanjur was being read by ten 'religious' gathered from here and there, two being the owners of other private chapels, three having come from outlying villages and the rest being Tibetan monks on pilgrimage. The owner of this chapel excused himself for his excessive show of reverence to the Buddhist scriptures by explaining that whereas he himself had little use for religion, his wife believed in it and so he was holding this ceremony to please her! To what a sorry pass has the 'Doctrine' come. In fact throughout the whole of the Kāli Gandaki valley the women have constituted themselves as the chief guardians of what little Buddhist practice remains. They at least are not ashamed of confessing it.

At the northern end of the little town is the Gomba Samba ('New Monastery'), next door to which we were staying. The walls are covered with large and beautiful frescoes of the sixteen arhats, a conventional set of Śākyamuni's early disciples. This must once have been the main monastery in Tukchä, providing for a community of monks with a presiding lama. But now there are no monks and just our host, the apostate lama.

Having thus seen all of Tukchä itself, I visited the surrounding villages, still attended by the faithful Takki Babu. We followed the main track down the right bank of the river, sometimes by the water's edge and sometimes along the rocks above. Further down the valley one sees the monsoon clouds, which have just enough strength to bring showers as far as Tukchä. The banks opposite are well covered with junipers and firs and among them we saw a small temple to be visited another day. In less than two hours we reached Narshang (SI: Khanti) and climbed up to the monastery. It contains some fine frescoes and a precious little white stone image of 'Glancing Eye' (*Avalokiteśvara*). It was difficult to see it properly, for it was carefully preserved in a glass casket and swathed in numerous silk garments, so that only the face was visible. Immediately below Narshang is Gophang Village (SI: Lārjung) with another temple. It contains a large image of 'Lotus-Born' and is cared for by local nuns. Hearing that there was a p'ön-po temple at the next village (Nabrikot) up the valley to the west, we climbed up to visit it. It was small and rapidly falling into disrepair, but certainly p'ön-po. The central image was that of Wäl-sä and there were paintings of the 'Tiger-God' and 'Composite Conqueror' (p. 49). Everything was dusty and ill-cared for. The next day we forded the river just above Tukchä and made our way down through the trees to the little red buildings we had seen there. The place is known as Sagaru Gomba and there are two small temples with a knowledgeable lama in residence. We found him seated reading in his kitchen beside an immaculate hearth adorned with shining brass pots. This as we had realized by now was typical of all T'hākāli houses.

Here and at Gophang (Lārjung) we seem to have reached the limit of Tibetan culture. I myself went no farther south, and Pasang returned now from his journey to Pokhara. He had been away for only ten days, travelling at his usual breakneck speed and sharing heavy loads with Karchung rather than employ porters, who would have delayed him another week and proved extremely costly. The monsoon was now at full force further down the valley and supplies expected by traders in Tukchä were already three weeks overdue. He had passed through Gurung territory, and although he had not seen them because they were off the main route, there are certainly a few scattered Buddhist temples of the Tibetan kind. Two for certain exist at Ghandrung and Ghālel, for later on we met Gurung villagers from these places who were visiting Muktināth to learn Tibetan. Such texts as they possess are all

Tibetan; they recite them at their ceremonies without understanding the meaning. In earlier times (8th to 13th centuries) this must have been one of the main routes by which Tibetan, Nepalese and Indian teachers travelled, painstakingly importing Buddhist teachings into Tibet. The Buddhism in this area was then of Indian inspiration, but of this not a trace seems to remain.[a] Like everywhere else throughout the Himalayas it is now Tibetan zeal which keeps the religion going and in witness of this we would refer above all to the Lama of Shang. Active hostility exists only at Tukchä, because it is here that the wealthy T'hākālis live and their sons return for holidays, having imbibed a little Western learning in the universities of northern India.

Now we had more letters to read and a fresh supply of provisions and films, and so could make ready for our return journey up the Kāli Gandaki. Shankarman Suba entertained us to a splendid meal in Tibetan style and presented us with tins of butter, cheese and meat, which had been given him by former mountaineering parties in the area. We entertained him in return the following day and Pasang supervised the cooking of delicious little patties filled with spiced mutton. One of the Tibetan monks whom we had seen reciting from the Tibetan canon (Kanjur) a few days before, visited us and said he would like to join our party; since he seemed a pleasant, willing fellow, we took him on as help-mate to Takki Babu. It was also very useful to me to have another member of the party besides Pasang, who was able to speak the regular dialect of central Tibet. Our provisions were also further increased, for having observed the joy with which we had accepted Shankarman's present, two villagers arrived with a large number of tins, containing yet more meat, cheese and butter, all of which had been left by previous mountaineering expeditions. The butter dated from the French expedition to Annapūrna in 1950. The cheese was less than two years old, for it had been brought by a

[a] Professor Tucci has followed the route right through to Lumbini near the present Indian frontier. See *Tra Giungle e Pagode*, pp. 89 ff.

German expedition the previous spring. There was enough, we estimated, to allow us one whole tin a week. The meat was also recent, having been brought by the Argentinians that same year. We agreed on a price and the lot became ours. We could now scarcely expect anything more of Tukchä itself.

There remained TSHEROK Monastery about four miles north, which we had glimpsed on the way down. Since it was on the far side of the river, it would be well off the Marpha track, so we decided to spend the next day visiting it. We crossed a bridge three miles up, passed through a small village and followed a line of prayer-walls to the grove in which the monastery stands.[a] Its isolated situation beside a stream is made altogether delightful by the surrounding trees and the tall hollyhocks that grow over the walls (pl. XXXIII*b*). To our chagrin the place was locked and deserted.

We returned to the little village by the bridge and learned from the villagers that the lama was away assisting at the Monastery of Ku-tsap-ter-nga (see p. 187) and that the key was in the keeping of a nun who lived up at Chimba (SI: Chimgāon). We climbed up to this village and found her house. She was working in the fields but came at the call of her parents, who were busy drying garlic on the roof. Just above the village we noticed a little shrine and so went up to investigate it. It contained two sacred tree-trunks standing some three feet high and swathed in yards of cotton cloth. They are known as Shä-bi Brother and Sister. The 'brother' has arms growing from the trunk and we were reminded of the 'dhauliya' protectors of the Tibrikot area (p. 28). We learned from the keeper of the shrine nothing except that they had been there 'a very long time', that six goats were sacrificed to them yearly and that the prosperity of the village depended upon this. We descended to the nun's house, bought two pounds of garlic from her parents, and then made our way down to Tsherok Monastery once more. She could tell

[a] The village is named after the monastery and appears on the Survey of India maps as 'Chhairogāon'.

us nothing more about the Shä-bi, but clearly disapproved of the goat-sacrifice.

We entered the courtyard of the monastery with great expectancy and were not disappointed. There is now not a single monk, although there would be room for thirty or so, but the whole place is well cared for, for the lama, whom we met later, is doubtless a worthy man. The main temple is about forty feet across. On the right wall are paintings of 'All Good' (*Samantabhadra*), flanked by the 'Fierce Master' and the 'Lion-Headed' Ḍākinī, and 'Glancing Eye' (*Avalokiteśvara*), flanked by two acolytes, making the gesture of giving with their right hands and that of explanation (*vitarka*) with the left. On the left wall are eight manifestations of 'Lotus-Born' (*Padmasambhava*), then the 'Holder of the Vajra' (*Vajradhara*) and Buddha Master of Medicine. On both sides below these main figures there is a frieze in the form of a row of Karma-pa lamas, thirteen on the left and eight on the right. On the back wall over the door is 'Adamantine Being' (*Vajrasattva*) with fierce 'defenders' to his left and right, two-armed, four-armed, six-armed. There is a second smaller temple containing a huge image of 'Lotus-Born' flanked by two great prayer-wheels. This is recent and impresses chiefly by its size. One ascends a kind of tower into the 'Defenders' Room' (*srung-khang* p. 36) where there are effigies of the fierce defender Ma-ning and a lama whom we could not identify. Both were concealed by curtains and the nun became very anxious when we peeped behind them. The general plan and mode of building is quite Tibetan in character, but the woodwork and most noticeably the doorways seems to owe much to Nepalese influence.

We returned to Tukchä for it was now evening and made preparations for our final departure the next day. We planned to travel to Dzongsam, for although this was only a short day's journey, it would give us time to visit the temples at Marpha, and by basing ourselves on the Dzongsam 'inn' for a day or two we would be able to see the other few places of interest in the vicinity. Thus the following morning we made our farewells and left with our belongings strapped on the back of three pack-horses which a friendly villager had pressed upon us. He had been so liberal with his arak whenever any member of our party had appeared within sight of his house, that we could not have refused his beasts without embarrassment, although they were rather ill-behaved. Two boxes were thrown off and tied on again more firmly and at last we were on our way.

We stopped by the 'inn' in MARPHA and while Takki Babu prepared a meal I went with Pasang to visit the monastery. It is small but well cared for by a lama and two or three reputable monks. The three presiding images in the temple are of 'Boundless Light' (*Amitābha*) at the centre, 'Glancing Eye' (*Avalokiteśvara*) to his right and 'Lotus-Born' (*Padmasambhava*) to his left. The frescoes on the left wall represent 'Lotus-Born' and 'Glancing Eye' with a third painting which is defaced by age. On the right wall is the complete set of the 'Tranquil and Fierce' divinities. The canonical commentaries (Tenjur) are arranged in racks the length of the temple, which is an unusual position. The canon itself (Kanjur) is kept in a private chapel at the southern end of the village. Up in the cliff behind the village there is a small rock temple containing some clay images of no artistic merit: Vajrapāni in the centre with Amitāyus on his right and the Lama *Rig-'dzin Nor-bu* on his left. The defender Ma-ning is concealed behind a curtain of rags in the corner. There are other small private chapels and although there can be little real learning in the place, the villagers still seem to hold the doctrine in respect; some of them expressed concern at the lack of religion in Tukchä. Having finished our meal and exchanged bantering remarks with the innkeeper's daughter, who spoke excellent Tibetan and with pretended and protracted regrets finally sold us a little arak-pot, made of wood and charmingly bound with silver, on which I had set my heart, we continued our journey. We passed by the bridge that leads to Ku-tsap-ter-nga and on by Shang (SI: Syāng), for we would be visiting both places the next day; then along the level route by the river-bank, across the bridge to Dzongsam and straight to the 'inn'. The host was there on this occasion and we learned that he was a cousin of Shankaman Suba and already knew much about us. In spite of our protests he vacated his own room for us and both he and his wife did all to make us comfortable.

The next morning we left Dzongsam by a track that continues down the left bank of the river and soon came to the village known as SOMBO in Tibetan and T'hin in Nepāli (SI: Thinigāon). There is a small p'ön-po temple void and deserted except for two large images of the 'Composite Conqueror' and Wäl-sä (pl. XXXIIIa). We were told that there had been a feud between the religious and anti-religious factions and that the latter had stripped the temple and thrown everything into the river except for these two images which were presumably too heavy to be carried conveniently. We noticed that they had also given vent to their fury upon a Buddhist prayer-wall on the way out of the village to the south.

We continued on our way and climbed up to the hill-top on which stands the Monastery named KU-TSAP-TER-NGA, 'Five Treasures of Bodily Representation' (sku-tshab gter nga). It is a place to which many Tibetan pilgrims come, for the five 'treasures' are said to have been brought from Sam-yä, the first Tibetan monastery, founded in A.D. 787. Their discoverer (gter-gton) bDud-'dul rDo-rje had given them to his disciple Urgyan dPal-bZang, who had subsequently founded Ku-tsap-ter-nga to enshrine them about two hundred years ago. They consist of a set of little terra-cotta images, two of 'Lotus-Born', one of his wife Mandāravā, one of 'Adamantine Sagging Belly' (rdo-rje grod-lod), who is another fierce manifestation of 'Lotus-Born', and one of the Buddha Master of Medicine. They are now kept wrapped up in a great deal of cloth and locked in a metal casket. There are also other interesting relics: namely one of Lotus-Born's slippers, which even if not genuine is a very fine replica of the type of slipper that he is always shown wearing; a miniature image of 'Supreme Bliss' cut in a dark brown stone and said to be self-produced, for it had been found in a cave near the monastery where a lama of great sanctity had meditated for many years; a section of the skull of another lama with the Tibetan letter A embossed as it were on the bone, for he had meditated so long on this basic vowel-sound, which lies at the root of all existence, that it had produced its written symbol miraculously inside his skull; lastly a Five-Buddha Crown represented in compressed form as one section of the five, cut from the same dark brown stone as the image of 'Supreme Bliss' and likewise said to be self-produced. These objects are in fact far more interesting than the five little clay images after which the whole monastery is named. We expressed our wonder, made a suitable offering and the box containing the relics was placed ceremoniously on our heads. The little temple in which the casket is kept, contains some good frescoes of Śākyamuni and the sixteen arhats and a collection of fine bronze images. We met here the lama of Tsherok Gomba, realizing suddenly that it was he who had shown us the relics. The main temple was being rebuilt, the Lama of Shang having contributed 15,000 rupees to this work. We found the painters at work on the left wall, which they were covering with the set of 'Tranquil and Fierce' divinities. The workmanship may well seem inferior, when one is acquainted with that of the older masters, but one can scarcely fail to be impressed by this great work of reconstruction. The villagers from the surrounding district were giving their services in exchange for just their daily food and all spoke with enthusiastic fervour of their chief benefactor, the Lama of Shang. We left them and descended the steep track to the bridge we had passed by the previous evening.

On our way back to Dzongsam we climbed up to SHANG.[a] There is a small temple in the centre of the village and a small monastery complete with living quarters; it was deserted.

At Dzongsam there is a small p'ön-po temple on the northern outskirts of the village, containing images of Wäl-sä, 'Composite Conqueror', 'Tiger-God' and 'Victorious One'. Inside the village there is also a minute Nying-ma-pa temple with

[a] Unconnected with the Lama of Shang, who comes from near Tashihlünpo.

images of 'Boundless Life', 'Glancing Eye' and 'Lotus-Born' and possessing a copy of the canonical 'Perfection of Wisdom' texts. This was carried in procession round the village during our stay and devout villagers came around to bow their heads beneath the massive volumes. It is first recited ceremonially and then carried round in this manner every year in order to ensure the prosperity of the village as a whole. Most of the reciters and carriers were women.

Leaving Dzongsam we kept to the right bank of the river and climbed up to the village of DANKAR-DZONG (SI: Dānkar-jong). The people here are classed as *bhotia*, viz. Tibetan, but T'hākāli is still spoken and even in the matter of race the change is not so sudden. One finds the true Tibetan type a further day's journey northwards—from Gyaga (SI: Keghagāon) and Samar onwards. Many of the people of Tshuk, for example our helper Karchung, might well pass as T'hākāli. But let it not be thought that they want to be taken for a higher caste by Nepalese standards, for they are proud enough just to be known as Tshuk-pa, 'men of Tshuk'. The people of Kāk (Kāgbeni) are known likewise as Kāk-pa and in spirit they still remain as independent as in the days when they had kings of their own.

Lo

The next morning the whole party, myself and Pasang, Takki Babu, Karchung and the monk Lopsang, set out northwards towards the Land of Lo (Mustāngbhot). We left most of our stores in Kāgbeni and were now sufficiently strong in numbers to need no extra porters for the things we carried. We stopped for a meal in Karchung's house at Tshuk, and having stayed too long, continued our journey belatedly. The route continues up the left bank of the Kāli Gandaki for less than a mile beyond Tshuk, and then crosses to the other side by a narrow plank bridge spanning the river just where it emerges from a great cleft in the rocks. Then it climbs up to Tshe-le Village (SI: Chelegāon) and over grey-brown mountainous desert to the gorge of a subsidiary stream. On the far side is Gyaga (SI: Keghagāon), which we had no reason to visit so we continued northwards out of this gorge and on to Samar (SI: Samargāon). We arrived late in the evening and a relative of Karchung's installed us in a small empty house in the village, where we spent a contented night.

There are alternative routes from Samar to Ge-ling (SI: Ghilinggāon), the longer one leading down through a deep ravine to a cave, known as the 'Self-Produced Place of Promenade' (*gcong-gzhi rang-byung*). We went by way of the cave which is a natural one with a small temple, now quite neglected, built at the entrance. It is still a favourite place of pilgrimage, for inside behind the temple there are a 'self-produced' chöten in the middle of the cave and four 'self-produced' images growing from the back walls. One is about two feet high, two about eighteen inches and the last about nine inches. They are curious pieces of work, very old and knocked about. It is commonly believed that if any part of them is broken off, it will grow afresh from the rock. They are modelled fully clothed but with garments not of a specifically religious kind. The 'self-produced' chöten is covered with a large number of small images of 'Lotus-Born'. Then there are four 'man-made' chötens with paintings of 'Boundless Light', 'Glancing Eye', 'Lotus-Born' and Śākyamuni (pl. XXXVa). In the porchway of the little temple there are small paintings of three Sa-kya-pa lamas, *Bya-bral kun-bzang brug-rgyas*, whose hands are in the attitude of meditation, *Drin-chen rtsa-ba'i bla-ma shā-kya rgyal-mtshan*, who makes the gesture of explanation with his right hand and that of 'earth-witness' with his left, and *Bya-btang kun-bzang 'phrin-las* who makes the same gestures but with the hands reversed. This place is visited by Tibetans on their way down from Mustang and also by Tibetans from other parts of Nepal. Later on we met a whole party of people from Nar who were on their way to this cave, where they burn juniper twigs as incense and place their heads reverently at the base of the chötens and the images. We climbed up out of the gorge and on across the brown barren landscape. Down on our right we saw the green fields and red temples of Ge-ling (SI: Ghilinggāon), but deciding to visit it on our return journey, we continued on and over a low pass and so down to Ge-mi (SI: Kehami).[a]

Like all villages in this strange land GE-MI appears from a distance as an oasis of green and red and gold in a mountainous desert of brown and grey, but when one reaches the houses, one seems as if surrounded by rocks, stone walls and ruins. We settled in the house of a friend of Karchung's family and I put up a tent for myself by the stream. Like other villages Ge-mi is also dominated by a massive castle, this one belonging to the King of Lo and in better repair than any we had seen so far. Inside there is a temple containing a few images and some very fine thankas, chiefly of the Buddha 'Imperturbable' (Akshobhya). But it was all quite uncared for and the floor-space was being used for drying onions. In the middle of the village there is a monastery, which has recently been repaired and was about to be repainted. The old frescoes had therefore been submerged beneath a preparatory coating of clay wash. There were said to be several monks, but they all seemed to be mere boys, and were monks only because the time had not yet come for them to marry. We noticed in the kitchen great copper cauldrons set over the hearths in Tibetan fashion for the preparation of vast quantities of Tibetan tea. There is another small temple at the eastern extremity of the village, which is looked after by nuns. We enquired about a route that descends to Ge-mi from Tsharka and learned that it was rarely used and was in any case quite impracticable in July and August because of the flooding of streams in some parts.

The main route to Mustang leads up through Tsarang (SI: Chārāng), but we directed our steps due north and crossed a low pass to the village of TR'ANG-MAR (SI: Tāhmar), which means 'Red Crag' (brag-dmar). The temple there is insignificant, but I shall always remember this place as we saw it at the end of

[a] Samar lies at about 11,000 feet, Ge-mi at about 10,000 and this pass is about 13,000 feet. We use 'low' in a relative sense.

July. It presented a most lovely blend of pastel shades: the great
red cliffs against a clear blue sky and at their foot the red and
white buildings amidst the green of the trees; nearby there
rushed a milky-coloured stream and all around was an expanse
of golden corn and the pink bloom of buckwheat. Beyond
Tr'ang-mar we climbed up again into the bare grey-brown
mountains and traversed the wilderness of their flanks (pl.
XXXIV*a*), descending at last to the head of another valley.
Here grass was growing and just ahead we saw a monastery
surrounded by trees. While we were resting a lama with three
attendants passed by; we hailed him politely and asked where
he came from. He replied that he came from Nup-ri and had
been on pilgrimage to Mustang. We answered his questions
about ourselves and said we would be visiting his country in due
course. This preliminary meeting with him proved to be of great
help later on.

We made our way down to the monastery, a great red and
white building with rows of new prayer-wheels round the outside walls and four new chötens at the corners (pl. XXXIV*b*).
We learned later that these were all gifts of the Lama of Shang,
who often stays here and has made this place his own. It is
known as LO GE-KAR, 'Pure Virtue of Lo'. The sacristan was
deaf and dumb, but two Tibetan monks and a nun were staying
there, as well as several ordinary pilgrims. We erected a tent
on the grass sward in front of the buildings and prepared a little
food before investigating further. Some of the pilgrims came
to beg alms and went away content with measures of tsamba and
small coins. One little boy stayed to eat some of our rice (pl.
XXXVII*b*).

Lo Ge-kar differs from all the other monasteries we have
seen in that it is planned inside rather after the style of a
private house. There is no main temple, but several rooms on
two floors, all more or less of the same size. Thus from a bare
entrance-hall one enters a room on the right. The walls are
painted pleasingly with the four kings of the quarters, the god-

desses of the offerings, the gods Brahmā and Indra, supported by a layman and a monk, all bearing gifts. The far wall opens into a deep dark alcove, in which with the help of our torch we discerned two life-size images, one seated on an ox and the other on a horse. They are fierce protective goddesses and the monk who accompanied us, identified the white-faced one on the horse as 'Mother with Good Things' (*ama legs-ldan*) and the blue-faced one on the ox as 'Fierce Lady with Good Things' (*legs-ldan drag-mo*). The nun opened a newly made and brightly painted cupboard (another present of the Lama of Shang) and displayed a set of sacrificial cakes (tormas) that she had made herself. From the doorway of the next room, where we now stood, we saw at the far end the brass tiers of an altar with butter-lamps illuminating the images of 'Lotus-Born' (*Padma-sambhava*) and his two wife-goddesses. The rest of the room was quite dark, but with the help of our torch we observed that the walls, once covered with frescoes, were now blackened from the smoke of the lamps that burn continually. There are other *terra-cotta* images of 'Lotus-Born', the 'Fierce Master', the 'Lion-Headed' Ḍākinī and of eight other special manifestations of 'Lotus-Born'. This dark shrine-room and its antechamber were altogether awe-inspiring. On the other side of the entrance hall there is a kitchen and a store-room. One then ascends to the first storey where there are four rooms, the walls of which are all covered with rows of small paintings on flat stones set within wooden frames. We had seen paintings of this kind before, but never in such great numbers. Thus one room contains all the 'Tranquil and Fierce' divinities and the set of twenty-five pundits (*rJe-'bangs*). Another contains the eighty-four great yogins (*siddha*) and the sixteen arhats. The third and fourth contain numerous replicas of 'Glancing Eye', 'Adamantine Being' and other buddhas. The first two rooms, where all the paintings are different, are the most pleasing, each painting deserving careful study (pl. XXXV*b*). There was a sense of living intimacy about this monastery and we understood why the Lama of Shang should come here often; of all the places we have seen in this whole area, it is here we would stay most readily.

The next morning our party separated. Pasang and Takki Babu continued northwards on a brief visit to the city of Mustang while Lopsang and Karchung accompanied me down the valley by Marang (SI: Māhārāng) to TSARANG (SI: Chārāng). This township, dominated by its fort and its monastery, is built on an eminence above the junction of this valley and another which descends from the direction of Mustang half a day's journey to the north. We approached through fields of pink buckwheat; the red and white buildings were silhouetted against yellow-brown cliffs beyond. Karchung led the way to the house of a family-acquaintance, where everyone was busy thrashing peas (pl. XXXVIIa). While we were setting up a tent and establishing ourselves in a corner of the courtyard, the 'incarnate' Lama of Tsarang came to see who we were. He was dressed for work in the fields and so was in no way distinguishable from any other well-to-do villager, but I recognized him from an earlier photograph of Professor Tucci's. He is the second son of the King of Lo (Mustāng-rāja) and now about thirty years old. After enquiring where I had come from, he invited me round to his house. It is a new one, which he has had built in the village, for having recently married, he lives in the monastery no longer. We sat and talked a short while and with Lopsang's assistance I explained where we had been and what we had been doing. His wife was meanwhile preparing enormous balls of moistened tsamba for the field-workers. She reheated the earthen tea-pot and served us with buttered tea. I asked to see the monastery, so the Lama summoned an old woman and handed her a key. She led the way up to the massive red building, which surmounts the bare ridge at the southern end of the village. The walled compound was guarded by a fierce half-starved mastiff, to whom she threw a ball of tsamba brought expressly for that purpose, followed by a well-aimed stone or two. The creature snarled and yelped and even though it knew

her, it made to get at Lopsang and myself. It was imprisoned on
the roof of an outhouse just above our heads, and one could
imagine it leaping upon its victim in a fury of madness. We
were glad to have passed through the courtyard and reached
safety inside the main doors. We ascended rickety wooden steps
to the lama's own apartments on the top floor. They are now
unused except when his father comes on a visit. There is a little
chapel, recently painted, with a number of fine images. The
living-rooms have large latticed windows in Tibetan style and I
reflected how pleasant a dwelling-place it would be. This is
certainly the largest monastery we have seen and must have
been occupied in former times by a sizeable community. But
now their kitchens and living quarters are bare and deserted.
There are said to be several monks in Tsarang, but here the term
'monk' (grva-pa) is used in the vaguest sense and is applied to
anyone who can recite religious texts when there are offerings
to be distributed. The old woman did not have the key to the
main temple, so we had to wait a long time while the sacristan
came in from the fields. But this main temple was the most
splendid we had seen on all these travels. The central image is a
most beautiful gilt bronze Maitreya, flanked by other smaller
images of Śākyamuni and the 'Holder of the Vajra' (Vajradhara).
There is a fine gilt chöten set with semi-precious stones, trumpets bound with chased silver and gold, well-sounding cymbals,
most beautiful thankas, all unappreciated by those who should
value them. Lopsang hastened to assure me that nowhere in
Tibet proper could a temple be abandoned like this one. The
frescoes are good and still unspoiled. In the alcove behind the
main images is a painting of the 'Holder of the Vajra' flanked
by Hevajra and 'Supreme Bliss'. On the left wall of the alcove
is Śākyamuni; the fresco on the right is spoilt. Śākyamuni
appears again to the left of the alcove, balanced by Buddha
Master of Medicine on the right. The Five Buddhas appear
along the walls to left and right, some appearing twice, some
three times. This temple overwhelms one with wonder and sad-
ness. At the far end of the monastery-compound there is another

temple, completely neglected and always unlocked, for there is nothing worth taking away. The frescoes were once good and with few exceptions are the same as those in the main temple.

We walked over to the fort (pl. XXXVIa) which is now one enormous ruin, but one can still make one's way through its collapsing portals and up dangerous wooden steps to a little chapel. This contains a copy of the Tibetan canon and some fine gilt bronze images, all deserving a better home. On the floor above is a 'Defenders' Room' (srung-khang) with a standing image of a drap-lha (dgra-lha—personal divinity protective against enemies), dressed in the Tibetan mail-armour of olden times. From the walls hang weapons and various other objects, the beak and claws of a pelican and a dried and blackened human hand, fierce reminder of the harsh punishments of former days. I left this place feeling as though I had had a vision of the last days of Tibetan Buddhism, its images and texts no longer understood or cared for, while the more horrific elements continue to exercise a powerful fascination on the mind.

I found the lama in his fields the next morning, watching over his men, who were busy watering (pl. XXXVIb). He is very friendly, sincere of speech and also perhaps rather pathetic, for there are few unhappier beings than a man of religion who has lost faith both in his religion and in himself. 'I really should live in the monastery, but now I am married, and what can I do, when no one believes in me.' The Lama of Tukchä had said much the same, but without this sense of tragedy. There is no doubt that throughout the whole valley of the Kāli Gandaki Buddhism is on the wane.

In the evening Pasang arrived with Takki Babu and a great deal to talk about; it is to him that I owe the following brief description of MUSTANG, known locally and by all Tibetan speakers as Mön-t'hang of Lo (blo smon-thang).[a] This petty

[a] The Tibetan name is given by the SI as Lho. Mantang. The aspiration of Lho is quite wrong and especially misleading as it suggests the Tibetan word for 'south'. I did not visit this city myself on this occasion, as there was

kingdom of Lo extends as far south as Ge-mi (SI: Kehami), but the actual power of the 'king' seems to consist only in the possession of property here and there throughout the area as well as certain magisterial powers, which are subject to the confirmation of the Chief District Magistrate at Bāglung, within whose province this part of Nepal falls. It is chiefly of interest as the last survival of a whole chain of petty kingdoms that used to extend along the upper Kāli Gandaki, perhaps rather like the strongholds of the old Rhineland barons. It has always been the largest and presumably the most powerful. Its past wealth is indicated by the splendid temples in the city of Mön-t'hang, most of which are now rapidly falling into ruin. The royal family is accorded the caste of T'hākāli. The king is given the rank of General of the Nepalese Army and his eldest son that of Colonel. In fact however their style of living is completely Tibetan and their houses are arranged like those of Lhasa noblemen. The present dynasty only dates from the end of the eighteenth century, the time of the Gorkha-Tibetan wars, when a younger son of the Gorkha Rāja was sent to this part of the frontier as General Commanding. He established himself as ruler and married a Tibetan wife. Since that time the family line has always sought wives from the Tibetan side, but the relationship with the present Nepalese royal family, although now so tenuous, is still recognized. It is since that time that these frontier areas have become part of the political unit of modern Nepal. We may also date from this same period all the destruction we have seen and the general decline of Tibetan religion.

Mön-t'hang (smon-thang), meaning 'plain of aspiration', is in fact built in a flat valley and so on a plain. Thus for its defence it has developed into a walled city, the only one of its kind in the whole area (pl. XXXVIIIa). Within the walls are the fort (now abandoned by the rulers for more convenient dwellings outside), the monastery, assembly-hall ('du-khang), several important temples and more than a hundred houses, all crowded close

recently trouble on the frontier and the Nepalese Government was concerned lest I should become involved in difficulties of a political nature.

together. The king with his youngest son lives at Tingkhar (SI: Tegār), a new residence about two miles NW of the city, while his eldest son who is now acting ruler, lives in a separate house just outside the walls. The second son is the Lama of Tsarang. Pasang stayed in the house of the eldest son and was impressed by the Tibetan furnishings, the like of which we had seen nowhere else on our travels, and especially by the private chapel and the carved altar-piece it contained (pl. XXXIX*b*).

Of the buildings inside the city the most impressive is the Temple of Avalokiteśvara, the Great Compassionate One (*thugs-chen lha-khang*), which is of enormous proportions, its roof being supported by six rows of seven pillars. These pillars with their elaborately carved capitals and the door-ways were once fine examples of Tibetan wood-craft. In the centre of the roof there is a cupola from which the heads of twenty-eight lions, carved of wood, survey the scene. The frescoes around the walls are also of unusual size and represent the motifs that we have learned to associate with Sa-kya-pa temples, viz. the Five Buddhas, 'Holder of the Vajra', Śākyamuni, etc. The main images are of Śākyamuni (centre), 'Glancing Eye' to his right flanked by a chöten and Maitreya to his left flanked by 'Lotus-Born'. Only Śākyamuni is of gilded bronze, the rest being *terra-cotta*. This temple was once the centre of a large monastery, but the living quarters of the monks are all now in ruins.

Close to the Temple of the Great Compassionate One is the Temple of Maitreya (*byams-pa lha-khang*). Although of smaller proportions, it rises to three stories with the great image of Maitreya reaching up to the top of the second floor. Since at present access is only possible to this floor, one looks down on to the enormous lotus-throne of Maitreya and the lower part of his figure on the floor below. The walls of this second floor are painted with the mystic circles (*maṇḍala*) of the 'Great Brilliance' (*Mahāvairocana*). Originally, this temple seems to have been in the care of the monks of the Temple of the Great Compassionate One, but since there are now no monks, it is looked after by laymen.

At the other end of the city is the Gomba Sarba, the 'New Monastery', so nicknamed because it has undergone repair in recent times (pl. XXXVIIIb). It is again a Sa-kya-pa foundation and its temple is painted with the regular motifs. The main images are those of the 'Holder of the Vajra', Śākyamuni and 'Lotus-Born'. It contains a large collection of smaller images, thankas and ritual instruments. Nearby is the assembly-hall which contains little else than the images of three Sa-kya-pa lamas. The frescoes have suffered here far more than in any other building. Between the monastery and the assembly-hall there is a small temple built around a large chöten (mchod-rten lha-khang). Behind the chöten Pasang noticed in particular a very fine painting of Hevajra, tutelary divinity (yi-dam) of the Sa-kya-pas.

In the old fort there are the remains of a chapel and a 'Defenders' Room' as in Tsarang. Half-way to the king's house to the NW is the Monastery of Victory (rnam-rgyal dgon-pa), which has recently been completely rebuilt and repainted. About two miles to the SW is the small Ka-gyü-pa Monastery of Sam-drup-ling, which Pasang had passed on his way from Lo Ge-kar.

This completed our brief visit to the Land of Lo and the next morning (August 7th) we followed the main route down from Tsarang to Ge-mi, where we stopped to cook a meal. Then continuing our journey we reached GE-LING (Ghilinggaon) by early evening, where once more we established ourselves in the courtyard of family-friends of Karchung. In the morning we visited the little monastery, which belongs to a Sa-kya-pa subsect (ngor-pa). It contained a few good images and thankas but nothing else impressive. There is a 'Defenders' Room' in the old fort, where hanging from the ceiling in front of the fierce images we noticed another blackened human hand. To the west of the village there is another little temple, which is looked after by nuns.

We continued across the barren mountains, passed the junction with the track that leads down to the 'self-produced' caves, and took the short route to Samar. There is a small group of houses just before one reaches there and one of these belonged to Karchung's elder brother, so we stopped to drink chang and cook food. There was a neat hearth in his kitchen after the T'hākāli style, but everything was rather grubbier in the careless Tibetan manner. We reached Tshuk in the evening and spent our last night in the house of Karchung's family. The next day, leaving Karchung to arrange for the purchase and grinding of a fresh supply of wheat, we went down to Kāgbeni and set up camp in a grove of willows just outside the town beyond the Muktināth stream. We spent the rest of the day organizing our supplies and loads for the journey eastwards to Muktināth and thence to other lands beyond.

DZAR-DZONG

The next morning, Friday, August 10th, we turned our backs on the Kāli Gandaki and set out for Muktināth. Since our arrival in Kāgbeni over a month before there had been no need of such a cavalcade. We climbed up high above the left bank of the Muktināth stream and within two hours came to the villages of Khyeng-khar (SI: Khingār) and Dzar (SI: Chāhar), which occupy the upper valley. Dzar dominates this southern side of the valley with its fort and monastery. Then passing through Purang (SI: Pura), we climbed on up to Muktināth. This place appears misleadingly on the Survey of India maps in very large type; in fact there is no village here at all. There are just two small sites of interest to pilgrims: the grove with the 108 water-spouts, after which the place is properly named Chhu-mik-gya-tsa, and the temple with the 'miraculous' fire, which burns from earth, water and stone.[a] A Hindu temple, built in the style of a Nepalese pagoda and containing an image

---

[a] *Tib.* classical spelling *chu-mig brgya rtsa* = 'Place of 100 Springs'. I use the Nepalese name of Muktināth because it is now so well established.

of Vishnu, now stands by the water-spouts, but this is a recent addition; everything else is Buddhist and Tibetan.

We set up our camp just below the grove of the 108 spouts, where there is a two-storied stone shelter for pilgrims, looked after by a nun. Although quite unlettered and with little enough knowledge of the religion she professes, she is altogether a remarkable person (pl. XL*b*). When we arrived, she was just setting out to visit her parents in Purang; she had never seen us before, but she handed Pasang her keys, telling him to take any supplies we needed from her room. Thus we helped ourselves to wheat-flour and tsamba, eggs and arak. Throughout our stay she kept us supplied with whatever was available, procuring meat and the little apricots that grow down the valley at Putra. Gradually we learned more about her. Her father had become indebted to one of the wealthy members of the Sher Chand family at Tukchä and since he was unable to pay, he and his whole family had gone into the enforced service of their creditor. When she was twenty years old the girl had run away and attached herself to a well-known lama (*Brag-dkar Rin-po-chè*) of Kyirong. She proved herself of extraordinary ability in business matters and began to trade first on his account and then gradually on her own, so that at last she had made sufficient money to repay her father's debts and so buy the freedom of her whole family. She is now thirty-two and of a jolly and vivacious disposition; she still goes trading as far as Calcutta and was planning to visit Singapore. She wanted to join our party and go to England with Pasang. If we had agreed nothing would have deterred her, but there were already problems enough on hand. Muktināth was pleasant and very quiet, being tired from the hectic travelling of the last month, we decided to delay there a week. There was much writing to be done and the whole upper valley to be visited.

Little needs to be said about the water-spouts. There is simply a stream above, which is fed through 108 spouts in the form of little brass animal-heads. Pilgrims should at least drink a few drops from each one; the more hardy bathe under all of them. The altitude is about 12,000 feet and the water extremely cold. The temple of the miraculous fire is Nyingma-pa and contains large and not very beautiful *terra-cotta* images of 'Boundless Light', 'Glancing Eye' and 'Lotus-Born'. The flames of natural gas burn in little caves at floor level in the far right-hand corner. One does indeed burn from earth; one burns just beside a little spring ('from water'); the one 'from stone' exhausted itself two years ago and so burns no longer, at which local people express concern. There are no less than five other Tibetan Buddhist temples in the immediate vicinity. Just below the grove is the 'New Monastery' (*dgon-pa gsar-pa*) containing a large image of 'Lotus-Born' behind a beautifully carved wooden screen. Just above the grove is the 'Temple of the Lamps' (*mar-me lha-khang*). To the north on an eminence is the 'Temple of the Encampment' (*sgar dgon-pa*) and below it is the 'Place of Mind-Perfection' (*bsam-grub-gling*), a small temple which has just been completely rebuilt and was being repainted by one of the monks of the Shang Lama. He was the only man of religion with any education whom we met in the whole area. All the other temples are cared for by nuns, who are mainly interested in mulcting pilgrims. There is a Hindu priest at the Vishnu temple, but even here the nuns have collecting rights, although the place is not of their faith.

More interesting than Muktināth itself is the whole valley below it. This is known as Dzar-Dzong-yül-druk (*Dzar-rDzong-yul-drug*), that is to say 'Dzar and Dzong and the other villages, six in all'. There are the three villages on the left bank of the river, through which we had passed on our way up Khyeng-khar, Dzar and Purang, and three more on the right, Chhönkhor (SI: Chhego), Dzong (SI: Chohang) and Putra in this order of descent. Dzong means just 'castle'. The original name of this township was 'Peak of Supreme Victory' (*rab-rgyal-rtse*). It is the largest of the six and the extent of the ruins of the fort and its dominating position leave little doubt that this was originally the seat of the 'king' of the whole valley (pl. XL*a*). Hence the local name of 'the castle', which now appears on SI maps in the garbled form of Chohang.[a] The monastery attached to this fort is also the largest in the whole area. It was once finely painted with frescoes, which are still just discernible; even now it contains a few good images and the remains of what were once good thankas. The whole place is forlorn and neglected, but it is worth clambering over the site in order to gain an impression of its former importance. There are also small monasteries at Dzar and Chhönkhor, but they contain nothing of special note. All the religious establishments in these villages are *ngor-pa* while those at Muktināth are generally Nying-ma-pa. About a mile SW. of Muktināth there is a small p'ön-po temple named the 'Monastery of Moral Law' (*tshul-khrim dgon-pa*).

Karchung parted from us, as he was unwilling to go on to Manang, saying that the Tshukpas and the Manangbas had been in a state of feud for some time and that his life would not be safe. Nor did he exaggerate the danger, but we were sorry to lose him. With the apricots from Putra and some extra sugar we had bought in Tukchä we made a few pounds of apricot jam for the weeks ahead. From our tents we looked across to the summit of Dhaulagiri and life seemed very tranquil It rained a little, for this upper valley unlike the Kāli Gandaki below us, was not protected from the monsoon.

On the 15th (full moon) of the 7th Tibetan month (September 21st) a great gathering was due to be held at the head of the valley. All the villages in the area were to send up parties on horseback dressed in their finest clothes. They visit the 108 water-spouts ceremoniously and then a great horse-race is held. Khyeng-khar and Dzar sent up rehearsal parties five days before. They met on the track, and since all were rather drunk and neither party would make room for the other, a fight developed.

[a] This fort used to belong to the family of the founder-lama of Shey Monastery, *bsTan-'dzin ras-pa* (see p. 150). It is referred to in his biography as the 'Fort of the Peak of Supreme Victory' in Lower Lo (*blo smad rab rgyal rtse mo'i rdzong*). The Kingdom of Lo then included the whole of the upper Kāli Gandaki Valley.

We met them coming down, one man with blood pouring from his face, supported by his companions and followed by wailing women. They were threatening vengeance. We had already heard accounts of the amount of arak consumed on the occasion of this festival, and with a feud between two of the villages just brewing, we decided that it would be more pleasant to leave before the event, for our tents would be surrounded by those of the revellers. Moreover no pack-animals would be available for two or three days afterwards and we were already far behind our schedule. So we made preparations to cross over to Nye-shang.

V

NYE-SHANG AND THE
NAR VALLEY

Very early on August 18th four dzos and two horses were brought to our camp by a man of Dzar and his son. I had decided to ride to the top of the pass. Probably the mounts of the wealthy T'hākālis which we had seen during the past month, had reminded me that there were other means of travel besides one's own feet. But we were at once involved in disputation with the owner, for he demanded a high daily rate for three days. Yet we would be able to ride only for the first day; it would be impossible during the steep descent on the second and on the third day the animals would be returning without us. Moreover on sober reflection it seemed absurd to ride, when we had already walked a thousand miles or so; we might as well complete our course in the same way throughout. We therefore refused the horses, at which the owner was not at all aggrieved, and having loaded the dzos and drunk some of the parting gift of buttered tea and arak, given by our friend the nun, we set out on our way. The track leads up behind the temple of the Hundred Springs, ascending a steep grassy valley beyond. The man of Dzar turned back, when we were well on our way, leaving his son in charge of the dzos. The weather became cold and wet and we were soon enveloped in heavy mist, as we moved gradually up into the familiar world of rocks and scree. Towards evening we reached the great summit-cairn and began the descent in heavy rain. After about two hours we reached a small stone building, where we intended to spend the night. Erected many years ago as a halting-place for travellers, it is now little more than a ruin. A party of Manangbas on their way to attend the festival at Muktināth, had already taken possession, so we had no choice but to put up the tents nearby. It was dark and very wet, but the house at least provided shelter for elementary cooking on a primus.

The next morning the sky was still overcast, but the rain had stopped. After a breakfast of tsamba, tea and biscuits we packed up our things, loaded the animals and made our way down to the stream. This is marked on the Survey of India maps as the Jargeng Khola and I wondered, as often, whence the surveyors had obtained this name. The people of these Tibetan regions never give names to the streams and rivers, referring to them all by the general appellation of *chu* ('water'). The Tibetan names for streams which appear on these maps are generally the names of villages and more rarely of districts, which have been arbitrarily applied to the streams, but here there is no village at all and the name Jargeng is quite unknown. Possibly it has been obtained in answer to a question where this valley led, for a villager may well have answered 'Dzar-dzong' and the enquirer would have written it down as he thought he heard it.[a]

We crossed this stream and continued down its left bank. The valley opened, shrubs began to appear, and having collected twigs, we settled down to prepare a morning meal. The clouds lifted and one of the peaks of Annapūrna became visible to the south. We followed the path down, crossed another stream and stopped to talk with two village-youths who were waiting on the bridge. They understood none of our Tibetan, for their own dialect was so different as to be a separate language; they spoke Nepāli willingly and fluently. One of them told us that his father had been in the Indian Army and that he himself had visited Malaya and Singapore. Later we were to learn that this was nothing exceptional for a man from these parts. Soon afterwards we came to the first small terraced fields, red with ripening buckwheat. Below us we saw the Marsyandi River, to which

[a] *j* on the SI maps of Nepal is to be pronounced *dz*. See p. 275. Dzar-dzong refers to the valley below Muktināth. See p. 201.

were now added the waters of our stream. Then we met village-girls, who stopped and stared and laughed. The track had become a well-trodden path between high stone walls and Tengi Village came into sight. We passed through the archway and hastened between the houses, down through their fields, across a stream and on towards MANANG, anxious to establish a comfortable place to sleep that night. Pasang, who was well ahead, had already found the headman's house and was talking to members of the family by the time we caught up with him. A crowd fast collected around us and we stood in the muddy lane, debating whether to accept the invitation to stay in the headman's house. I had no intention of doing so, for it looked very dirty and was doubtless infested with fleas, but where else to stay was a problem. After wandering around, followed by a crowd of laughing children, I saw a possible camp-site below the village down by the river. By this time the whole village was concerned in our doings and we could not expect a moment of peace in its vicinity. Fortunately the site was suitable, although rather stony; the loads were brought down and our camp was established.

Early next morning two patients arrived, a man with a three-year-old sore on his leg and a boy with a festering thorn in his foot. We gave them both penicillin injections, removed the thorn and applied dressings as best we could. Then we went up to visit the temple, which stands in the middle of the village. There are two central images of 'Lotus-Born' with 'Glancing Eye' and 'Boundless Light' on the right and the 'Fierce Master' and a small bronze 'Lotus-Born' on the left. The walls are unpainted except for the eight signs of good fortune, which the Lama of Shang had recently paid to have done. We noticed, as something unusual, long pendants of Chinese silk of various colours, which hung from the ceiling and all seemed quite new. These, we learned, had been brought back from Singapore by some of the villagers.

We looked around the village, visiting another patient who had sent a boy begging us to come, and talking to various people.

Those we had helped with medicine were certainly the most friendly, especially the man with the three-year-old sore, for he undertook to supply us with wheat. In general, however, these people made an unpleasant impression upon us. They are not pure Tibetan, as may be discerned at once from their features and from their language, which is too far removed to be considered a Tibetan dialect. They are extremely dirty without the compensating Tibetan virtue of zeal for their professed religion. They are keen traders and travellers—Burma, Singapore and Hongkong are all known to them—and yet they are of an ungenerous disposition towards foreigners who visit their country, whether Tibetans or Europeans. Lopsang had visited Manang before and although he had friends here, he disliked these *Manangbas,* telling us how they ill-treated his fellow-countrymen who passed through their country and how the Tibetans enjoyed nothing more than thrashing a Manangba whenever they met one in India. Since these people never seem to go to Tibet, there is no chance of getting even with them at home. As for our party, they often tended to treat us in a surly manner, but at the same time there were notable exceptions, or our stay in their country would have been difficult indeed.

On the Survey of India maps Manangbhot appears not only as the name of this village, but of the whole region as well, and this is very misleading, for it suggests a single cultural group.[a] In fact there are three distinct units, properly known as Nye-shang, Nar and Gyasumdo. We were now in Nye-shang which embraces all the villages in the upper Marsyandi Valley down as far as Pi (SI: Pisāng). The three largest are Manang, Drakar (SI: Brāga) and Bangba (SI: Ngāwal) and these are referred to as Manang-tsok-sum, the 'Three Manang Communities'. Little love however seems to be lost between them, for Manang and Drakar had been waging a feud for the last five years and woe betide any villager who found himself in the hands of his neighbours. Fortunately they had made peace in the year of our visit. Both are large villages of about three hundred houses.

[a] Concerning *-bhot* see p. 276.

Bangba has somewhat less. Then there is the smaller village of Tengi just above Manang and the two villages of Gyaru (SI: Ghyāru) and Pi (Pisāng) a day's journey downstream. We visited them all in due course, lest anything of interest should be missed. It proved quite impossible ever to obtain reliable information about places ahead, which would have enabled us to decide without more ado that such and such a village was not worth a long detour. When we make enquiries on any matter whatsoever, the spelling of a name, the identification of an image, etc., we always cross-check and judge what is plausible and what is not. But when it comes to estimating the merits of a place we have not seen, we find ourselves quite unable to make sense of the different accounts we receive. In the whole of Nye-shang there are only two monasteries worth visiting, Bo-dzo Gomba, less than an hour's walk below Manang, and Drakar Gomba. The other village-temples are not to be compared with them, but since no Manangba, not even those who were friendly and helpful, seemed aware of this, we had no choice but to go everywhere and see for ourselves.

We were told that the oldest monastery of the whole region was TA-HRAP (*rta-srab*) Gomba beyond the little village of Ngaba (SI: Khāngsar), so the following day we went to see it. We crossed to the right bank of the Marsyandi and followed the track up through a pine-forest. This in itself was a delight, for it was a long time since we had walked beneath so many trees. The track recrossed the river, ascending steeply to Ngaba village; we visited the bare temple with its poor clay images, and then went on to Ta-hrap. This monastery consists of a small stone building, entered through a high-walled courtyard. Here a man was at work making small bells for religious use. He proved to be a Tibetan who had been earning his living in this way for many years, obtaining bell-metal by melting down old broken bells. He was happy enough and showed us the ways of his craft, but the sight was a forlorn one. The temple inside had a bare earth floor and bare walls unadorned. Some threadbare thankas were hanging from the wooden pillars and an untidy collection of images covered the dusty altar-tables. It seemed to be the kind of place which some lama might have established long ago as a hermitage. In fact later on we heard that it had been built by a former lama of Drakar. On the way back we were joined by a young man from Ngaba who told us about his trading activities.

These people can reach the Indian frontier in about two weeks, whence they go by train, with or without ticket, to Calcutta. Here at some government office well known to them, but which they are quite unable to specify, they obtain a pass, which enables them to buy a ticket and take ship to Burma or Singapore. They carry paper money and buy chiefly semi-precious stones and silks, which they trade in India on their return. They remain quite vague about the details of these journeys, such as the nature of the 'pass' or even of the paper currency that they obtain in exchange for their Nepalese rupees. Our young friend mentioned that a party of his acquaintances had gone all the way to Calcutta in vain, because they had found the 'pass' too expensive. He had noticed he said, that it was becoming more and more costly. He knew about customs officials and said that they lost much of their profit to them. He seemed to be quite unobservant and could describe nothing of the places he had visited. This trading habit must have been started by a few intelligent adventurers comparatively recently, and now Tom, Dick and Harry all follow suit. He begged us to come to his house and have some food, but being anxious to reach our own camp, we declined.

As we left the village, we met another of its inhabitants, who recognizing me as a Westerner (and therefore as British because he knew of no other kind), blocked our way in the narrow track and insisted that we should go to his house. He had been to Singapore, he said, and knew what splendid fellows the British were; they would soon be leaving and what a great pity it would be! Would we come to his house and have something to drink? Again we declined despite his insistence. Our refusal might perhaps seem churlish, but it would have been totally impossible to refuse the fierce spirit which he would most certainly have pressed upon us. He was already rather drunk. We therefore thanked him in the friendliest terms and manœuvred past him.

Returning happily through the pine-forest and along the river to our camp, we found a small crowd of friendly spectators and the man with the unhealed sore awaiting us. He wanted another dose of penicillin and had brought us thirty eggs and a bag of potatoes, which were very welcome, as so little food was available. We eventually obtained the wheat we needed, but the Manangbas themselves live mainly on buckwheat. Some rice, as a great luxury, is carried up from the lower valleys. There was no shortage of potatoes, but butter was scarce and very expensive; we learned later on that local trade restrictions were responsible for this (p. 227). They eat meat occasionally, but there was none palatable enough for us. Their staple food is buckwheat tsamba and tea prepared in Tibetan style. It is significant that we neither gave nor accepted hospitality in this region. Except for a Tibetan monk at Drakar and the Lama of Shang whom we met at Pi, there seemed to be no one who knew enough about his own religion to understand what we were doing. Thus in their ignorance they remained suspicious of us, wondering what our real intentions might be.

The following day we visited BO-DZO Monastery, about an hour's walk downstream from Manang. It stands on the summit of a rocky ridge beside the fort-like residence of former lamas. We approached through fields of flowering buckwheat, crossed a stony ravine with a turgid stream and ascended the steep path up the ridge. Some villagers were busy by the stream cutting up an animal they had killed and burning the unwanted parts. We walked round the temple, admiring its fine position and regretting only that heavy cloud across the valley concealed from us the snow-peaks of Annapūrna. In reply to our calls a woman appeared with the key and we entered by a tumbledown porch into the dark interior, only to discover that we had forgotten our torch. At Pasang's request the woman brought some butter and smouldering ash; thus having lit several butter-lamps, we deposited some on the altar and then each carrying one, set about examining the walls. The paintings were marvellous. Beginning on the back-wall to the left and continuing along the side-wall we saw nine buddhas, all yellow in colour, but distinguished by their different gestures and the different animals that supported their thrones. Since I was unable to recognize them as making up any conventional number, we noted their distinctive marks carefully.

Gestures *right hand — left hand*	Supporting Animals
1. contemplation with bowl	(defaced)
2. both hands preaching	harpy
3. earth witness—explanatory	seated lion
4. explanatory — contemplation	elephant
5. both hands explanatory	{ fore-quarters horse { rear-quarters lion
6. giving — contemplation	horse
7. contemplation with bowl	peacock
8. both hands preaching	harpy
9. earth witness—contemplation with bowl	rampant lion

The series may have continued along the wall behind the altar, but here everything was defaced except in the far corner, where a painting of the 'Saviouress' (*Tārā*) was visible. Continuing along the right wall we saw:

'Holder of the Vajra' (*Vajradhara*) with partner,

'Boundless Light' (*Amitābha*), new and garish, the only painting of such a kind in the whole temple,
A Sa-kya-pa Lama,
'Jewel-Born' (*Ratnasambhava*),
'Buddha Master of Medicine' (*Bhaishajyaguru*),
'Boundless Light' (*Amitābha*)

Then came:

	right hand—left hand	Supporting Animals
another yellow buddha,	explanatory—contemplation	harpy
an image much defaced		
another yellow buddha,	both explanatory	horse

Around the corner on the back wall were the Buddhas of past, present and future, 'Light-Maker' (*Dīpankara*), Śākyamuni and Maitreya. On the other side of the door were the 'Great Black' divinity (*Mahākāla*) with six arms, Jambhala, the god of wealth; then the series of unidentified yellow buddhas began.

The size of this temple and the fine quality of the frescoes suggest the existence of a well-established community, but now there are no monks and no true lama. There was also a large collection of images, Śākyamuni, Maitreya, 'Boundless Light', 'Holder of the Vajra', 'Lotus-Born' and his two spouses, the Buddhas of the Three Times and Sa-kya-pa lamas. After seeing Bo-dzo Monastery we had hopes of finding more such places in Nye-shang, but it proved to be the only one of its kind.

We returned to our camp early in order to make arrangements for departure on the morrow, for we now planned to move down to Pi (Pisāng), looking for anything of interest on the way. Our purposes would have been served best by establishing one camp just below Drakar (Brāga), whence we could have visited with ease everything of note in Nye-shang and then started on the journey into Nar. But we had no means of knowing this at the time; moreover we hoped to meet the Lama of Shang who would soon be on his way down to Pi from Gyaru. In any case we needed a full complement of transport, which Pasang now went in search of. No animals were available and no men were free or willing to come, but some women were prepared to discuss terms; by slightly raising the rates which we had been paying up till then, Pasang persuaded them to accompany us. Since Takki Babu and Lopsang would be carrying their normal loads, five women seemed sufficient. Alert as ever in these matters, they reminded us that we had had three dzos with us from Muktināth, which would have carried six man-loads, so that we were clearly scheming to overload them in order to reduce our costs. Pasang argued rightly that we had consumed a fair proportion of food in the last three days and that there was a great difference between a load suitable for carrying over an 18,000 foot pass and one for the easy walk down to Pi.

Thus the following morning we set out according to plan and passing below Bo-dzo, soon came to DRAKAR (SI: Brāga). The houses are built in tiers down a steep slope at the foot of precipitous crags; the monastery, painted white, rises above the other buildings with its topmost temple in the form of a chöten set against the cliffs of the summit-rocks. I was reminded of a Tibetan altar loaded with offerings and surmounted by the pointed tormas of the main divinities; thus it seemed that man and nature had combined to perfect a symbol of their unity, acknowledging the pre-eminence of the religious sphere. The scene was adorned with little groves of junipers and the fore-ground was a red sea of waving buckwheat. The size of the monastery indicated that here too there had once been a flourishing community; the first settlers had of course built their houses against the protection of the rock, leaving the fertile land below free for their crops. But the present generation at Drakar gave us no great reason to love them; we only gained access to their monastery thanks to the presence there of a wandering Tibetan monk, whom we met quite fortuitously as we climbed up to the village. Pasang addressed him in Tibetan and he showed great pleasure at meeting us. We discussed places along our route, rejoicing to have found a man of like spirit. He invited us forthwith to the house where he lived, and offered to get the keys of the monastery. The houses of Drakar are small one-storied affairs. The ground-floor, where the animals are kept at night, is partly open to the sky; a knotched tree-trunk ascends to a flat roof, towards the back of which more rooms are built, leaving the house open to the front. We unburdened ourselves of rucksacks and cameras and with a village-boy as guide Pasang went to the house of the temple-keeper; meanwhile the monk set about brewing tea. He had lived there for several months, he said, helping with ceremonies in the temple, but these Manangbas were so parsimonious in their offerings, that life was indeed difficult for a practiser of religion. In reply to my questions he told me that this monastery was not more than fifty to sixty years old and represented no particular order of Tibetan Buddhism, as the villagers themselves were quite undiscriminating. These statements proved to be wrong; we learned later from further questions and from the actual images that it must be 400–500 years old, and while it is only too true that the villagers are quite ignorant about their religion, this monastery is manifestly a Ka-gyü-pa establishment. His reply was typical of the lack of thoughtful observation among these people and one more lesson in the necessity of seeing for oneself. Pasang returned with the news that the keeper of the temple, supported by other villagers, refused to let us enter the monastery, for they were afraid that we would take photographs and profane it. They complained that other 'gya-mi' (presumably members of the recent German expedition to Dhaulagiri) had tried to gain access that year and had been taking photographs indiscriminately.

This was the first time we had encountered an objection to photography. In Dolpo we had used a camera while ceremonies were in progress without causing offence. Nevertheless there are grounds for theoretical objection: these people fear that the camera may not only capture the outer form, but also absorb part of the 'grace' (*byin-brlabs*) of a sacred image or revered person. The villagers of Pi voiced this fear to us with regard to the Lama of Shang. A new image is regarded as quite lifeless, but it is empowered at the time of its consecration and continues to derive power as the focus-point of so many ceremonies. Thus, if photographs continue to be taken, the image will eventually become 'powerless'. One can meet the objections of these suspicious villagers, in terms which they understand, for even if 'grace' were extracted, they could always 're-empower' the image. In any case we had no intention of taking photographs on this occasion, for our electronic flash was broken. Accompanied by the Tibetan monk, Pasang now went to make a second attempt to gain access. They met the keeper outside and his abusive shouts were raised for all to hear. But the monk brought him to reason, made him listen and explained that both Pasang and I were Tibetan-speakers, that we had no intention of taking photographs and that it was wrong to prevent men of religious disposition from visiting a temple. Gradually these arguments made themselves felt and the general mood of the by-standers changed in our favour, so that at last this troublesome man gave the keys to his son and told him to show us in. Rather saddened by all this un-pleasantness, we made our way up to the monastery, but our spirits revived as soon as we found ourselves inside.

The monastery consists of a main temple of the usual rect-angular shape with a second three-storied temple and the 'Defenders' Room' built separately higher up the mountain side. There are no frescoes in the main temple, but it contains a remarkable collection of more than a hundred small images arranged in a double row around three of the walls. They are of *terra-cotta*, each about two feet high and though individually of no great artistic merit, altogether of great historical interest. The series begins on the left of the door as one enters, con-tinuing round the back wall and the left-hand wall. By the door at the lower end of the bottom row a Ka-gyü-pa lama, *rGyal-dbang bsTan-'dzin,* is represented and thereafter one passes before the whole Ka-gyü-pa hierarchy, lama by lama, ending with *Ras-chung, sGam-po-pa,* Mila Räpa, Marpa, Tilopa, Näropa and finally the 'Holder of the Vajra' (see p. 77), a total of thirty-nine images. In the upper row the Five Buddhas appear over and over again with 'All Good' (*Samantabhadra*) among the last set. At the very end come the Red Ḍākinī (the only standing figure) and finally two images of the 'Saviouress' (*Tārā*).

In the corner there are the Buddhas of past, present and future, the Goddess of Wisdom (*Prajñāpāramitā*) and then along the right-hand wall:

lower row	*upper row*
'Lotus-Born' and his two spouses;	'Holder of the Vajra'
Phag-mo grub-pa and two lamas, the one on his right inscribed *bla-ma zhang;*	and Five Buddhas crowned
Lama Karma-pa and two lamas, red-hatted and black-hatted;	and six
Atīśa and two lamas, the one on his left being the Great Sa-kya-pa Pandit.	feminine partners.

Behind the table of offerings is a fine bronze image of 'Light-Maker' (*Dīpankara*), Buddha of the past. In the far right-hand corner of the temple behind the book-cases is a bronze image of Maitreya of similar workmanship. In the far left-hand corner, however, there is a large and rather ugly *terra-cotta* Maitreya. One wonders if this place were once occupied by a bronze Śākyamuni, thus completing the set of the Buddhas of the Three Times.

To the right of the main Dīpankara there are images of the founder-lama of the monastery, *mKhas-grub Karma sLob-bzang*, then of the 'Holder of the Vajra' and Mila Rāpa.

The wooden pillars are carved and painted and long silk Chinese banners, brought from Singapore, hang from the roof.

The main images in the 'Defenders' Room' above are those of Ma-ning, four-armed Mahākāla and the 'Great Goddess' (*dpal-ldan lha-mo*).

One then ascends a steep slope to the three-storied temple above, which is known as the 'chöten'. Steps lead up into a shrine containing a large image of Maitreya. The walls are painted with the Five Buddhas and numerous small buddhas. On the floor above, which is entered by climbing round the back of the building, there is a second and far smaller temple containing an image of eleven-headed Avalokiteśvara.[a] The walls are painted with the Five Buddhas, Avalokiteśvara (four-armed), the Buddhas of the six spheres (p. 168 fn.) and the goddesses of the offerings.

The little top-shrine contains an image of the Buddha 'Boundless Light' (*Amitābha*).

The whole forms a remarkable complex of buildings and imagery. It was impossible to see everything on this first visit, so we resolved to come again. A small group of villagers followed us around, noting all we said and did, but by this time Pasang had established friendly relations and there was no reason to expect difficulties on a second visit.

Our porters were now well ahead, so we followed rapidly in their tracks. Just below Drakar there is a fork; one path continues along the left bank of the river and then ascends to Bangba (SI: Ngāwal), the other crosses to the right bank by a bridge and leads gently down to Pi. This valley with its pine-forests, overhanging crags and neat fields of pink buckwheat was one of the pleasantest parts of our journey; but it still showered a little and heavy monsoon-clouds obscured the higher summits. In spite of the apparent lack of interest in religion in Nye-shang, there are many prayer-walls along the tracks. We were told that they were all the work of wandering Tibetans, for the Nyeshangbas could never have spelt classical Tibetan or cut the letters so well. I would not doubt the truth of the latter statement nowadays; yet earlier generations must certainly have practised Tibetan religious arts. How else should one explain the existence of these two large monasteries of Bo-dzo and Drakar? But Manang is within reach of the main Nepalese townships to the south (Pokhara is eight days distant), and now that it is politically part of Nepal, there is no apparent advantage in maintaining the far more difficult connections on the Tibetan side.

[a] The eleven heads represent Avalokiteśvara ('Glancing Eye') as universal lord. The number eleven is obtained by counting the four points of the compass, the four intermediate points, the zenith, nadir and centre. See also p. 88.

We found the porters resting by a wall. There were shrieks and laughter from the women and mild protests from Takki Babu. They were telling him, it seems, that as he had been separated from his wife for so long, here was a chance not to be missed. When he resisted their joking advances, they threatened to band together and remove his trousers. Takki Babu was certainly pleased to see us, for skilled as he was at repartee, the odds were weighed heavily against him. We continued downstream through the forested valley. There was one brief steep climb where the river entered a gorge and then PI (SI: Pisāng) became visible above the far bank. We descended to the bridge, where there is a small group of houses on the right bank of the river, and debated whether we could hope to find anywhere better to camp on the other side. I insisted on continuing across the bridge and so we ascended a track to a pleasant meadow, enclosed by the tree-covered mountain-side behind and with a little stream in a copse nearby. It proved to be one of our best sites; while Pasang and I erected the tents, Takki Babu and Lopsang collected wood for our fires. Our women-porters sat in a group and watched us, still calling out ribald remarks to Takki Babu. But Pasang soon paid them off and they wandered up to the village to seek shelter for the night. By this time a number of villagers had assembled to find out who we were and what our intentions might be. Among them was a young fellow, who hearing Pasang and me talking Tibetan together, addressed himself to us in the same language. To my surprise he then produced a testimonial given him by the German mountaineering expedition, which had been in that region earlier during the year. His name was Nam-gyel and he was Tibetan. Having wandered here in search of work, he had married a local girl and settled down. He had little liking for his new fellow-countrymen, but said they were preferable to the Manangbas higher up the valley. It is typical of the staunch independence of the Tibetans, that he should live calmly alone amongst people who feel no sympathy for him. He was certainly the only man we met in the whole of Nye-shang who seemed to relish the prospect of assisting us. We warned him that he would not be paid as well as he had been in the past and promised to discuss the matter in the morning. That night we made an enormous fire between two great tree-trunks, which Takki Babu hauled into position, cooked cakes of unleavened bread and prepared some form of curry, enjoying the comfort and peace of our new site to the full.

The next morning Pasang went up to the village to see what food he could find and returned with a side of fresh mutton. The Lama of Shang was expected to come down from Gyaru that day, and since no animal could decently be slain while he was staying in the village, the men of Pi had made haste to supply themselves with meat in advance. GYARU (SI: Ghyāru) is built on the same side of the river as Pi, but about 2,500 feet higher up. A track leads round the mountain-side above our camp, crosses a small stream, and then ascends steeply to the upper village. Just by the stream there is a small grassy place and here one of the Gyaru villagers had built a new prayer-wall. It was arranged that the 'Precious Lama' should consecrate this on his way down and that the leading villagers of Pi should meet him there ceremonially. Already villagers, some on horseback, some on foot, were going along the track above our camp; we followed in their wake, intending to climb up to Gyaru to visit the temple there and so meet the Lama on his way down. The villagers crowded around us and warned us in an unfriendly manner that we were not to take photographs. Pasang retorted that if we took photographs in the presence of the Lama, it would be with the Lama's consent and no one else's. Someone shouted out: 'He is our Lama, not your's,' to which we made the obvious reply that a Lama is nobody's property. We passed by the new prayer-wall, noting that they had combined the colours and the hand-gestures of the Five Buddhas quite wrongly. Having made a 'respectful circumambulation', we left them to their preparations, and crossing the stream, ascended the steep mountain-side beyond. We met the Lama about half-way up. He was descending slowly, assisted by two retainers and surrounded by some twenty more, all members of his permanent cortège, and a throng of the Gyaru villagers. He received us with great wonder and delight. He did not remember our brief meeting by the Kāgbeni bridge, and although he had seen Europeans before, he had never met one who could speak Tibetan. He nodded his head with great pleasure and instructed the keeper of the purse at his side to give each of us a rupee for chang. I did not refuse on this occasion and having exchanged more compliments, we promised to pay our respects when he was settled at Pi, explaining that we were on our way up to visit the temple at Gyaru. 'The keeper is there,' his followers said, 'he will let you in.' The welcome given us by the lama set the tone for the rest of the party and everyone now smiled upon us as though we were the best of friends. We continued the steep and hot climb up to the village above and stopped to ask a group of men who were rebuilding a house, where the keeper of the temple might be. They stared and asked us where we came from; others quickly joined the group. We answered their questions politely enough and repeated ours. 'He has gone down to Pi with the Lama,' they said, 'and taken the key with him.' This bare-faced lie and their unfriendly and insolent manner, combined with memories of other unpleasantness we had experienced in this inhospitable land of Nye-shang, strained our patience to its limits. Pasang, however, merely replied that we had heard from the Lama's party, that the keeper and the key were here, and that if they pleased, they could show us in. There was more surly talking and laughing; then one of them said, that as the Lama had blessed the temple, they did not intend to open the doors to anybody for three days. This was a more plausible reason; we met with a similar problem in Pi later on, and would have accepted it calmly if they had told us so politely at first. But now Pasang threw care to the winds and addressed them as sternly as he could. 'How would they feel if they went to visit shrines in India and had the doors closed against them? Was this the way to treat travellers from afar? What did it profit them to entertain a renowned lama, if they could not keep the simplest precepts of the religion he represented?'

They were reduced to a sullen silence, while we, consumed perhaps with over-righteous indignation, left them and descended the steep way we had come. In all our seven months of travel this was the only occasion on which we failed to enter a temple we had come to see.

When we reached the new prayer-wall the ceremony of consecration was nearing its end; we were invited to take our seats behind the Lama, who turned and whispered a few friendly words. When Pasang explained that he had not been able to enter the temple at Gyaru, general regret was expressed. There was no doubt that so long as we were in the Lama's presence, we were surrounded by seeming friends. A few laymen from the two villages walked round and round the wall, carrying smouldering juniper and chanting. Meanwhile the Lama's monks were busy distributing the general offerings and the Lama himself insisted on our accepting a jar of chang and a large sacrificial cake, of which Lopsang and Takki Babu ate most. Having just spent a strenuous three hours climbing up to Gyaru and back, we were not only tired, but also extremely hungry. It was now long past noon, so we took our leave of the Lama, admiring his wondrous patience. He too was tired, and for the rest of the day he would remain the chief centre of attention. Women and children were now walking round the wall, singing secular songs.

We returned to our camp, where fresh mutton awaited us. It might seem to some of our readers that we were at least as guilty as the villagers of Gyaru in our neglect of elementary Buddhist precepts, for had we no pity for the unfortunate sheep that had been killed? Although not a Buddhist, I never had an animal killed after we left Dunyer (p. 31) out of deference to the religion of the people, through whose lands we were travelling. Moreover whatever the villagers themselves might do, our reputation as peaceful pilgrims would have been ruined by such an act. But we had no scruples when meat was offered us; our party had to be fed and there was little enough food at the best of times. Meat such as this was a rare luxury indeed and we feasted that day as perhaps never before on this journey.

A small deputation arrived from the village, asking if they might borrow our Aladdin lamp and inviting us up to the temple. The Tibetan Nam-gyel also came to offer his services and we discussed the project of visiting the Nar Valley (SI: Naur—Phu Kholā). We did not want to make this journey un-necessarily, but as usual it was impossible to discover in advance whether it would be worth while. Nam-gyel insisted that it was and offered to come with us. It would mean travelling via Bangba or Gyaru and crossing a 17,000–18,000 foot pass over to the valley that runs SE down to the village of Lower Nar (SI: Naurgāon).[a] From Lower Nar we would then turn up-stream to Upper Nar (SI: Phugāon[b]). Everyone present agreed that there were temples worth seeing at both Lower and Upper Nar, especially the latter; one villager added that the monastery there was perhaps not so well cared for as that of Drakar, but there were many more images. This sounded quite convincing. Later one of the Lama's monks told us that there was little of interest as all the frescoes were old. This finally persuaded me that it was worth the journey and I began to envisage a temple like Bo-dzo, covered with fine old frescoes, which might help us to identify with certainty those on which we had doubts. We therefore planned to leave the next day.

But now it was evening, time to visit the Lama in the village monastery and take up the lamp. The temple was crowded with men, women and children; the doorway was completely blocked and dogs waited hopefully outside. Way was made for us and we were pushed inside. The walls were quite plain and the images of no special interest; there was a large *terra-cotta* Maitreya above the centre of the table of offerings and 'Lotus-

---

[a] The surveyors were unaware that Nar, which they write 'Naur' is primarily that of a district and not just of a village or even a stream.

[b] Tib. *phu* means 'head of a valley', any valley, and so by careless question-ing the surveyors established a new name, ignoring the proper one.

Born', the 'Fierce Master' and the 'Lion-Headed' Ḍākinī to the sides. The Lama sat patiently on a high raised throne beside the altar and we were motioned to a mat just below him. Conversation was difficult as he had to talk up and across a burly monk who served as bodyguard. For our part we said how amazed we were at the great number of monasteries and temples which he had set about repairing, while he expressed great pleasure at the interest we were taking in Tibetan religion and his admiration at the distance we had travelled in the last six months. All the places we had visited were well known to him, for it may be remembered that we had first heard of him far away at Tichu-rong (p. 37). In effect we had been visiting the lands in which he personally had taken so great an interest. We made an offering of rupees, accompanied by a white scarf, and while Pasang stayed, I made my way down to the camp, regretting that we could not speak with the lama at ease. I sent Lopsang and Takki Babu up to receive their share of merit and offerings and settled by the fire in pleasant solitude. Unless one has been on a journey of this kind, it may be difficult to understand why one should sometimes want to slip away from the very people one has come to see. Day in, day out, one is a centre of interest, followed everywhere by wondering eyes. This was perhaps more wearying than all the physical effort of our seven months of travel.

We were very late in starting the next day. Since we were taking with us as little as possible, we packed the boxes and carried them up to Nam-gyel's house. Then we called on the Lama, who had spent the night in the temple and was now being served with a meal by some of his attendants. The place was not as crowded as the night before, but preparations were being made for the day's ceremonies and although the Lama himself appeared quite calm, he was continually being approached on one matter or another, so that it was impossible to converse properly. We expressed the hope of seeing him again on our return from Nar and took our leave.

We had decided to travel by way of BANGBA (SI: Ngāwal), since this village would be new to us. The path from Pi follows the left bank of the river, separating from the Gyaru track just beyond the new prayer-wall and the stream. Then it ascends high above the cliffs of the gorge, giving fine views up and down the upper Marsyandi valley. But the peaks of Annapūrna were still hidden in cloud. It began to shower slightly and soon rain was falling heavily. The way to Bangba seemed unexpectedly long. There was a pleasant sward by a chöten just on the outskirts of the village, but we were not then equipped to establish a camp in such weather. We walked through the village and on to the temple at the further end, feeling rather forlorn. Just then a man appeared from a neighbouring house, friendly and talkative, saying that he had also travelled and knew how difficult it often was. He pushed open the door of a stone-built outhouse by the temple and suggested we settled there. It was a monastery-kitchen, such as we have often stayed in, so depositing our loads, we set about making ourselves at home. The friendly villager brought dry wood and a large water-pot, while we wrestled with camp-beds in the gloom and undid wet bedding-rolls. As soon as a fire was lit, the room filled with smoke, so I began to look elsewhere for a subsidiary shelter. There was nowhere nearby where one could pitch a tent, so I investigated the monastery. The temple itself was locked, but by way of the entrance-porch one could ascend to an upper storey which had the form of an interior balcony, looking down into the temple below. It was now quite dark and rather eerie by the light of a torch; while the others were cooking I arranged beds for myself and Pasang. The rest of the party would sleep in the kitchen. Thus we passed a tolerably comfortable night and awoke late in the morning. When we had cooked and eaten a meal, Namgyel declared that it was already too late to attempt to cross the pass and we had better wait till the morrow. We upbraided him for not having warned us the previous night, since he was now guide; but I was glad of the opportunity to visit Drakar again, which can be reached in a couple of hours from Bangba.

XXXIII.

a. dBal-gsas *in the temple at* T'hin. (*pp. 49 & 186*)
b. Tsherok Gomba. (*p. 183*)

XXXIV.

a. View southwards from the arid hills above Tr'ang-mar. (p. *191*)
b. Lo Ge-kar. (p. *191*)

XXXV.

a. 'Man-made' chötens at gCong-gzhi rang-byung. (*p. 189*)
b. Painted stone-plaques at Lo-Gekar. (*p. 192*). These stones are incised, painted and set in wooden frames. The six upper plaques portray six of the set of 25 Pundits (rJe-'bangs), which continues along this wall. The three lower ones are three of the Fierce Divinities.

XXXVI.

a. Tsarang Fort. (p. 195)
b. The Lama of Tsarang. (p. 195)

XXXVII.

a. Villagers of Tsarang, threshing peas. (p. 193)
b. Beggar-boy. (p. 191)

XXXVIII.

a. Mustang, general view (taken by Pasang). (p. 196)
b. Gomba Sarba, Mustang (taken by Pasang). (p. 198)

XXXIX.

a. *Maitreya in the cave-temple near Tshuk.* (p. 171)
b. *Carved altar-piece in the private temple of the Prince of Mustang.*
(p. 197)

XL.

a. The ruined fort of Rab-rgyal-rtse. (*p. 201*)
b. Water-spouts and our 'nun' of Muktināth. (*p. 200*)

We had no difficulty in entering the monastery on this occasion and there was time to observe everything carefully.

By early evening we were back at our hovel in Bangba. The temple contained nothing but a few rough clay images; the son of the keeper came once to light a lamp, burn some juniper as incense and recite a few prayers. Religion counts for as little here as elsewhere in Nye-shang. While the rest of us were away and Takki Babu was alone, someone found the opportunity of stealing our electric torch and a tin of pepper. The torch was the last of three and so a most inconvenient loss, as well as being the first theft we had experienced in all our months of travel. In spite of the friendly villager who had helped us on our arrival in Bangba, we thought even less of these people of Nye-shang. The theft was repaid, however, in an unexpected and most happy manner. On our way back from Drakar, we were followed by a rather pathetic black dog. He belonged to the fierce breed of the Tibetan mastiff, but was a mere puppy of six months or so. He settled outside the door while we were cooking our evening meal; at first we took little notice of him, but when one of the inquisitive villagers, who were hanging around, drove him away with a kick, he attracted my attention by a pathetic little yelp. We fed him that evening and the next morning he was still at the door, having slept outside in the rain. I fed him again, and when we left he followed at a respectful distance. When we stopped far up on the wet, misty mountain-side to eat a lunch of cold stewed meat and potatoes, he came and shared it with us, and I decided that unless an owner claimed him, this dog should be ours. This was not going to be easy, for food was scarce and it meant giving him food that the rest of the party could all too easily have eaten themselves. The others realized this from the start and when out of humour tended to resent his presence. The pass was indeed a long and difficult one, for relatively it is far higher than the one above Muktināth. Moreover the rain of the previous days had brought snow on the higher reaches and it was far colder than we had been used to for a long time.

NAR

At the top of the pass the weather cleared to reveal fine snow-summits across the valley which now opened below us. A few blue delphiniums (*Delphinium brunonianum*) grew between the rocks and we plunged down happily on the steep scree to the stream that would lead us to Nar. There was still a long and slow descent before us, but grass soon made the going easier, and the black dog leaped along with us, showing not the slightest exhaustion.

LOWER NAR (SI: Naurgāon, pl. XLI*b*) consists of some thirty houses, most of them arranged along the sides of a wide track. Entering the village, we had to run a gauntlet of staring eyes and barking dogs. Our own dog made no response to this noisy welcome and we passed through to the upper end of the village where there was a pleasant site for camping on the edge of the grass-covered mountain-side, which encloses the scene to the north. A snow-covered range now separated us from the Marsyandi Valley to the south whence we had come, and a stupendous mass of rock and snow limited our world to the east (K'ang Guru—22,997 feet). On the far side of that great mountain flows the main eastern tributary of the Marsyandi (Dudh Kholā), up which we would soon be travelling on our way to the land of Nup-ri (Lārkya). It would be a mere twenty miles across to that other valley, if one could go direct; but the actual journey requires five to six days of circuitous and difficult travel. It is no wonder that these regions along Nepal's northern frontier remain so remote from one another.

While we put up the tents, Pasang went to the village to see what food could be found, returning with eggs, potatoes and buckwheat tsamba. I now discovered that our stock of wheat-flour was very low, scarcely enough to last us on this journey through Nar and back to Pi and certainly not sufficient for the journey down the Marsyandi. The only place where we could get more was Manang Village, so there seemed no alternative but to send our new helper Nam-gyel back the next morning. He would then be able to arrange for porters as well; thus by the time the rest of us arrived in Pi, everything would be ready so that we could continue our journey without further delay. We had to find a local man to replace Nam-gyel and after the usual argument an old man at last volunteered to come on condition that he would have only a light load to carry. Pasang bought two pounds of butter from a Manang trader who happened to be in Nar, for which we had to pay the sum of nine Nepalese rupees (about the equivalent of nine shillings). We then learned from the villagers that Manang, Bangba and Pi forcibly monopolize the butter-trade of Nar, buying cheap at rates comparable with those we had paid in Dolpo and selling dear at Tukchä prices. This Manangba had in fact resold us butter at the very place that he himself had bought it, and at twice the price that he had paid. But there was no help for it, as the villagers of Nar would not sell to us direct, afraid that the Manangbas would impose a heavy fine upon them. They fear and dislike their more powerful neighbours of Nye-shang, but since their summer-routes lead perforce through Bangba or Pi, they have to accept dictated terms. They are not even allowed to trade cigarettes in their own country, it seems, for this too is monopolized by the men of Nye-shang.

There are three temples at Lower Nar and the next morning we sought out the keepers of each one in turn and went to see what there might be of interest. They contained a large number of *terra-cotta* images of varying artistic merit; 'Lotus-Born' was the most common, for the Buddhism of Nar is that of the 'Old Sect' (Nying-ma-pa). In one temple situated below the village in the midst of terraced fields, there are three large impressive images of 'Lotus-Born' and his two goddess-wives and another set of the Buddhas of the Three Times, Dīpankara, Śākyamuni and Maitreya. There was also a small notice of repairs which gave us for the first time the correct classical spelling of the name of Nar (*sNar*). There was far less of interest than we had been led to expect, but we had already learned not to be disappointed.

227

We could now see the end of our journey and it was already certain that the best parts lay far behind us in Dolpo and Lo. Nye-shang had affected us adversely, for the villagers there were generally difficult to deal with. Moreover we were far more tired than we actually realized, for we had now been travelling for close on six months. At this stage interest was sustained mainly by my determination to complete the planned journey and thus collect enough material for a general survey. Perhaps this determination gave us new strength, for we were happily resigned to whatever the future might hold for us; thus we were altogether proof against the subtle pangs of disappointment.

We left Lower Nar by an easterly track and passing by terraced fields and several ancient chötens, descended steeply to the Nar River (Naur—Phu Kholā). The towering ruins of a fort watch over an old neglected bridge, spanning a deep and narrow gorge, through which the water surges some 200 feet below. It is known as the 'Sacred Fort of the Bridge' (*zam-pa chos rdzong*) and must have served in the past to protect the whole upper valley, which we were now about to enter. A little way below the fort there is a large chöten built on a small grassy clearing just above the right bank of the river and enclosed by great rock-cliffs behind. This place is known as Yung-kar-lha-chö.[a] Further downstream high up on the opposite bank one sees a deserted village of some fifteen houses. Crossing the trembling bridge, we followed the path up the far bank. After walking for about two hours, we came to another small group of deserted houses, known as Dzu-nam. We passed beyond, and having waded through a torrent soon came upon yet another deserted village, called Cha-go, with about thirty houses. The terracing below the village was still intact and the ground must have been worked within the last ten years or so. This was confirmed by our porter, who told us that villagers from Lower Nar

---

[a] Since no classical spelling is available, various interpretations are possible; e.g. 'Divine Worship of the White Swastika' (*gYung-dkar lha-mchod*), which seems the most likely or 'of the White (i.e. Virtuous) Village' (*yul dkar*).

used to come up and work the fields, but that the village itself had been deserted before his time. All the inhabitants were said to have died of disease (? smallpox) and no one has wanted to live there ever since. We continued upstream and by evening reached another deserted village, known as Kyang, where we resolved to spend the night. We clambered through the empty broken houses, cutting through the tall weeds that grew in the courtyards, until we found one that would offer us sufficient shelter. Takki Babu had thoughtfully added a few dried branches to his load lower down the valley; there was also some wood nearby, so we lit a roaring fire and settled in cheerfully for the evening.

The next morning we continued up the valley, which had now become a narrow gorge. The track kept close above the river for about five miles and then suddenly ascended steeply by roughly cut steps high up onto the cliffs of the gorge, leaving the river flowing through a deep ravine below. We passed under a gateway adorned with three small chötens and observed how in earlier times the track had passed over a bridge guarded by a fort, just like the one further down the valley. This fort is now totally ruined and the bridge destroyed. The present track continues for a while above the right bank of the river and then descends to cross by a less impregnable bridge further on. In the days of bows and arrows this upper valley must have been safe from all foes. From the second bridge the path leads upstream for about half a mile, where one suddenly comes upon the village of UPPER NAR, built onto the cliffs above.

The monastery to which we directed our steps, is situated on a hill-top on the other side of the stream (pl. XLI*a*). It is a splendid position at the head of the valley enclosed by high mountains on all sides.[a] The yellow and grey-brown cliffs and the deeply eroded river-beds of this weird treeless landscape reminded us of the upper valley of the Kāli Gandaki, which we

[a] For the SI name of the village see p. 222. Concerning the routes beyond see H. W. Tilman, *Nepal Himalaya*, pp. 180 ff.

had left six weeks before. I felt content that our journey had been worth while, whether the monastery itself proved a disappointment or not. It was in fact far smaller than we had been led to believe and contained very little of interest. There is a small temple, the walls of which have been recently painted with the thirty-five Confessional Buddhas, thus obscuring older and presumably more interesting frescoes. Three images, 'Lotus-Born', 'Fierce Master' and 'Lion-Headed' Ḍākinī, stood above the table of offerings. In fact there was nothing of iconographic interest in spite of what Nam-gyel, the Shang Lama's monk and the villager of Pi had told us. But we could only know this by seeing for ourselves.

From the dark bare ante-room that enclosed the temple on two sides, we ascended by a knotched ladder to the upper storey. Here a party of men and women were engaged in preparations for the Ceremony of the 'Tranquil and Fierce' divinities, which we learned was to be performed that evening. They showed little surprise at our sudden appearance at the top of the ladder and we sat down to rest and to talk with them. They were melting a great pot of butter while tea was made ready in a larger cauldron. The women attended to the fire and the pots, while the men sat busily moulding sacrificial cakes (tormas). In hope of food our black pup clambered up the ladder to join us. Pasang shared their buttered tea, while Takki Babu prepared a clearer brew for me. These people were spontaneously friendly and even if we had been oblivious to the changed landscape outside, we should have known at once that we were in a very different land from Nye-shang. The village-lama and his son-in-law, the headman, were both present. There was the headman's wife, assisted by another village-woman, two monks and two other young laymen. The monks belonged to the Shang Lama's party and had come up from Gyaru a few days before with funds for the ceremony which was now being prepared. Thus the benefactor was the Shang Lama himself. I asked how old the monastery was, and receiving a vague reply, asked further if there was no local history. One of the laymen left the cake he was moulding, went down below and returned with a dusty volume. It was a manuscript copy of the biography of the founder-lama, who was named *Urgyan lhun-grub rgya-mtsho* and had been a contemporary of the founder-lama of Drakar Monastery. My companion was very well informed and showed the greatest pleasure at having someone to read with. Meanwhile the village-lama and the headman were busy asking Pasang who we were and how we had learned to read classical Tibetan, nodding their heads at his replies with evident satisfaction. Pasang gave some rupees towards their general offerings and then in the midst of the reading I heard him mention at last the prosaic subject of butter. Butter was indeed a serious problem, for it was the only fat we could use and since leaving Dolpo we had never been able to get enough of it. Yet here was a great pot of butter all ready melted for feeding innumerable lamps.

'We cannot normally sell butter', the headman was saying.

'Can you not let us have some for offering in lamps?' Pasang replied, 'then you could allow a little extra for our own use'. The headman was persuaded by this happy turn of phrase, for even the black-hearted Manangbas would scarcely regard a religious act as a breach of contract. Thus we acquired a generous supply of butter at reasonable cost, and having fed a few butter-lamps, replenished our own empty pots. The lama offered us the use of a small subsidiary kitchen, on the flat roof of which there was just room to pitch one tent. Now we were indeed in the midst of the ceremony, for all the villagers who came up to pay their respects at the monastery on this auspicious day, inevitably included our kitchen and tent on their rounds. There was another small temple besides the one we had seen, but we were unable to go inside, since two members of the small community were performing a vow of undisturbed meditation. Expressing regret, the lama added that he trusted we would not peep in the window. Knowing how these villagers delighted in lifting our tent-flaps for a peep inside, we were not surprised at being credited with the same insatiable curiosity.

The ceremony began in the early evening and the small temple was soon crowded with the celebrants and as many villagers as could get inside. We were familiar with the liturgy, which was an invocation of the complete set of 42 Tranquil and 58 Fierce Divinities. The tranquil ones consist of the supreme Buddha 'All Good' (p. 47), the Five Buddhas and their feminine partners together with attendant bodhisattvas and goddesses, the buddhas of the six spheres of existence (p. 168 fn.) and four protectors with their partners. The fierce set consists of fierce aspects of the Five Buddhas, known as Herukas, eight attendant *yoginīs*, who delight in gruesome rites, and several sets of beast-goddesses with heads of animals and birds. The monks and religious laymen sat in two facing rows down the centre of the temple, while other villagers crowded to the sides and around the door. Light and heat came from the hundreds of little butter-lamps, arranged in rows round the lower tiers of the altar. On the top tier were three large sacrificial cakes (tormas), dedicated to 'Lotus-Born', the 'Fierce Master' and the 'Lion-Headed' Ḍākinī, who as the 'Union of the Precious Ones' embody all the divinities, tranquil and fierce, who are invoked in the ceremony. Next down are placed the cakes of various 'defenders', moulded of tsamba and butter, painted red and adorned with patterned disks of more butter, which soon began to droop and melt from the heat of the lamps. Then there were little bowls containing the conventional offerings of washing water, drinking water, flowers, incense, perfume and food, for the divinities must be treated as though they were honoured guests. The celebrants were intoning the liturgy, beseeching each buddha to be present in turn together with his entourage of bodhisattvas and goddesses, imploring them to accept the offerings and regard the congregation with compassion. The liturgy is repeated a large number of times in order to produce an increasingly beneficial effect, in just the same way that individual prayers are repeated, so that a worshipper's thought may be concentrated on a single chosen divinity. In this general ceremony the aspirations of the community were directed upon the whole company of buddhas and lesser beings, all envisaged as manifestations of one buddha, 'Lotus-Born'.

Long after midnight I retired to the tent, exhilarated but none the less exhausted by the events of a very long day. The general offerings were distributed some time before dawn and the villagers continued dancing until day-break in the ante-room of the temple. This was no religious dance, but simply spontaneous merriment, for in these lands holy days and holidays are still one and the same thing. By morning the monastery was again deserted, for everyone had gone down to the village—to work, if they had to, and to sleep if they could. There was nothing else to delay us in Nar, and so counting ourselves fortunate to have arrived on such a day, we repacked our chattels and set out on the return journey.

We descended the gorge, passed by the deserted villages and reached the 'Sacred Fort of the Bridge' by early evening. Rather than climb up to Lower Nar and arrive there at night-fall, we decided to stay at the chöten of Yung-kar-lha-chö, for there was a convenient shelter nearby. Water was difficult to get from the gorge below, but it proved to be a delightful site. We rose early and so reached Lower Nar in time for our morning meal. We had already discussed our plans of continuing that day at least to the foot of the pass leading over to Gyaru and Pi. The old man who had been assisting us, refused to come any further. We hoped to find someone to replace him during our halt in the village, but discovered that no one would be available before the following day. We decided, therefore, to shoulder our own loads and set out at once. Takki Babu and Lopsang, to whom the greater share would necessarily fall, viewed this plan with some despondency, but they showed no unwillingness. Pasang was so determined to leave as soon as possible, that we were allowed no doubts in the matter in spite of the rain-clouds that swept along the valley. So we set off on our wet and overladen journey, not even certain where the track turned off towards the pass. There are two passes connecting Nye-shang to Nar, the one from Bangba by which we had come, and the other, shorter and steeper, which climbs directly up from Gyaru and descends with even greater steepness to a point about half-way along the valley we had previously descended. We were now looking for this point and thanks to Pasang's extraordinary mountain-sense we found the place without difficulty and a large overhanging boulder nearby, which would provide sufficient shelter for the night. A loose stone wall had been built around it as a protection for travellers; by draping ground-sheets and rugs about and lighting a fire inside with the dry wood which we had remembered to bring from Nar, we made ourselves comfortable enough. The black dog was now accepted as a member of the party and food was always somehow provided for him. In our present straitened circumstances it usually consisted of a bowl of buckwheat broth fortified with a lump of butter. Lopsang, noticing that he had a little spot of white on his breast, had called him playfully Nying-kar ('White Heart') and so this became his name.

The ascent to the pass was very steep, but always delightful with views through the clouds of the valley below and snowy summits above. We reached the cairn at the top, a height of about 18,000 feet within two hours. A party of Manangbas was ascending from the other side together with a little yelping dog, which wanted to befriend Nying-kar. Neither of them showed the slightest exhaustion, for in these lands dogs are of necessity good climbers.

We descended through the snow and scree down to grassy slopes where yaks were grazing, then still further down to Gyaru Village and again down the steep track to our camp-site below Pi. On this long descent we had dropped about 8,000 feet. Our tents were soon erected and the boxes brought down from Nam-gyel's house. It was now Saturday, September 1st; we had planned to rest here on Sunday and leave on Monday with the porters that Nam-gyel had arranged for us, but Nam-gyel himself arrived with a bag of wheat and a tale of new

234

trouble. The Lama of Shang, who was still in the village-temple, was performing a final ceremony of general blessing and the villagers were insisting that no person and no object whatsoever that happened to be in Pi, should leave the village before three days had passed. They feared that such a departure would provide a means of escape for a part of the blessing, and that they would never know how much had been lost to them. Our boxes had been stored in Nam-gyel's house and his neighbours had permitted them to be carried down to our camp on condition they went no further before the three days had passed. Nam-gyel was clearly very anxious; the porters he had ordered in Manang were due to arrive on Monday morning, so there would be nothing to prevent our going. The men of Pi would not use physical force against us; they had simply told Nam-gyel that if our boxes went, he would be expelled from the village. He was very upset and told us how he was always getting into trouble for befriending foreigners, which we could well believe in this unfriendly land. We assured him that he need have no fear, for if we left on Monday, it would only be with the agreement of the Shang Lama himself, so that the villagers would not be able to say anything against it. 'If they make our porters wait a day,' Pasang added, 'they will have to provide them with food, and that will not please them overmuch.' An extra day's delay made not the slightest difference to my plans, but in such circumstances small affairs sometimes seem of great moment and there would be some satisfaction in getting the better of these troublesome men of Nye-shang.

The next day we went up to visit the Lama who was still seated in the temple (pl. XLIIa). On this occasion we were able to sit close to him and so converse rather more freely. Having told him of our travels, we observed that he had stayed in Pi for a very long time. He smiled gently and said: 'These people are like children. If one does not do just what they want, they show their displeasure at once, and nothing is gained by causing them displeasure.' We told him of the obstruction to our plans of departure and he assured us that there would be no difficulty.

235

He asked the headman to come and explained to him that they would lose none of their blessings by allowing our party to leave, for he would see to it that we were blessed in our own right for the journey ahead of us. There was still one request to be made of the Lama, for the villagers had forbidden us to take his photograph. He assented at once, but some of his followers demanded a copy for themselves. As often before, we had to explain that we could not produce a photograph on the spot and that we would have to send it later. They were disgruntled at this reply, interpreting it as an evasive refusal. Three months later I despatched these photographs from Kathmandu, but we have no means of knowing whether they reached their destination. After making an offering we left the Lama and promised to visit him again the next morning just before our departure.

Early on Monday morning six women porters from Manang, some of them old acquaintances, reported for duty. Nam-gyel said he was not coming with us, which caused us neither regrets nor inconvenience. In spite of our warnings, he had refused to believe that we would not maintain the standard of living which he expected of Western travellers. He told Pasang that he had looked forward to an abundant supply of tea well dosed with condensed milk and sugar, but we had no tinned milk and little enough Indian tea, so that Tibetan buttered tea was our regular drink. In fact we were rather pleased at his harmless criticism and merely reminded him that he had been warned. There remained only the problem of the dog, for we had heard that his owner was a man of Bangba who was away on a journey to Kathmandu. It would therefore be unwise to induce him to follow us, and I was persuaded to give my consent to the following plan. We were to feed him unseen by any villager that morning and otherwise to ignore him altogether. When he began to follow us, he was to be driven off with sticks and stones, but without actually being hit. Pasang and Takki Babu were sure that he would persist in following us, but the villagers would see that it was entirely against our will.

It was a splendid morning; for the first time since our arrival in Nye-shang the clouds were lifted right off the face of Anna-pūrna. We went up to the monastery to say good-bye to the Lama. He gave us his blessing, placing his hands on our heads, and then ordered one of his monks to prepare little charms for us. These consisted of written benedictions, folded up into small squares and neatly bound with coloured threads. He blessed these too and then gave us one each. The villagers of Pi beamed with goodwill upon us, but how would we have fared in their midst if this Lama had not still been there? We took leave of him most gratefully and hastened down to the bridge where the porters awaited us. The plan for the guiltless abduction of Nying-kar having worked just as Pasang had foretold, the whole party was soon advancing cheerfully down the right bank of the Marsyandi on the way to Gyasumdo.

GYASUMDO

Gyasumdo, 'Meeting-place of Three Highways', is the local name of the whole area which centres on Thangjet (SI: Thonje), extending up and down the Marsyandi and up the Dudh Kholā which joins the Marsyandi at this point. These river-names mean nothing to the Tibetans who inhabit this region; they envisage this junction as the meeting-place of three waters (*chu*) and of the three routes that make their way along the valleys as best they can. Gyasumdo is in fact significant regional name, for when one descends from Nye-shang one is aware of a sudden and rather surprising cultural change, all of which is hidden from the map-reader by the general district-name 'MANANGBHOT'.

We had not descended the Marsyandi far below Pi before we were totally enveloped in forest. About four miles down the river makes a majestic turn towards the south, flowing through an open V-shaped rock-basin of such smooth regularity that it might have been specially laid down by titans. Here we crossed to the left bank and followed the track ever further down. By early evening we reached the first village, named Tr'ak-lung ('Village of the Crags'), a group of some twenty houses, stone built and roofed with wooden boards, approached through fields of ripening maize, all wedged between the high rock-cliffs above and the deep gorge below. We met three villagers in the middle of the track. They looked like Tibetans and when I addressed them in that language, asking how far it was to Tshä-me (SI: Chame), they replied in terms as close to the dialect of central Tibet as to make little difference. It seemed incongruous indeed to find pure Tibetans at 5,000 feet and less below sea-level, living as true 'valley-men' in a monsoon-climate, especially when the hybrid men of Nye-shang live so far up the valley above them. They told us that it was but a short way down to Tshä-me and that we would find a good camping-site just beyond the village across the bridge.

TSHÄ-ME is a village of about thirty houses; there are fields round the main group of buildings on the left bank, as well as others across the river, terraced up the bank beyond. We found the suggested site to our liking and were soon established there. Several villagers came to see us, all talking good Tibetan and expressing wonder at this Westerner who knew it too. One of them who was anxious to put my literary knowledge to the test, proved to be the village school-master. We learned that he was really a Sherpa by birth, for his parents were folk from Shar-Khumbu, who had come here to trade and then settled permanently. It was indeed remarkable to discover that the children in this village were learning to read and write classical Tibetan, for one would have to travel a long way northwards to find the same again; we wondered even more at the difference between these people and the men of Nye-shang. They gladly sold us peas, potatoes, broad beans and arak and came with the usual requests for medicine and dressings. They were as well travelled as the Manangbas, for many of them had visited Calcutta, Rangoon and Singapore. Hearing that Pasang had been to England, they enquired about the possibility of carrying their small trade to the British Isles. They possessed of course only the vaguest ideas

238

of geography, and he dissuaded them by describing the vast distance they would have to travel. The next morning we visited the small village-temple with its clumsy frescoes and ungainly *terra-cotta* images, and then continued on our way with friendly memories.

The valley now began to open out and soon we could see beyond to the forest-covered slopes of the Dudh Kholā, where lay our route for the following day. We passed through Dzong-gyu (SI: Thāngja), which proved to be a Gurung village, then through Tshap (SI: Bagarchhap) and down to Thangjet (SI: Thonje), both of which are peopled with Tibetans like those of Tshä-me. We stayed the night at Thangjet just above the junction of the two rivers and the next morning, crossing to the left bank of the Dudh Kholā, set our steps towards the high mountains once more. We passed through one more village, that of Tiljet, which is peopled both by Gurungs and Tibetans, and by evening reached a small settlement of two or three houses, known as Karjet, where we found a pleasant camp-site for the night. We continued upstream all the next day and towards evening a steep ascent brought us well above the tree-line amidst a great wilderness of rocks and stones. Crossing this, we came at last to a small sandy, grassy plain overlooked by a little group of stone-built houses. This is Bim-t'hang, 'Plain of Sand'.[a] It is simply a small trading mart, occupied only during the summer months like Babuk (Lārkya) across the pass eastward. From Tibet via Babuk come yak-loads of salt and wool, and from the Nepalese side rice and other food grains, cotton cloth, cigarettes, matches and other useful oddments. One meets here Tibetans from across the political frontier, Tibetans from Gyasumdo and Tibetans from Nup-ri, all seeking to make profit out of the loads they have brought. Yaks and sheep graze on the mountain-sides round about. Our porters were very slow, arriving tired and complaining; they refused to accompany us

---

[a] The correct Tibetan spelling is *bye-ma-thang*. On the SI maps it appears as Bimtakothi. The ending *-kothi*, 'settlement', seems to be the gratuitous addition of some Nepāli informant.

over the pass to Nup-ri and said they would return to their homes the following morning. We accepted this news with equanimity, established a camp and relied upon finding an owner of yaks to come to our assistance. To our surprise Lopsang said he was tired and would come no further with us. We were sorry to part with him, but he was of no special service to us. Our party was thus reduced to myself, Pasang, Takki Babu and the black dog. We were delayed in Bim-t'hang the following day, but transport in the form of three dzos was duly arranged for the next, and we were content to rest and cook food at our leisure. Pasang had collected a large number of little red mushrooms on his way up the valley, which he intended as a special delicacy. They were excessively bitter but fortunately not poisonous. The weather was uncertain. A clear morning with superb views of Manaslu to the SE was soon enveloped in cold mist and rain. It was a forlorn place, much as one might imagine the limits of the inhabited world to be. The next morning the dzos were duly loaded and we set off on our way. But Nying-kar would not come. Twice Takki Babu went back for him and twice he ran back to the houses to keep company with the other dogs that were there. We could not force him to follow and so continued rather sadly without him.

VI

NUP-RI AND TSUM

NUP-RI

The track was steep, but the dzos continued at an even pace without a halt and we followed in a silent world of mist. Lopsang had left us and so had the dog; we supposed that both had just grown tired of this interminable walking. But after some three hours or so the dog appeared once more beside us and to reward his faithfulness we shared our meagre lunch with him forthwith. The dzos disappeared ahead and no more was seen of them until we found them resting with their owner just beyond the summit-cairn. This was our last great pass (17,102 feet) and also the easiest in spite of the fearful descriptions given by the people of Bim-t'hang. The mist cleared for a while; two small lakes became visible below us and then gradually the great snow-covered flanks of the mountains north of Manaslu. We were entering the land of Nup-ri, the 'Western Mountains', of which we had heard long ago in Dolpo. At that time it had been quite impossible to identify it with certainty, but now we were soon to understand the reason for the name. The villages of the upper waters of the Buri Gandaki represent one cultural unit, but there are two main streams. The western part is Nup-ri and the eastern is known as Shar ('East') as well as by its proper name of Tsum.[a]

We passed the little lakes with their banks of ice and the boulder-track gradually became an easy mountain-path. Lower

[a] Nup-ri appears on the SI maps as Lārkya, the Nepalese name for the trading-centre of Babuk. The last village in Nup-ri is Bartsam (SI: Barcham), which in fact means 'Boundary'. Thereafter one is in Kutang, although Nup-ri seems to be used vaguely for the whole region as far as the last Tibetan village of Drang (SI: Deng). The SI spelling 'Shiār' (for Shar) is another example of cumbersome transliteration.

down we skirted another lake with waters of brilliant blue, set between steep grass-covered slopes. If we wanted wood for our fires, there would be no place to camp before Babuk, still many hours distant. Porters cannot possibly make the whole journey from Bim-t'hang in one day, so the enforced change of carriers had spared us a wretched night just below the pass with neither paraffin nor petrol to burn in our stoves. The dzos, urged on by their owner who feared that night would overtake us, led the way down the stony path, while the rest of us followed tired and listless. Then just below on the right we saw a powerful torrent, shooting dramatically out of the mountain-side, and I realized that this was the source of the Buri Gandaki. We were soon enveloped in wet mist, which gradually turned into rain, and it seemed that this journey would never have an end. At last in the gathering dusk we suddenly came upon some nomads' tents; with work to be done animation returned. We put up our tents beside the others, arranged the boxes on stones under the shelter of the large fly-sheet, bought a small bundle of brush-wood from our wondering neighbours and began to prepare a meal.

Rain fell heavily during the night and continued inter-mittently throughout the morning. BABUK (SI: Lārkya) appeared as a depressing place, consisting of a group of some twenty stone shacks surrounded by a few tents. Pasang and I went to visit the headman, who had already sent down word that with-out a pass we would not be allowed to continue. It seemed that I had been taken for a Chinese, but once again it was impossible to be sure because of the confusing use of the term 'gya-mi'. Friendly relations were soon established, however, for the head-man was a lama, who had once been teacher to our friend Nga-wang Yön-ten of Jiwong.[a] He is known generally as Shap-ruk De-wa (*shar-brug bde-ba*), meaning 'Happiness of Shap-ruk', which is a title rather than a name, for Shap-ruk, his family-home, is a village in the Trisuli Valley, south of Kyirong. He also has a house at Chhö-khang in Tsum, where we were later to stay. Like Nyi-ma Tshe-ring of Dolpo he is primarily a

[a] Concerning this monk see *BH*, pp. 221–2.

trader and man of property, owing his local influence to the confidence that people have placed in him. The greater part of the year he lives at Chhö-khang, coming to Babuk just for the trading season, which lasts from July to October. During our brief stay trade was at its height; from Tibet came salt, wool and butter, from the Nepalese side rice and other grain. There were also a few Sherpa traders, who had come to sell dzos. They brought a large jar of chang and a pot of buttered tea, joyfully exchanging news with Pasang in their own Sherpa dialect. Inquisitive crowds collected all around us and it was past noon before we could leave. During a lull in the rain we packed our wet tents and said good-bye to Shap-ruk De-wa, who made us a welcome present of some sugar and tea, given him by Japanese mountaineers. Our own stock of presents was exhausted, but we suddenly remembered a new poplin shirt, which Pasang had bought for me in Aden and was too large round the neck. Shap-ruk De-wa was more sturdily built than either of us, so we offered it to him and he seemed delighted, insisting that on our way through Tsum we should stay in his house, even though he would still be away trading.

We crossed the bridge below Babuk and continued down the right bank of the Buri Gandaki, reflecting that this river would eventually lead us to within a few days' journey of Kathmandu. Thoughts turned most readily to home, for this was the wettest and most dismal of our days of travel. There was no doubt that we had at last entered an area fully affected by the monsoon. It will be remembered that the general plan of our journey had been conditioned by the weather. We had crossed into Dolpo before the coming of the monsoon and by keeping to the northern side of the main Himalayan range we had met with very little rain until now. There had been some as we left Dolpo, none at all along the upper valley of the Kāli Gandaki and only two wet days in Nye-shang. But now it rained with a depressing suggestion of permanence. We could only hope that the monsoon would keep to the rules of the geography text-book and relax its hold by the middle of September; it was now the 9th.

We reached Sāma[a] by late afternoon and went up to the monastery in search of some shelter other than our tents. The monastery consists of a main temple, surrounded by thirty small one-storey dwellings, mainly occupied by nuns. Several of them were in residence and one invited us to make use of her house for the night, adding that it really belonged to the Lama, who was staying down at the village. She therefore begged us not to stay more than the one night, lest he should be offended at her presumption. Thus we made ourselves temporarily at home, unpacking the sodden boxes and arranging the contents round the open hearth. The room was dark but comfortable, for the hooded smoke vent in the ceiling was large enough to keep the atmosphere smoke-free; we sat around the fire, drinking tea, eating our last Garibaldi biscuits and feeling that life was pleasant after all. Moreover Pasang had bought half a sheep at Babuk, so we could look forward to a feast of fresh curried meat and turnips.

The following day it was still raining, so having moved our belongings to the monastery-kitchen, a large and better lighted room, we made a survey of the whole monastery-group. The buildings are of stone. The temple, like all temples east from Manang, is painted white, while the houses are left a natural grey. Particularly noticeable are the thickly packed eaves of brush-wood, which not only top the temple-walls, but also the main door and windows (pl. XLIIb). Inside we saw a large *terra-cotta* image of 'Lotus-Born' (*Padmasambhava*) occupying the central position, and another quite as large in bronze to the left. This second one is the recent work of craftsmen summoned from Pātan in the Nepal Valley. These are three other smaller images, again of 'Lotus-Born', of eleven-headed 'Glancing Eye' and of the Boar-Headed Goddess (*Vajravārāhī*). On the left wall are paintings of the sixteen arhats, the eight manifestations of 'Lotus-Born', the 'Lord of the Dead' (*gshin-rje*) and other fierce defenders. On the right wall are the 'Union of the Precious Ones', the 'Unity of All the Blessed', 'Boundless Life',

[a] The local Tibetan name is Rö (*ros*).

'Glancing Eye' and 'Lotus-Born'. This monastery is manifestly Nying-ma-pa. The frescoes are all painted on wooden panels and set against the wall. This is a feature of all the temples east from here, for wood is easily available. Nearby is another small temple containing the canonical texts.

During the afternoon the Lama came up from the village. We recognized him at once as the pilgrim-lama who had exchanged a few words with us by Lo Ge-kar (p. 191) and this earlier acquaintance with him did much to strengthen our position locally. There was greater need of this than we had realized at first, for the monks and villagers who crowded into the room after the Lama, were soon engaged in telling us about the evil deeds of other 'gya-mi' and Sherpas who had visited their country before us. In this case the 'gya-mi' were the Japanese mountaineers, who have made four expeditions to Manaslu between 1953 and 1956. They are generally believed to have been directly responsible for an outbreak of plague, for the loss of cattle and sheep who died of some unspecified disease and, most serious of all, for the destruction of Pung-gyen Monastery where eighteen lives were lost. Pung-gyen (*dpung-brgyan* = 'bracelet') is the local Tibetan name of Manaslu and of the god (*gzhi-bdag*) who resides upon it. He had clearly shown his wrath at this uninvited trespassing into his sanctuary, they argued, by hurling down a fearful avalanche on a scale unknown in living memory during the very winter that followed upon the departure of those first 'gya-mi' mountain-climbers. The monastery was in fact completely destroyed, and all the occupants, mainly nuns, lost their lives. We suggested tentatively that had this really been the cause, it would have been more reasonable for the god to vent his wrath upon the Japanese themselves. But this was not so, it seemed, for the villagers of Sāma and Lö were the keepers of the temple and it was their duty to keep unknowing foreigners away. This explained their flat refusal to allow the Japanese anywhere near the mountain when they arrived again the following year, as well as all the subsequent ill-will and trouble, when these persistent mountaineers finally climbed

Manaslu in 1956. Their success was gained at the cost of such bitterness, that it seemed to us they might more wisely have climbed elsewhere. The villagers still remained unappeased despite a most generous contribution which the Japanese had made towards the rebuilding of the lost monastery. We observed that Japan was a Buddhist country and that the doctrine flourished there no less than in Tibet, but the villagers were not convinced, for they cannot conceive of anyone being a Buddhist unless he can speak Tibetan.[a] How can one read the sacred canon (and they know of no canon except the Tibetan one) unless one knows Tibetan? We pretended to accept this contention, as argument was futile and they were clearly willing to include us among the blessed. The Lama, who kept his peace in this assembly, later asked us why foreigners came to climb mountains. Did they really hope to find jewels on the summit, as some people suggested, or were they merely hoping to receive titles from the Government at Kathmandu? We explained the sport of mountaineering as best we could, and then asked the Lama if we might see his private chapel, to which he led us at once. It was a low room some twenty-five feet square and had been completely and most effectively redecorated. Arranged in finely carved book-cases against the opposite wall were the sixty-three volumes of the *Precious Treasury* (*rin-chen gter-mdzod*), an important set of extra-canonical Nying-ma-pa books.[b] The wooden panels of the left wall showed paintings of the fierce divinity Ka-gyä (*bKa'-brgyad*) and the six followers of his entourage; those on the right showed four different cycles of divinities and lamas representing four main Nying-ma-pa rituals.[c] 'Lotus-

[a] These mountaineers were accompanied in 1952–3 by a party of scholars, who have since produced the results of their researches in three volumes: *Fauna and Flora of the Nepal Himalaya* (1955), *Land and Crops of the Nepal Himalaya* (1956) and *Peoples of the Nepal Himalaya* (1957), ed. H. Kihara, Japan Society for the Promotion of Science, Tokyo.
[b] In Europe copies of this work exist in Professor Tucci's library in Rome and in the School of Oriental Studies, London.
[c] These are the *klong-chen yang-thig*, the *bar-chad kun-sel*, the *dkon-mchog spyi-'dus* and *yan-'dus*.

Born' appears as the central divinity in every case. The paintings were brightly coloured like all modern Tibetan painting, but were certainly well drawn. The painter-carver is a man of Lö.

Having seen this fine example of his work, we decided not to visit the newly rebuilt Pung-gyen Monastery, for after the total destruction of the place, there could be nothing of historical interest there. Even in Sāma there seem to be no past records and the Lama explained that everything had been lost long ago in a fire.

The following day it was still raining too hard for the transport of our boxes, so leaving most things behind, we made a short trip to Naktsa Gomba (*gnag-tshal dgon-pa*), the 'Grove Monastery', taking one villager of Sāma with us to carry what was needed for the night. We had to travel via Lö (SI: Lho), about two hours distant downstream. The track wanders away from the bank of the Buri Gandaki and three miles below Sāma one finds oneself amidst typical Himalayan valley scenery, great pines, junipers, rhododendron bushes, rocks and clear rushing streams. One might be in Khumbu or Sikkim or in any of the upper valleys of east Nepal. Lö is about the same height above sea-level as Kāgbeni, but the two places could scarcely be more different. Around Kāgbeni and all the way up to Mustang the land is bare, dry, fantastically eroded. But this village of Lö was a mass of mud from the monsoon rains and its fields were filled with stalks of Indian corn. To the north are Sāma and Babuk with their shrub growth and grass-covered slopes and then the great deserted mountains. Only in west Nepal where the main river-valleys are raised so much higher or where they are sheltered from the monsoon can one find lands such as Dolpo, Lö and Nar.

There is a small temple at Lö containing two complete sets of the Tibetan canon (Kanjur) in the Narthang and Lhasa prints. They are arranged against the left and right walls while to the centre above the main table of offerings is a fine gilded *terracotta* image of Śākyamuni. The back-wall is panelled with paintings of the Five Buddhas and of 'Lotus-Born' with different

ritual cycles of divinities and lamas. Along the top is a row of
Ka-gyü-pa lamas; the temple is in fact Karma Ka-gyü-pa
(p. 77).

Crossing the bridge below Lö, we climbed high up the opposite bank to NAKTSA Monastery. It was quite deserted except
for a suspicious old woman who remained in charge. The
painted panels on the right wall may be about seventy-five years
old; the drawing is well-executed and the colours are pleasing.
We saw the Buddhas of the Three Times, Buddha Master of
Medicine, 'Glancing Eye', 'Lotus-Born' and 'Lord of Death'
with his entourage. The panels on the left wall show the complete set of the 'Tranquil and Fierce' divinities and are newly
painted. Ceremonies are performed in this temple once a year
by members of the community at Drong (grong) just below
Naktsa; thus a minimum of interest is maintained. We set up
our camp-beds by the altar, which was covered with a jumble of
old clay images. Rain fell continuously outside and the atmosphere within was heavily pervaded with the smell of onions
which had been spread out to dry on the temple-floor by the
old woman-keeper.

The following morning we made our way down the steep and
slippery track to Drong, a small religious community consisting
of some nuns and a few families. There are two small temples,
one containing little images of 'Adamantine Being' (Vajrasattva)
arranged in tiered shelves around three of the walls; the other,
fitted with the usual painted panels, was of special interest
because all the sets of divinities and lamas were individually
named. While I was noting these and photographing, Pasang
prepared a meal. Then we returned to Sāma, well content to be
settled comfortably around our hearth once more. The weather
was indeed the worst that we had encountered in six months of
travel. Six men from Sāma had already agreed to come as porters the following day, so we decided to leave if only the rain
would lessen.

Our route would follow the Buri Gandaki through Nup-ri and

Kutang and down as far as Tara-Dodang (SI: Setibās-Philim) where there is a rope swing bridge across the river. Here we would leave our main luggage and then ascend the eastern valley (SI: Shiār Kholā) to Tsum. Then returning by the same route, we would collect our luggage and continue down to Arughāt. The six loads of luggage forced this plan upon us. Otherwise we could have crossed straight over from Kutang to Tsum by a route ascending eastwards over the mountains from Bi. In a better season this would give superb views of Manaslu and Himāl-chuli to the west and of Ganesh Himāl to the east, but there was little cause for regret in early September when everything was enveloped in mist and rain. In no way, however, did the valley-routes provide an easier alternative. On the morning of departure we were delayed by fresh negotiations with our porters. They had contracted to come as far as Jagat half a day below Tara-Dodang, for at that place there is a customs-post with officials, where we could have conveniently left our boxes. Now they said that they would be sure to catch malaria and refused to go beyond Tara. At that time we did not possess our later knowledge of the route, and so were trying to locate the Tibetan place-names, used by the villagers, on a map which proved to be inaccurate. They told us for instance that Tara was the same as Setibās and also that the only bridge available was at that place, so that we should have to cross the river there in order to ascend to Tsum. Yet our map showed no bridge by Setibās and so we doubted if Tara really were the same.[a] Eventually it proved to be so: the Survey of India maps had simply misplaced the bridge. For the present, however, we could only come to terms with our porters and accept their services so long as they were prepared to give them.

They now promised to come as far as Tara-Dodang, accepting a nominal reduction of their wages because of the shorter distance. Thus both sides were satisfied and we agreed that there should

[a] The place-names on the upper Buri Gandaki often have two forms, one Tibetan proper and one Gurung (a language of Tibetan origin) or Nepāli. The alternatives are given in the list of place-names pp. 279–84.

249

be no further disputation. We made our way down between the wet undergrowth that surrounded the monastery and through the mud of the village lanes. The houses are all built of grey stone with a single storey and roofs of wood. People called out to know if we were finally leaving and to enquire how far our porters would accompany us. Thence we passed through the chöten-exit and out onto the grass track which follows the river. Half a mile further we crossed the raging torrent that descends this side of Manaslu, and our men pointed the way up to the monastery which had been destroyed by the wrathful god. Thereafter the track leaves the bank of the Buri Gandaki for a while, joining it again just below Lö, which holds a commanding position high up on the bank. We halted here to await the porters and to eat our lunch of bread and meat and cheese. Nying-kar was in especially good spirits and Takki Babu suggested that maybe he knew we were on the way to Kathmandu. There was no doubt of our own anticipation in this respect; we were even wondering whether it would prove worth the effort to make the extra journey up to Tsum. There was really no doubt that we would go, but somehow we all wished that we might be spared it.

Still descending the right bank we passed through the villages of Sho and Li, visiting their little temples on the way. The painter of Lö had been employed in both of them, so we had occasion to admire his work again. Just below Bartsam the river-bank widened and there was a cave for the porters and a sward for our tents. Takki Babu went to buy dry wood in the village and returned with some French beans as well. They were the first ones we had seen this summer and were welcome indeed.

KUTANG

The next day we continued through Namdru Village and down into the narrowing gorge. Dense jungle now enclosed the track and our boots slid dangerously on slippery rock and clay. We crossed to the left bank of the swollen torrent by a firm wooden bridge, but returned very soon to the right bank by a bridge of natural rock. The whole Buri Gandaki forced itself foaming and roaring through a narrow chasm below. We were now entering Kutang and a mile further on the valley began to open out. The track left the gorge and we could see villages high up on the mountain-slopes, surrounded by steeply terraced fields. We came to another bridge, leading across to the first village, Tsak; our porters went that way, because the track down the left bank was more level. Pasang and I followed another path, climbing steeply up the right bank to the village of Prok, where we had heard there were temples worth seeing. We stopped to admire a splendid rock-painting of the Buddha 'Lotus-Born' near the top of the cliff, then passed through an entrance-chöten and made our way slowly up between fields of dead maize-stalks. We saw no one until we reached the centre of the village, where a Tibetan tent was set up just above the track. A small fierce dog rushed out at us barking, followed by a little boy, who stared in amazement. We asked him the way to the temple and he pointed in its direction without hesitation. 'Are you pilgrims?' we asked. 'Yes', he replied, 'we come from Kyirong and are making a pilgrimage to Nepal. Where do you come from?' A woman appeared in the door of the tent and threw a stone at the dog in a vain effort to stop its barking. 'We come from India,' we said. 'Are you also pilgrims?'—'Yes we are pilgrims'—'Then go in peace.' 'Remain in peace,' we replied and walked on up to the temple, pleased by the ready retorts of the little Tibetan boy and strangely affected by his greeting, although the actual words were quite conventional.

A wide veranda in front of the temple was filled with baskets of maize and piles of corncobs. Two men sat amongst them, breaking the corn off fresh cobs with their hands. They looked up at our approach and we asked if we could see the temple. 'Certainly,' the older man replied, 'my wife will show you in,' and he called out to her to bring the key. We explained briefly where we had come from and the lama (for so he proved to be) asked if we had visited Naktsa Gomba on our way. He was delighted to hear that we had been there and told us that his grandfather had been one of the founders of the community at Drong just below the monastery. Meanwhile his wife had brought the key and opened the door for us. Inside there was a complete set of the Tibetan Canon (Kanjur) arranged in racks against the left wall, while the right wall was painted with frescoes of the 1,000 buddhas. The central image was of Śākyamuni, flanked by 'Boundless Light' and 'Glancing Eye'. The lama was more pleased than ever at our appreciative interest and told his wife to roast us a dish of maize. We paid for the lighting of two butter-lamps and while resting on the balcony, asked him to name the villages across the valley and point out the high-level route to Tsum. The maize was too hard for my teeth, but it was welcome grist for Pasang's mill, although he complained of thirst as we climbed up the steep slope to the upper temple.

A little house, surrounded by a garden, stood at the top of the slope. A nun appeared in response to our call and led us gladly into the temple, which was painted with frescoes of the 'Tranquil and Fierce' divinities. Several images were set above the altar, 'Lotus-Born' and his two goddess-wives, 'Boundless Life', 'Glancing Eye' and Śākyamuni. We offered some butter-lamps and then followed the nun into her two-roomed house, where she gave us little bowls of arak and a bundle of greens from her garden, apologizing that there was nothing else that would help us on our way. She told us how many years she herself had spent on pilgrimage, and that she well knew how difficult it often was to find shelter and food. We had received sympathy of this kind before, but welcome as it was, we could scarcely claim to be worthy recipients. When this nun went on pilgrimage, she would probably be carrying all her requirements on her own back, while eight sturdy men, slowly wending their way down the valley below, carried ours. But compared with other more lavish expeditions, we were certainly experiencing privation, for was not the party of ten Japanese who climbed on Manaslu, accompanied by some 600 porters? In any case we were grateful for fresh greens.

Another track descends from Prok towards the south, so we followed this, passing the village water-mills and crossing another torrential stream. We found some mushrooms on the way down of the kind commonly cultivated in England and looking more palatable than Pasang's pink variety. We reached the banks of the Buri Gandaki by another bridge and could not be sure whether our porters had continued down the left-hand bank or recrossed to where we now were, for there were tracks on both sides. Deciding to follow the better track above the far bank, we crawled one by one over the very rickety bridge. The first wayfarer to meet us, put our minds to rest, for he had met eight loaded men and one black dog. We caught them up within an hour and continued together past the two or three houses, known as Koya, and then down again to the banks of the river, which we crossed once more. The track continued along the narrow gorge and we soon found a place to halt where the overhanging rock would give protection and a space could be cleared for one of the tents. A party of villagers, returning home late, found themselves caught amidst guy ropes and nettles.

The following day we continued down the gorge for a while and then climbed up high above it, thence we could look across to the other gorge of the east river (SI: Shiār Kholā), which, descending from Tsum, joins the Buri Gandaki at this point. But one has to descend a full day's journey in order to reach a possible crossing-place. Within an hour we reached NYAK (SI: Ngyāk), the first Gurung village; although it was barely three in the afternoon, we followed the advice of our porters and set up camp for the night. The only flat places were the threshing-grounds and while we were unpacking the tents on one of these, an ill-tempered old woman appeared, admonishing us not to make the place dirty. For months now we had been travelling through villages, where hygiene was never considered, yet re-

maining ourselves paragons of cleanliness, and now we were
admonished to be clean by a cross old woman whose personal
standards fell far short of ours even at the end of our day's
journey! Pasang spoke quietly to her and she was sufficiently
reassured to bring us supplies of fire-wood. She later looked into
the tents with the sleeping-bags spread over the light camp-beds,
and at last exclaimed, as many had exclaimed before, how clean
everything looked. Yet everything was, in fact, as our readers
would expect it to be after six months of such travel. A girl
brought us a pumpkin and two delicious cucumbers, the first
we had seen this year, and after first demanding an absurd price,
she agreed to barter them for one box of matches. The villagers
crowded around the tents, comparing us and our ways with the
Japanese mountaineers, who were the only other 'gya-mi' that
most of them had seen. We thought it might be advisable to
take a villager from here, who would then stay with us, when
the other porters returned home. He could accompany us up to
Tsum and come down to Kathmandu, if he felt inclined to
carry a load so far. This suggestion initiated interminable discussion amongst the bystanders, but it led nowhere, for nothing
would convince them that our money-bags were not as full as
those of the Japanese had proved to be.

In appearance these Gurungs are easily distinguishable from
the Tibetans of the higher villages we have left behind. One
observes at once their softer features, which are enhanced by a
rather higher standard of cleanliness. But their way of life is
the same, for it is set within the same physical conditions. They
practise Tibetan religion and speak Tibetan as well as Gurung.
There is a small village-temple just above the village, differing
in no way from those of Kutang, and the few religious texts they
possess are regular Tibetan block-prints.

We left late the following morning, for the journey before
us was not a long one. It was raining slightly and the village-
lanes were a miry morass; we were dismally aware of the fact
that although approaching Kathmandu that day, we should be
travelling away from it on the morrow, clambering up the oppo-

site bank of the Buri Gandaki, which certainly looked very unpleasant. There is joy in making one's way along a river-gorge,
when one can place one's feet confidently forward and delight
in the high crags and the swirling river below, but there is little
pleasure, when all is wet and slippery and one must be wary of
every step. Beyond Nyak we descended precipitously to the
stream that surges down from Himāl-chūli, crossing it by a
natural rock-bridge; this side-valley was filled with writhing
leeches, and we regretted the monsoon the more. The date was
now September 16th, time for the rain-clouds to disperse. In
any case we would have to delay at Tara until our tents and
boxes were dry. We envisaged ourselves running the gauntlet of
leeches for much of the remainder of our journey. Another steep
ascent and a long traverse brought us above Pang-sh'ing (SI:
Pāngsing). This is the lowest Gurung village on the right side of
the river to possess a Tibetan Buddhist temple. In the late afternoon the weather began to clear, so that by the time we reached
TARA (SI: Setibās), we had decided to camp away from the
village. Our porters would be leaving us, so there was no need
to give thought to their welfare. We found a place on the sand
beside the river, and rapidly sorting out the things needed for
the week's journey up to Tsum, we repacked the rest and left it
in the headman's house. Meanwhile the awaited transformation
took place: the sky became blue and we saw the sun for the first
time since we had crossed over into Nup-ri. Exclaiming that
this must be the end of the monsoon, we no longer envisaged
the visit to Tsum as the last section of an exhausting journey
which it would be cowardly to omit, but as one more delightful
expedition into high mountains. I confess to little understanding of those mountaineers who commend mountain-travel,
whatever the weather. There is a visual magic in high snow-
peaks and ridges, but to climb across mountains without seeing
them would seem to profit a man little. The Tibetans certainly
know of more beneficial forms of asceticism. That night we
slept beneath a clear and starry sky.

Thus on the morning of September 17th we were able to

bathe and wash our clothes in brilliant sunshine; everything was dry by the time our fresh porters from the village were ready to leave. Meanwhile Nying-kar was lying panting in the shade, unaccustomed to such heat. We had descended to 6,000 feet above sea-level, where cacti and plantains were flourishing, but during the dismal weather of the past days we had been little aware of our surroundings. We crossed the swinging rope-bridge just above our camp-site and climbed up to DODANG (SI: Philim). This village is also peopled by Gurungs and is the lowest to have a Tibetan Buddhist temple on the left side of the Buri Gandaki. Their fields were filled with growing millet and the fruit of the plantains was not yet ripe. Pasang looked in vain for a few early ones while the rest of the party rested under a tree above the last house. Nying-kar followed very slowly because of the heat, and we wondered if he would manage the journey to Kathmandu. The track climbs high above the river north of Dodang and for several hours there was no water, so that he looked very pathetic. Then we passed through Serchung and Anwang (SI: Philam) and on to Lokwa above the junction of the east and west rivers. This is the first Tibetan village on the eastern side and we decided to stay the night, as there seemed to be little hope of finding another site before dark. Even here it was difficult enough, but we managed to erect one tent at a slight angle. The villagers offered us accommodation, adding that there were not many fleas. One however is enough for me, so Pasang and I slept in the tent and the rest of the party in a house nearby. They seemed to be immune to these insects. The weather had been superb and now we looked westwards across the Buri Gandaki and up the leech-infested valley opposite which we had crossed the previous day. The sky was clear and at the head of the valley we saw the great rounded summit of Himāl-chūli. In the morning light it looked even more splendid with the drooping red heads of ripening amaranthus hanging in the foreground

Tsum

From Lokwa we descended into the gorge. Although the weather was so delightful, the track was still dangerous from all the past rain. Nying-kar was happy again, for there was no shortage of water. We cooked lunch by the river with the mountains of the Kutang Himāl towering above the rock-cliffs of the gorge, feeling as contented as at our first meal in the mountains over six months before. The track continued to be difficult and tiring, for we were now skirting the steep sides of Ganesh Himāl, but by evening we emerged from the jungle onto a pleasant grass sward just by HRIP-CHE. In the morning I visited the temple, observing the same type of frescoes on inset wooden panels as in Nup-ri. Also the houses are left grey and the temples whitewashed in just the same way. Meanwhile Pasang went vainly searching for butter and returned with a party of villagers who were asking for medicine and trying to persuade him to sell Nying-kar, whose physique impressed them greatly. We gave them medicine and continued merrily on our way. The track became easier and we halted for lunch just below Rinsam where another large stream flows down from the east. First this had to be crossed and soon afterwards the main river itself, followed by a long ascent high above the right bank. We were all affected by torturing thirst, but the river was left ever further below us and there was no sign of any stream ahead. We continued thus for three hours or so until we heard the sound of voices above the track. Climbing off through the undergrowth, we found two boys from Chhö-khang sitting by a spring of water which trickled over a rock and disappeared again under ground. It seemed the most delicious water we had ever tasted. We continued climbing, and the river, which descends here by a series of rapid falls, appeared once more only just below us. We passed through a grove and entered an upper valley; the banks began to widen and the trees gradually lessened, until once more the scenery was typically Tibetan.

We reached CHHÖ-KHANG (SI: Chhukang) by early evening and asked for the house of Shap-ruk De-wa. Entering a courtyard, we climbed up wooden stairs onto a veranda, where the headman's wife came forward to meet us. She showed us at once into their little temple, lit lamps and incense and served us with buttered tea and biscuits. Since the temple serves as the best room of the house, we were invited to make ourselves at ease for as long as we cared to stay, so I arranged beds and sleeping-bags while Pasang supervised the preparation of a meal in the kitchen. Our charming hostess provided us with eggs, turnips, potatoes and a little meat, and while the cooking was in progress, cheered our spirits with little cups of arak.

We left early the next morning, intending to reach Ra-chhen Monastery in time to cook a meal. There is a small temple above Chhö-khang and another prayer-wheel temple by a stream just beyond the village towards the north. Then one climbs even higher across grass slopes and by prayer-walls, reaching Nga-chhu (SI: Ngāchu) in about an hour. We passed through the village and crossed its spacious fields, which spread across the wide right bank of the river. The whole village seemed to be at work, for the buckwheat harvest was in its last stages and the planting of the wheat had begun. The villagers shouted across to ask who we were and where we were going, some crowding around to observe us from close quarters. In half an hour we had crossed their fields, and passing by Nga we crossed to the left bank of the river by the hamlet of Khangsa. In twenty minutes we had reached RA-CHHEN Monastery. The main gate was open, but except for a fierce mastiff the place was deserted and the temple-doors were closed to us. The group of temples is built in the centre of a rectangular courtyard, the sides of which are formed by the single-storied houses of the community (pl. XLIIIa), which, as we were soon to learn, consists entirely of nuns. We were wandering around disconsolately, wondering how we might find the means to cook a meal as well as gain access to the temples, when two nuns arrived from the village. While we were explaining what we wanted, other nuns began to appear

258

on the scene. Fearing that we were 'gya-mi' and unable to speak Tibetan, they had gone into hiding at our approach. Now hearing Tibetan being spoken, they all re-emerged. Three of them led us to the monastery-kitchen and supplied wood and water, while the keeper of the temple went to get the keys.

The main temple is entered through a porch, decorated in the regular manner with paintings of the Wheel of Existence and the four kings of the quarters. One then enters a large, square, pillared hall. The back and side-walls are covered by row upon row of small *terra-cotta* images of eleven-headed 'Glancing Eye' (*bcu-gcig zhal*). Along the facing wall are fitted finely carved and painted cases, containing various images and the hundred odd volumes of the Tibetan canon. Dragons and lotuses, twining foliage and jewels, frame the glass of the image-cases. In the centre there is a large gilt eleven-headed 'Glancing Eye' and to left and right images of Śākyamuni, 'Lotus-Born', the 'Saviouress' and 'Boundless Light'. The capitals of the pillars and the ceiling beams are similarly carved and painted. Next to the main temple there is a small one containing a large prayer-wheel and beyond this again there is the private chapel of the head-lama, where a fine image of the 'Holder of the Vajra' is set behind glass. The head-lama is the chief hierarch of Bhutān ('*brug-pa rin-po-che*), who in his previous incarnation founded this convent, Mu Monastery and another monastery at Kyirong just across the political frontier. We had already met the present incarnation, who is still a boy, when he was on a visit to the Nepal Valley. The rooms are always kept as his, but the last incarnation merely made brief visits and the present one has not yet had occasion to come at all.

We returned to the kitchen, where Takki Babu had finished the cooking; after our meal we made an offering to the nuns and went on our way. We continued up the left bank through Lar and Phur-be Village, where we stopped to see the little temple and light a butter-lamp. We went on past prayer-walls to Pang-dön and across the fields to CHHU-LE (SI: Shule). Another stream flows in here from the east; there is an old stone bridge with the houses rising up behind and the little village-temple high on the hillside above. The track crosses the bridge and skirts the village by keeping close to the river. Another bridge takes one across to Nyi-le village. These two names are interpretable as 'water-side' (*chu-le*) and 'sun-side' (*nyi-le*). They are the two last villages of Tsum.

Mu Monastery is visible further up the valley and we were cheered by the thought that this was our last objective. Like Ra-chhen it consists of a central temple surrounded by the little houses of the inmates, but it is built in an isolated position on a ridge high above the river (pl. XLIIIb).[a] It appears to be the very head of the valley, but in fact streams meet at this point from the east and the west and tracks lead to the political frontier of Tibet in both directions.

'Why do you not go on to Kyirong?' we were asked, and although we tried to explain the political reasons, none of these people could really understand. They travel freely themselves and assumed we travelled likewise. O happy innocence!

The monks had seen us clambering up the last part of the ascent and a group of them gathered in the courtyard to learn who these strange visitors might be. Pasang explained in the usual terms, that we were pilgrims and begged room to stay that night, for there was no flat space outside the monastery compound, where one could have erected a tent. We received not a word in reply and they indicated by gesture that they were under a vow of silence. We told them more about ourselves, while they stood nodding their heads; then after pointing and more nodding they conducted us in a throng to one of the houses. Meanwhile other monks had arrived and also a boy,

[a] Mu Monastery appears on the SI maps as 'Chum Gompa'. 'Chum' represents 'Tsum' (see p. 275), the name of this whole region. Since it is the most important, this monastery is also known as 'Tsum Gomba' as well as by its proper name of Mu Gomba. 'Gomba' is preferable to 'Gompa', as it comes closer to the actual Tibetan pronunciation of *dgon-pa*. The SI maps of Nepal write Gömpa and Gömpā as well as Gompa. There are many Tibetan words in which the vowel sign ö can be used with advantage, but this is not one of them.

who was either free of the vow or had been freed for our benefit. He explained that we could use this house and he would bring wood and water for us. The monks were observing silence and a fast that day, but they would be free after the culminating ceremony which was to be performed early the next morning. We thanked them and gave money for a general tea-offering, which it was arranged should take place later the following morning. The fast with its accompanying ceremony is known as Nyungnä (*smyung-gnas*) and was so arranged that it would come to an end of the 16th of the Tibetan month. It provides a solemn occasion for the reaffirming of the regular rules by which the monks are bound and is thus a developed form of the general monastic confession (*pratimoksha*). We had arrived just in time for the final ceremony by no special design, and Pasang was delighted at the auspicious combination of circumstances. He argued that we had endured months of difficulties and privations and if we had decided to have a ceremony performed at the last of the many monasteries we had visited, we could have chosen nothing more suitable than the Nyung-nä Ceremony. Now we had arrived here to find the monks bringing this very ceremony to its conclusion. The least we could do, he said, was to contribute generously to the general offerings (*tshogs*). I suggested a sum, which in his enthusiasm he promptly doubled and handed over to the monks. This money represented the purchase-price of butter, flour and salt, used in the preparation of cakes and biscuits, which are piled up below the sacrificial cakes and distributed to everyone present after the ceremony. Now we turned to our own affairs and after drinking the buttered tea that had been specially prepared, succeeded in erecting one tent by the door of the house, which was too small for all of us. Our stocks of food were low, but the monks let us have some wheat-flour, butter and potatoes. We slept peacefully, reflecting that this really was our journey's end.

The ceremony began in the early hours of the morning and I awoke to the sound of trumpets, drums and cymbals. Nothing essential was missed, however, for the main part of the liturgy was repeated so many times. The temple was arranged inside just like the one at Ra-chhen Gomba. A fine bronze image of eleven-headed 'Glancing Eye' stood above the altar and the walls were covered with little *terra-cotta* images of the same divinity. The altar had been piled high with tormas, butter-lamps and dishes of offerings. About thirty monks were present, seated in the customary facing rows down the centre of the room. Two 'neophytes' were moving along the rows, replenishing the monks' bowls with buttered tea. We sat at the end of the right-hand row and bowls of tea were soon placed before us. Meanwhile there was no interruption in the ceremony; parts of the liturgy were recited rapidly in a low monotone, others were sung in the deep haunting melody of Tibetan religious chant and every so often the trumpets, cymbals, drums and bells gave forth their eerie and daemonic sounds. We borrowed a spare copy of the text, so as to follow the words. The liturgy consisted of an introductory statement of the general intention, namely to perform the rite of confession as it has always been performed in the past, then the invoking of buddha-names and lamas, in whose presence the words of confession were pronounced; next came the special invocation of 'Glancing Eye', his description and praises, then the presentation of the offerings and prayers for succour. A Tibetan ceremony, well performed, is one of the most impressive experiences, but one's reaction to it, as to all fine things, is so personal that no adequate description is possible. The terse Tibetan syllables of the regular verses cannot be translated effectively, for to convey the sense in a European language one needs far too many words. Moreover many of the phrases have a codified significance, only understandable within the terms of Buddhist philosophy. Buddhas, saviours, lamas, gods are conjured forth, as it were, from an ineffable state of absolute 'nothingness', receiving substantial form merely for the purpose of the rite. Yet they may be treated as real by their worshippers, for even their apparitional forms seem permanent compared with the transitory nature of all phenomenal things. At the same time the ceremony is pervaded by so positive a moral quality and such faith in the saviour's power to save, that the source of all things, that absolute 'nothingness', becomes revealed intuitively as an all-embracing ultra-positive good.

'Those who gained enlightenment in the past, those worthy ones, those perfect buddhas, all-wise, mighty elephants of men, who did what ought to be done, doing well what they did, having put off their own burden and gained their real objective, free from all attachment to the world, pure in speech, free in thought, free in wisdom, even they performed the rite of confession for the sake of all living creatures, for their benefit, for their salvation, for the removal of famine and sickness, for the perfecting of qualities conducive to enlightenment, for the sake of achieving supreme and perfect enlightenment. Thus may we do likewise from now on till the sun no longer gives light; for the sake of all living creatures and their final enlightenment let us perform the rite of confession!'

'There shall be no taking of life,
        no robbing of others,
        no sin of impurity,
        no speaking untruth,
        no drinking fermented liquor,
    which brings many faults in its train,
        no sleeping on fine beds,
        no eating at unallowed times,
        no using of scents or garlands or finery,
        no frivolity at parties and dances.'[a]

'Even as the worthy ones of old refrained from these things, may we, doing likewise, achieve supreme enlightenment!'

[a] This is the ancient conventional set of prohibitions for Buddhist monks. The tenth item, 'no acquiring of money or property' is omitted. These and the following brief extracts are translated from a short ritual text entitled 'The Rite of the Practice of Abstinence which relies on the Compassionate Lord and is known as the Essence of Benefit to Others' (*jo-bo thugs-rje chen-po la brten-pa'i smyung-bar gnas-pa'i cho-ga gzhan phan snying-po zhes-byas-ba*).

'May our moral practice be free from defect!
May our moral practice be perfectly pure!
With our moral practice free from all pride
Let us attain perfection of morality!'

———————

'In power of passion, anger, ignorance,
Whatever evil I have done
In thought or deed or word,
Each sin I separately confess.

All buddhas and their spiritual sons,
All holy hermits, monks and laymen,
Whatever merit each has gained,
I rejoice in sympathy.'

———————

'May all beings be happy, possessing the cause of happiness!
May all beings be freed from suffering and the cause of
suffering!
O may they know happiness unalloyed by suffering!
May they abide in equanimity, free from aversion and attach-
ment!'

———————

'Noble Lord "Glancing Eye", Treasure of Compassion!
May you and your whole circle be pleased to listen to us!
Save us, we beseech you, from the ocean of existence
Together with all beings, close to us as parents!
Quickly plant in us, we beg you,
The seed of enlightenment!
With the water of compassion wash quickly away
Defilements amassed from beginningless time!
Stretch forth your hand in compassion, we beg you,
And lead all beings to the land of the blessed.'

VII

RETURN TO THE NEPAL VALLEY

Although our visit to their land was so short, the people of Tsum accepted us there with little surprise and no hesitation. As we passed through the fields of Nga-chhu, the villagers stopped from their work to greet us as friends and enquire how we had fared at Mu. We stayed again in Shap-ruk De-wa's house at Chhö-khang; now no longer strangers, we were received with spontaneous goodwill. Descending the next day through the gorge, slippery with slimy stones and mud and overgrown with dying vegetation, I realized how far autumn was advanced. We slept by the river, where the snow-covered ridge of the Kutang Himāl towers above the great cliffs of the gorge, rejoicing to come this way again and pass through the well remembered places. Our return to Kathmandu no longer seemed so urgent and as I lay awake in the tent, recalling to mind the various stages of our long journey, I suddenly conceived the idea of this book. The next day we stopped below Lokwa to prepare a meal and while Pasang and Takki Babu busied themselves with the fire and the pots, I lay looking westwards towards the Land of Nup-ri, my mind still going back over the way we had come.

Yet however changed our feelings might be, the journey must now come to its end. Not only had we reached the last stage of our planned route, but our energy and means were well-nigh exhausted. Pasang was already using my spare pair of boots, since his were quite worn out; my own would be beyond repair if I continued to wear them much longer. Our stocks of food were almost gone and Takki Babu, although still the most resilient member of the party, longed to reach the lower valleys, where rice would be plentiful once more.

We stayed on our old camp-site just above Tara (Setibās) and negotiated with the headman for porters. He insisted that it would take quite two weeks to reach Kathmandu, but I measured the distance as about seventy map-miles and hoped we might get there in eight or nine days. In fact it took just eleven. I had heard frightful stories about the route down the Buri Gandaki from two friends who had descended the gorge in 1954. For sheer terror Ekai Kawaguchi's description of the Sangdak Pass into Dolpo is more likely to excite the spirit of adventure, but neither account exaggerates.[a] Nimbleness of movement and sureness of foot are indispensable accomplishments in both places. However there are many sections of route through Nepal of a similar standard; I would hesitate, for instance, to grade the route along the Bheri gorge between Anā and Tibrikot as less difficult than the Buri Gandaki.

We left the following day, September 24th, with five Gurung villagers as our porters; three were men of Tara (Setibās) and two came from Uyak Village, which we would pass on our way down. These two had come up trading on their own account, but willingly deposited their loads to come to our assistance and earn some extra rupees. We were delayed by the resorting of our luggage and remaking of loads, and could not leave until midday. The route made a long detour sweeping up and down a side valley to reach a crossing-place of the tributary torrent that adds its waters to the main river just north of Jagat. We arrived in this place only to be further delayed by the officials of the frontier check-post, but gratefully accepted their offer of hospitality for the night, although we had only travelled for three hours that day. The next morning we left at eight, descended to the river's very edge and clambered again for hours to the summit cliffs of the gorge. This was followed by an unusually long section, which gave us the rare satisfaction of having neither to climb higher nor to lose the height gained. But eventually another ridge had to be crossed; having reached its summit, we had the choice of a long detour round the mountain-sides or a steep descent of some 2,000 feet towards the river with another

[a] see Showell Styles, *The Moated Mountain*, London 1955, pp. 199 ff. Reference to Kawaguchi is given in the preface, p. xv fn.

equally steep ascent beyond. We left the decision to the porters, who chose the descent as being more rapid. From the mountain we descended through terraced fields, set at such steepness that they seemed rather like an interminable flight of giant steps. We climbed and slid down the uprights and stumbled and slipped through the millet which carpeted the treads. The peasants who were working in these little fields, stopped to watch our progress with curiosity and amusement. Their tiny houses were overgrown with cucumbers, but we could find no one indoors to sell us a few. At last we reached a track and crossing a stream, came suddenly upon a resting-place for coolies. It consisted of stone supports to receive their loads and a small expanse of flat cropless land behind, which provided just enough room for our tents. Along more frequented routes these resting-places (chautara) are so numerous as to offer a constant temptation to delay, but this particular one presented itself as a single oasis in a sloping maze of stones, mud, growing crops and stubble. We had been travelling for nine hours, so it was time to call a halt. Uyak Village was not far distant and since we would traverse below it on the morrow, our porters shed their loads and hastened there at once, so as to replenish their own stocks of food and sleep in greater comfort.

The next day we traversed more fields and reached the top of the main gorge again, only to plunge down once more by a precipitous track to the water's edge. Here we were enclosed within great cliffs of rock, and the route became a stony track. Thus we continued pleasantly for hour after hour, stopping only to wonder at a little stream of hot water which ran from under the rocks to be lost in the cold roaring torrent of the Buri Gandaki. At last the cliffs on our side began to recede and suddenly we emerged from jungle into little fields. So we came to Khorlak Village and I stopped to delight in the smell of champak blossoms, while Pasang went to buy guavas, which he had noticed hanging ripe on the trees. Just below Khorlak another raging tributary pours into the main river. The first half of this stream was fordable, although the water was waist-deep and swift flowing. Ten yards of such a crossing led to a small island of rocks in mid-stream, whence a pole-walk offered the only way to the far bank. A hand-support in the form of a waving stick projected from the far end of this bridge, but it only reached half-way across. A slip would result in almost certain death; below the water roared and surged as it hurled itself against the rocks. The use of our nylon rope would have been a wise precaution, but no one was interested in it. Four of the porters carried their loads across quite unconcernedly. The fifth was unwilling, so one of the others returned to bring his load, followed by Takki Babu who went back for the dog. While we were waiting, two shepherds arrived and began to carry their sheep across one by one (pl. XLIVa). Nobody seemed to be concerned about the bridge, although it probably claims several victims every year. Beyond this stream the main gorge closed in upon us and the track led up to a narrow cat-walk, consisting of small trunks pegged against the rocks. This was interspersed with sections of slippery mud, where the only handholds were tufts of grass. With as much surprise as relief I found the whole party still present when we reached the safety of a firmer route beyond. This led us through densely growing wormwood, reaching high above our heads, and when we finally emerged on the bank of the river, all were agreed that seven hours of travelling sufficed for that day.

The next morning began with another cat-walk, but thereafter the route became easy enough. More habitations began to appear and more and more paddy fields. But we still had to negotiate long sections of rocky track up and down the steep sides of the wooded valley. It was in such a place that the first casualty occurred on the following day. We had come to a splendid water-fall, which plunged into a clear rock basin just beside the route, so we stopped to have a bathe. On the other side of the track there was a drop of about thirty feet down to rocks and shrubs. While bathing in the pool, we suddenly heard cries from Nying-kar, who had fallen down the precipice. He must have checked his fall, for he suffered nothing worse than a sprained back-leg, but even this made progress slow and difficult for him. He was very unhappy and clearly blamed us for his sufferings, since he refused to accompany us and would only follow at the heels of the last of the porters. If one of us kept to the rear, he would lie down and refuse to move. Thus we could do nothing but leave him to follow. He limped in late at our lunch-time halt and even later when we stopped for the night. The next day we tried to encourage him, but with no better results, and could only trust that he would continue to follow. By noon we reached Arughāt and great was our excitement, for here we would join the main route through central Nepal, which connects the district headquarters of Pokhara, Gurkha and Nawākot with Kathmandu; it seemed we were already at our journey's end. We cooked a meal in one of the village houses, but although we stayed more than two hours, still Nying-kar did not appear. Sending the porters on with Takki Babu, I waited in the village while Pasang returned the way we had come. He went back four miles before he met a man and boy, who told him that they had seen a black dog limping northwards. Since it was too late to follow that evening, he returned to Arughāt. We caught up with the porters, who had been travelling very slowly and established a camp about two miles beyond the village. The next day Pasang went back on the search, while the rest of us continued on our way.

The track now led along the sandy bank of the Ankhu Kholā and it was very hot indeed. For months we had been accustomed to living at 10,000 feet and more; now we had arrived at a mere 2,000 feet in the heat and moisture that always follow the monsoon. It was irksome and oppressive as no other part of our long journey had been. Relief was afforded by plunging into water, but the pleasing sensation was so transitory that it availed very little. Takki Babu bought rice and eggs in the next village, and cooking a meal, we left a share for Pasang in the hope that he would soon follow with the dog. Then we crossed a bridge and ascended slowly and laboriously to Katunje Village, where our porters said they could go no further. We settled in

269

the lower storey of a house, which the owner put at our disposal and set about the preparation of a meal, leaving all other problems to Pasang. He arrived late in the evening leading the unhappy Nying-kar, whom I had scarcely expected to see again. By good fortune he had been found by two soldiers from the check-post at Jagat, who were on their way down to Gurkha. They recognized him and he consented to be led on a rope, an act of servitude to which he had never submitted before in spite of our well-meant efforts. Thus Pasang had met them and joyfully received his charge. We now turned our attention to the porters, who insisted that they were too tired to continue with us the next day. Replacements were found in the village without much difficulty and we added to the number a small boy who was willing to carry the dog (pl. XLIV*b*).

From above Katunje we had our last view back across the foothills to the summits of Dhaulagiri and Annapūrna, the two great massifs beyond which we had been travelling all these months. There were no more mishaps, but the way to Kathmandu seemed surprisingly long. Now we had reached rather easier tracks, I expected to increase our daily mileage but we covered no more than eight map-miles a day, although we were travelling from seven in the morning until four or so in the afternoon. Thus we continued travelling for four more days, descending from hill-top to valley, only to reascend once more, and then again came the inevitable descent. The track seemed crowded after the solitude of the past months. One meets a continuous succession of coolies, loaded with a variety of articles. The chief item of trade must be cigarettes, for the people of Nepal are inveterate smokers. Next in importance is cotton cloth, mostly of Indian manufacture. Others carry great balks of timber across their shoulders, thus blocking completely the narrow path. Again and again they have to stand aside with their loads turned lengthways along the track, so that those who meet them may pass. It must be one of the most laborious means of earning a livelihood. A few coolies carry salt, and even fewer carry such luxuries as sugar, condensed milk or tins of biscuits. Even at the low rates for porterage that are payable in Nepal, items carried in such a way soon become very costly. We saw a lady being carried in a specially shaped basket on the shoulders of a single porter, while her husband followed on foot. A gentleman hastened past us in a litter carried by four. But such sights are rare. One may save one's energy if one can afford to be carried, but there is no comfort at all in riding on another man's shoulders.

We passed through Trisuli Bazaar, marvelling at the existence of shops and stalls, which we had not seen for so long. Nawākot we avoided by taking a short cut and crossing the Tādi Kholā in a boat. At last on October 4th we reached Kaulia Village and shouted with joy at the first glimpse of the Nepal Valley between the last of its surrounding hills. We could just see its western end and distinguish the little Newār town of Kīrtipur. Pasang hastened ahead, so that he could get a jeep and bring it to meet us at Bālāju, where the motorable track begins. Meanwhile Takki Babu and I came along with the porters. We paused in Kakani on the rim of the Valley, and then began our last rapid descent into the heart of Nepal, the real 'Nepal' of history with all the traces of its own splendid culture. We reached Bālāju, famous for its recumbent image of the god Vishnu, who manifests himself in the kings of Nepal. Near the pool in which the image lies submerged, there is a long row of water-spouts. Here we removed our heavy boots and ragged garments, bathed under the cold jets and dressed in unironed cotton clothes, which we had kept ready for this occasion. The jeep stood waiting with Nying-kar by its side, and as we came to take our places in it, I was pervaded with a sense of happy fulfilment. The last two miles into Kathmandu seemed like a ride on a magic carpet and I was welcomed at our house in Dilli Bazaar by another friend and colleague, Lt. Col. T. W. Clark.

A whole country can never be reduced to a single concept and perhaps the name of Nepal evades concise definition more than

RETURN TO THE NEPAL VALLEY

any other. To those who live in the Valley, the Newārs and the Gorkhas, 'Nepal' still means little more than the Valley itself. They scarcely think of the people from the surrounding mountains as their fellow-countrymen. Likewise those who live in the mountains refer to the Valley as 'Nepal', for they also live as though their separate communities were entities in themselves. How could it be otherwise, when villagers half a day's journey away speak with a variation of dialect and the people beyond the head of the valley belong to a different race?

While waiting for Pasang at Arughāt, I had wandered up the bank of the Buri Gandaki with the village school-master as companion. 'Where does this track lead?' I asked him. 'To Tibet', he replied. 'To nowhere else on the way?'—'To nowhere else.' 'We have come that way,' I said. He showed no interest. You who have read this book, now know where we came from, but to the Nepalese of the lower valleys those lands of the great mountains might be part of another world. This is not really surprising, for the Himalayas form a barrier between two cultures, which are as different from one another as Europe from India. In fact a Tibetan is almost as much a foreigner in the Valley as an Englishman, even though he may live within the political frontier of Nepal. This is not only because he speaks another language, for there are many local languages besides Tibetan still used throughout the country, but because his whole cultural background is radically different. His society is caste-free and his religion of the special Tibetan kind, either Buddhist or p'ön. It matters not to him that as a 'bhotia' he is relegated by Nepalese caste-laws to one of the lowest castes. He lives and travels freely, and for his own part tends to pity the 'valley-men' (rong-ba) as unfortunates who have no religion.

On the southern side of this cultural watershed live caste-conscious societies often of great complexity. They too have their religious cults, but without the cohesion and universalism of Tibetan religion. Moreover while our 'bhotia' friends had the vaguest ideas about places outside their cultural area, the different districts and chief monasteries were well known to them

XLI.

a. Upper Nar. (p. 229) The photograph is taken from just above the gomba, looking across the deeply eroded valley to the village on the other side. We have pitched a tent on the roof of the kitchen.
b. The terraced fields of Lower Nar. (p. 226)

XLII.

a. *The Lama of Shang in Pi Gomba.* (p. 235)
b. *Sāma Gomba.* (p. 244)

XLIII.

a. Ra-chhen Gomba. (p. 258)
b. Mu Gomba. (p. 260)

XLIV.

a. Bridge below Khorlak. Takki Babu is carrying our dog across.
(p. 268)
b. Tamang boy and the wounded dog. (p. 270)

all the way from Dolpo to Tsum. They know them by the names used in this book, not by the Survey of India names. Such mistakes were made just because the surveyors and their informants found themselves in alien areas. When we reached the lower valleys, it was by no means easy to explain where we had been, for the only names of 'bhotia' places at all familiar south of the watershed seem to be Manangbhot, Mustangbhot and Muktināth. Indeed we might well have come from another world.

The Buddhism of the Nepal Valley, identical with Tibetan Buddhism until the end of the thirteenth century, began to diverge ever further from it under the influence of Hinduism, which seems to have been actively fostered by the ruling families. The monks gradually disappeared, having been transformed into the highest orders of a rigid caste-system, modelled on the Hindu pattern. Then came the Gorkhas with their militant Hinduism, determined on the destruction of what little real Buddhism still remained. Whether the surviving Buddhist cults, conceived in the Hindu pattern, are to be called Buddhist or not, depends on one's definition of terms.[a] They certainly differ considerably in intention and form from Tibetan cere-monies and seem to have lost touch altogether with the funda-mental philosophical ideas, which alone can finally distinguish Buddhism from Hinduism.

Yet all this time one small section of Newar society, namely the traders (udās), were maintaining close connections with Lhasa, where there has been a small Newar community for centuries. Many of them married Tibetan wives, and being already Buddhists, all of them were readily influenced by Tibe-tan religion. The wives were debarred from entering Nepal, but it was no such easy matter to exclude incorporeal ideas. The ritual bath, to which they were forced to submit on their return to the Valley, certainly did not wash them away. Supported by some artisans, producers of significant items of trade such as images, ritual instruments and vessels, they formed a nucleus of

[a] see *BH*, ch. III, 'Buddhism in Nepal'.

Nepalese Buddhists, who realized that the practice of their religion could not be circumscribed by local caste-laws. These ideas continually brought them into conflict with the upper castes of their own society, but since trading is an essential occupation for a civilized community, they could never be finally repressed.

Since the revolution of 1950 and the ousting of the Rāna régime, their position has been suddenly strengthened out of all proportion to their numbers. For the ideas of democracy and personal freedom, which are now spreading throughout the country, must eventually undermine the whole caste-system and so vindicate those who claim that the Buddhism of the Valley is properly part of a universal religion. Nowadays other Nepalese Buddhists, besides the traders, may be heard expressing admiration for the superiority of Tibetan religious practice. The Tibetan monks and pilgrims, who come in winter to visit the splendid shrines of the Valley, far from being regarded as strange beings from another world, are even welcomed in some circles as religious brethren. Perhaps after all the great cultural barrier, which, unacknowledged by its rulers, divides Nepal lengthways into two mutually incomprehensible parts, is beginning to resolve itself in the very heart of the country. Perhaps too the 'bhotias' with their caste-free society and their practice of a universal religion may be regarded as the token of a new caste-free Nepal, united in a common culture.

APPENDIX

TIBETAN PLACE-NAMES IN WEST NEPAL

The place-names throughout the northern frontier districts of Nepal are Tibetan, but they appear on the Survey of India maps in a strange Nepāli ·garb. Those of us able to work out the method of transcription used by the surveyors, can sometimes approximate to the correct pronunciation, but for the most part the spellings of these names are quite misleading. An entirely different method is used by the Survey of India for all other Tibetan regions, not only political Tibet, but also districts such as Ladākh, Spiti and Lahul, and the small states of Sikkim and Bhutān. This is set out in 'Rules for the phonetic transcription into English of Tibetan words' by Charles Bell and W. F. O'Connor (India, Foreign Dept., P/W 441, Delhi 1903). On the sheets covering the northern regions of Nepal all place-names on the Tibetan side of the frontier are transcribed in accordance with these rules. The numerous Tibetan place-names inside the Nepalese frontier, however, appear in barely recognizable forms.

I quote a few place-names as they appear on the Survey of India maps of Nepal (1931 edition, scale 1:253,440) together with 'corrected' spellings based on the rules of Bell and O'Connor:

Thyangboche (Khumbu, District no: 3 East)	'Teng-bo-che'
Syā Gömpā (Chharkābhot, Palpa District)	'She Gompa'
Jomosom (Thākkhola, Palpa District)	'Dzong-sam'
Chhairogāon (Thākkhola)	'Tse-ro'
Chharkābhotgāon (Palpa District)	'Tsarka'

In these Nepalese spelling of Tibetan names:

ya is to be pronounced as *e*	
j	as *dẓ*
ch	as *ts*
s followed by *y, e* or *i*	as *sh*

But all too often there is complete lack of system, for the surveyors have given the names just as they thought they heard them:

Chohang (nr. Muktināth. — intended for 'Dzong' (meaning: fort)
District no: 4 west)
Chhego (nr. Muktināth) — intended for 'Chönkor'
Thangja (Manangbhot) — intended for 'Dzong-gyu'

It is lamentable that some of these falsified names are beginning to gain currency now that foreigners are travelling more freely in the remoter parts of

Nepal. When I was checking the route ahead with our assistant Nam-gyel, he once remarked: 'That place is Nar-tö but the sahibs (viz. some German mountaineers he had been working for) call it Phugāon'.[a]

A special cause for regret is the omission of nearly all the local district-names of these Tibetan regions and the invention of new ones covering different areas which represent no sort of cultural unity. Elsewhere the Survey of India has not banned from its maps such names as Ladākh, Lahul, Spiti or Zangskar. Thus I have deliberately reinstated all the district-names of the regions through which we passed, marking my maps accordingly.

The new district-names were often formed by adding the suffix -bhot (meaning 'Tibetan') to the more important towns and villages. Thus we find MUSTANGBHOT instead of the proper district-name LO, CHHARKĀBHOT invented from TSHARKA, MANANGBHOT from MANANG, altogether ignoring the proper district-name of NYE-SHANG. Sometimes the district-names appear in garbled forms as the names of rivers, e.g. Naur Kholā (from the district-name NAR), Pānjāng Kholā (from PANZANG). One district-name, TARAP, is allocated just to a village in the district and its true significance lost altogether.

These criticisms seem so radical, that I can imagine some of my readers being sceptical. My small party, however, was the first one proficient in the three languages of Nepāli, Tibetan and English to have visited these regions.

It is not only irksome to find incorrect or misleading names on existing maps; they have already gained such currency, that one has no choice but to continue using them as a means of reference. I have therefore quoted them in brackets whenever I refer to these villages for the first time, e.g. Ting-khyu (SI: Tingjegāon), Tsharka (SI: Chharkābhotgāon). (The suffix -gāon attached to so many of these names, means 'village' and is quite superfluous on maps.) Elsewhere I adhere to my amended spellings, which are all listed below.

Amended Method of Transcription

I have followed the method of Bell and O'Connor, simply introducing for greater exactitude certain distinctions, which they decided deliberately to omit. 'It is useless', O'Connor writes, 'to attempt to discriminate in English characters between such sounds as unaspirated and aspirated *p*.' If we were preparing our transcriptions for English speakers only, I would not hesitate to

---

[a] For some well known places there are two forms of the name, one Tibetan and one Nepalese. In these cases I have not hesitated to use the Nepalese one e.g. Muktināth (*tib.* chhu-mik-gya-tsa), Mustang (*tib.* Mön-t'hang), Sāma (*tib.* Rö). These of course appear quite properly on the existing maps. Concerning 'Phugāon' see p. 222 fn.

agree. But the Indian travellers who now increasingly visit these Tibetan areas, can and do distinguish perfectly well between such sounds, as can also many other Europeans. Should we therefore conceal a distinction of sound just because an untrained English ear cannot hear the difference?

In the following list the sounds omitted by Bell and O'Connor are marked by asterisks and their equivalent transcriptions given in square brackets.

Pronounce: a — like *u* in s*u*n,
[e] * ä — like *e* in sc*e*nt,
    b — as in English,
    ch — unaspirated rather like *ch* in pit*ch*er (= Sanskrit: c),
[ch] * chh — aspirated rather as in *ch*urn (= Sanskrit: ch),
[ch] * ch' — as in *ch*urn but with the voice on a low pitch,
    d — as in English,
    e — like *ai* in rain,
    g — always hard as in *g*et,
    h — as in English,
    i — like *i* in tw*i*g,
    j — always hard as in *j*et,
    k — unaspirated as in French *c*abane,
[k] * kh — aspirated as in English *c*abin or even more strongly as in York-*h*am,
[k] * k' — as in *c*abin but with the voice on a low pitch,
    l — as in English,
    m — as in English,
    n — as in English,
    o — like *o* in c*o*ld,
    ö — like *er* in f*er*n or even more closely like *eu* in French p*eu*,
    p — unaspirated as in French p*eu*,
[p] * ph — aspirated as in English *p*urr or even more strongly as in top-*h*eavy,
[p] * p' — as in *p*urr but with the voice on a low pitch,
    r — as in English,
    s — as in English,
[s] * s' — as in English but on a low pitch,
    sh — as in English *sh*eep (= Sanskrit: ś),
[sh] * sh' — as in English but on a low pitch,
    t — unaspirated as in French *t*able,
[t] * t'h — aspirated as in English *t*able or even more strongly as in goat-*h*erd,
[t] * t' — as in English *t*able but with the voice on a low pitch,
    tr — rather as in English *tr*ee but with the *r* barely sounded.

[tr] * trh — rather like *tr-h* in *Traherne* when pronounced as one syllable,

[tr] * tr' — as *tr* above but with the voice on a low pitch,

ts — like *ts* in *tsetse-fly*,

[ts] * tsh — like *ts-h* in ca*ts-h*ome,

[ts] * ts' — like *ts* above but with the voice on a low pitch,

u — like *oo* in w*oo*d,

ü — rather like *u* in y*u*le or like German *ü*,

w — as in English,

y — as in English.

Most of the consonants are pronounced as in English, the only ones to cause the English speaker any difficulty being the sets:

ch	chh	ch'
k	kh	k'
p	ph	p'
t	t'h	t'
tr	trh	tr'
ts	tsh	ts'

One must ensure that the first vertical row is quite free from aspiration, that the second is fully aspirated and that the third, besides being slightly aspirated, is pronounced on a low pitch. *ph* is properly just aspirated *p*, but it is sometimes pronounced as *f*. Aspirated *t* is written *t'h*, so as to ensure that it is not confused with English *th*.

The simple vowels, a, e, i, o, u, and the modified ä, ö, ü, are all pronounced much as in German.

Very occasionally I have 'improved' the transcribed spellings. For example there is an important monastery which I spell 'Shey' (rhyming with English 'they'). According to our rules the spelling should be 'She', but the classical spelling is in fact *Shel*. This final *-l* produces a slight liquid sound, well represented by *-y*.

Also in the case of Phijor Village I have made an exception, retaining the Survey of India spelling in preference to a regular transcription 'Phi-tsher'. After an initial syllable ending in *-i*, *tsh* tends to be pronounced as *j*.

In the names Kāk and T'hāk I have introduced a long vowel sign.

The syllables of Tibetan names are all properly separable and thus it would be logical to insert hyphens between them. But as a regular practice this would be cumbersome and unnecessary. Thus I have inserted them only when it is desirable to keep certain vowels clear or to avoid awkward clusters of consonants.

278

The classical spellings given below in the third column represent a letter by letter transliteration of the correct Tibetan written forms. Ideally Tibetan place-names should be regularly shown in this way, but it seems scarcely likely that such a method will commend itself to the Survey of India. Perhaps one day the Tibetans will insist on it, if ever they become nationally minded. After all we do not produce maps of France with all the names in phonetic spellings; we learn to pronounce French. Curious as Tibetan spellings must appear at first sight, the rules of pronunciation can be learned with little difficulty and there are far fewer irregularities than with English place-names. In some remote villages, however, where there is no proper literary tradition, the correct spellings have been forgotten and replaced by *ad hoc* phonetic spellings. One can sometimes find them in earlier historical records, which account for quite a number of those quoted below.

The names given to the districts in the fourth column are those used throughout this book. They are listed below on p. 285.

(*nep*) after a Survey of India name indicates a Nepalese name, alternative to the local Tibetan one and valid in its own right. I use 'Nepalese' in a wide sense embracing all the languages and dialects of Nepal. In the present cases these names will be Magar, Gurung or Nepāli (viz. Gorkhāli).

I have listed below all the places in the Tibetan-speaking areas of West Nepal through which we passed (chs. II–VI of this book). In a political sense these names also are Nepalese, but since they are Tibetan linguistically, it is only as Tibetan that they can properly be spelt.

NAMES OF VILLAGES AND MONASTERIES

Survey of India	Amended Name	Classical Spelling	District
Atāli	Tok-khyu	*Tog-'khyu*	DOLPO (Tarap)
Bagarchhap	(Bagar-)Tshap[a]		GYASUMDO
Baijubāra (*nep*)	P'ar-lä	(*Bar-slad*)	
Barcham	Bartsam	*Bar-mtshams*	NUP-RI
Bih	Bi		KUTANG
Bimtakothi	Bim-t'hang	*Bye-ma-thang*	GYASUMDO
— —	Bo-dzo		NYE-SHANG
Brāga	Drakar (Brakar)[b]	*Brag-dkar*	NYE-SHANG
— —	Bur-shi		TSUM
Chāhar	Dzar	*'Dzar*	DZAR-DZONG

[a] Tshap is the local Tibetan name, Bagartshap the Nepalese one. Note the Nepāli use of *chh* to represent the sound *tsh*.

[b] Brakar is the local dialect form, now giving way to Tibetan Drakar.

279

Survey of India	Amended Name	Classical Spelling	District
Chame	Tshä-me	(*Tshad-med*)	GYASUMDO
Chārāng	Tsarang	*gTsang-brang*	LO
Chelegāon	Tshe-le	*Tshe-le*	Upper Kāli Gandaki
Chhandul Gömpa	Sandul Gomba[a]	*Sa-'dul dgon-pa*	Upper Bheri
Chhāng	Serang		KUTANG
Chhairogāon	Tsherok	*Tshe-rog*	T'HĀK
Chharkābhotgāon	Tsharka	*Tshar-ka*	DOLPO (Tsharbung)
Chhego	Chhönkhor	*Chos-'khor*	DZAR-DZONG
Chhukang	Chhö-khang	*Chos-khang*	TSUM
Chho	Sho		NUP-RI
Chhukgāon	Tshuk	*Tshugs*	Upper Kāli Gandaki
	Tr'a-kar	*Brag-dkar* ⎫	
	Tse-kye	*rTse-skyes* ⎬	(Tshuk)
	Kyang-ma	*rKyang-ma* ⎭	
Chimgāon	Chimba		T'HĀK
Chohang	Dzong	*rDzong*	DZAR-DZONG
Chum Gompa	Mu Gomba[b]	*Mu dgon-pa*	TSUM
Chumje	Tsumjet		TSUM
Dāngarjong	Dankar-dzong		Upper Kāli Gandaki
Deng	Drang		KUTANG
— —	Doro		DOLPO (Tarap)
Dunaihi	Du-ne		Upper Bheri
Ghilinggāon	Ge-ling	*dGe-gling*	Upper Kāli Gandaki
Ghyāru	Gyaru	(*rGya-ru*)	NYE-SHANG
— —	Hrip		KUTANG
Jomosom	Dzongsam[c]	*rDzong gsar-ba*	T'HĀK
Kāgbeni (*nep*)	Kāgbeni (Kāk)[d]	*bKag* or *sKags*	Upper Kāli Gandaki
Karāng	Karang		DOLPO (Namgung)
— —	Karjet		GYASUMDO

---

[a] Concerning 'Gomba' see p. 260 fn.

[b] Also known as Tsum Gomba (p. 260).

[c] This is the local form of the name. By Tibetan speakers it is known as Dzong-sarba, which represents the classical spelling.

[d] Kāk (long vowel ā) is the local Tibetan name, Kāgbeni the recognized Nepalese form.

Survey of India	Amended Name	Classical Spelling	District
Keghagāon	Gyaga		Upper Kāli Gandaki
Kehami	Ge-mi		LO
Khāngsar[a]	Ngaba		NYE-SHANG
Khānīgāon	Ka-ne		Upper Bheri
Khanti (nep)	Narshang		T'HĀK
Khingār	Khyeng-khar		DZAR-DZONG
Komāgāon	Koma		DOLPO (Panzang)
	Koya		KUTANG
Krok	Gak		KUTANG
— —	Ku-tsap-ter-nga	sKu-tshab-gter-nga	T'HĀK
— —	Lang Gomba	Glang dgon-pa	DOLPO (Namgung)
Lar	Lar		TSUM
Lārjung (nep)	Gophang		T'HĀK
Larkya (nep)	Babuk		NUP-RI
Lho	Lö	Slod	NUP-RI
Lho (= Mustang-bhot)	Lo	Blo	
— —	Lo Ge-kar	Blo dGe-dkar	LO
Lidanda (nep)	Li		NUP-RI
LOKWA	Lokwa		KUTANG
Lurigāon	Lhori	lHo-ri	DOLPO (Panzang)
Māhārāng	Marang	(Ma-brang)	LO
Mājhgāon	Mä	Mad	DOLPO (Panzang)
Manangbhot	Manang	(Ma-nang)	NYE-SHANG
Mārphā	Marpha	Mar-phag	T'HĀK
— —	Mö		DOLPO (Panzang)
Muktināth (nep)	Chhu-mik-gya-tsa	Chu-mig brgya-rtsa	DZAR-DZONG
— —	Murwa		PHOKSUMDO
Mustāng (nep) ⎫ (Lho Mantang)⎭	Mön-t'hang	sMon-thang	LO
— —	Naktsa Gomba	Nags-tshal dgon-pa	NUP-RI
Nāmdogāon	Namdo	gNam-mdo	DOLPO (Namgung)
— —	Namdru		KUTANG
— —	Namgung[b]	gNam-gung	DOLPO (Namgung)
Naurgāon	Nar-mä (Lower Nar)	sNar-smad	NAR
— —	Nga		TSUM

[a] Khangsar is the name of the grazing-ground above the village.

[b] This name appears on the SI maps attached to the river (Nāngung Kholā) which flows through the district of Namgung.

Survey of India	Amended Name	Classical Spelling	District
Ngāchu	Nga-chhu		TSUM
Ngāwal	Bangba		NYE-SHANG
Ngile	Nyi-le	*Nyi-le*	TSUM
Ngyāk	Nyak	*gNyag*	KUTANG
Nisālgāon	Nyisäl	*Nyi-gsal*	DOLPO (Panzang)
— —	Päl-ding Gomba	*dPal-lding dgon-pa*	DOLPO (Namgung)
— —	Pang-dön		TSUM
Pāngsing	Pang-sh'ing	*sPang-zhing*	KUTANG
— —	Phalam		PHOKSUMDO
Phijorgāon	Phijor	*Phyi-mtsher*	DOLPO (Namgung)
Philam[a]	Angwang		KUTANG
Philim	{ Philön { Dodang	*'Phi-slon*	KUTANG
Phugāon	Nar-tö (Upper Nar)	*sNar-stod*	NAR
Phulbe	Phur-be		TSUM
Pisāng (*nep*)	Pi		NYE-SHANG
Prok (*nep*)	Prok (Trok)[b]	*Krog*	KUTANG
Pudāmigāon	Pungmo	*sPung-mo*	PHOKSUMDO
Pura	Purang	*sPu-rang*	DZAR-DZONG
— —	Putra	*sPu-tra*	DZAR-DZONG
— —	Ra-chhen Gomba	*Ra-chen dgon-pa*	TSUM
Ringmigāon[c]	{ Ringmo { Tsho-wa	*mTsho-ba*	PHOKSUMDO
Ripche	Hrip-che		TSUM
— —	Sagaru		T'HĀK
— —	Säl Gomba	*gSal dgon-pa*	DOLPO (Namgung)
Sāldānggāon	Saldang	*gSal-mdangs*	DOLPO (Namgung)
Sāma (*nep*)	Rö	*Ros*	NUP-RI
Samargāon	Samar		Upper Kāli Gandaki
— —	Samling	*bSam-gling*	DOLPO (Namgung)

[a] This 'Philam' seems to be a false duplication of 'Philim', for not only is the name unknown at Angwang, but the bridge shown here on the SI maps should be located at 'Philim'.

[b] The Gurung pronunciation is 'Prok'; the local Tibetan pronunciation 'Trok'. The classical spelling although surprising, it well vouched for. One would expect *Prok*.

[c] Ringmi (-gāon) is incorrect for the proper Nepalese name Ringmo. The Tibetan name 'Tsho-wa' means just 'lake-side'.

Survey of India	Amended Name	Classical Spelling	District
Sangdāh	⎰Sangdak	gSang-dag	Upper Kāli
	⎱P'a-ling*a*	Ba-gling	Gandaki
— —	Serchung		KUTANG
Setibās (*nep*)	Tara		KUTANG
— —	Sham-tr'ak Gomba	Shel-brag dgon-pa	DOLPO (Namgung)
— —	Sh'ip-chhok Gomba	Zhib-phyogs dgon-pa	DOLPO (Tarap)
Shule	Chhu-le	Chu-le	TSUM
Simengāon	Shimen	(Shing-man)	DOLPO (Panzang)
Syā Gömpa	Shey Gomba	Shel dgon-pa	DOLPO (Namgung)
Syāng	Shang		T'HĀK
— —	Ta-hrap Gomba	rTa-srab dgon-pa	NYE-SHANG
Tāhmar	Tr'ang-mar	Brag-dmar	LO
Tāngbe	Tangbe		Upper Kāli
			Gandaki
Tārakot (*nep*)	Dzong	rDzong ⎫	
	Sartara—Ba	⎪	
	Tupara—Tup	⎬	TICHU-RONG*b*
	Densa—	⎪	
	Dri-k'ung	'Bri-gung ⎭	
Tarāpgāon	Do	mDo	DOLPO (Tarap)*c*
Tegār	Tingkhar		LO
— —	Tengi	sTeng-skyes	NYE-SHANG
Tetāng	Te		Upper Kāli
			Gandaki
Thāngja	Dzong-gyu	(rDzong-rgyud)	GYASUMDO
Thinigāon	⎰T'hin		T'HĀK
	⎱Sombo		
Thonje	⎰Thangjet		GYASUMDO
Tilje	⎱Tiljet		GYASUMDO
Tingjegāon	Ting-khyu	gTing-'khyu	DOLPO (Panzang)
Tirigāon	Ting-ri	gTing-ri	Upper Kāli
			Gandaki
— —	Tr'ak-lung	Brag-lung	GYASUMDO
— —	Tsak		KUTANG
— —	Tshoknam		Upper Kāli
			Gandaki
Tukuchā	Tukchä	sPrug-chad	T'HĀK

---

a Concerning these two names see p. 163.

b Concerning Tichu-rong and this group of villages see p. 33.

c Concerning Tarap as a district and not a village-name see p. 154 fn.

Survey of India	Amended Name	Classical Spelling	District
Tumje	Rinsam		TSUM
Yānjar Gömpā[a]	Yang-tsher Gomba	gYas-mtsher dgon-pa	DOLPO (Panzang)
	Sh'ung-tsher Gomba	Zhugs-mtsher dgon-pa	
— —	Yab-yum Gomba	Yab-yum dgon-pa	DOLPO (Namgung)

[a] On the Survey of India maps this monastery is marked where Sh'ung-tsher Monastery should be. Yang-tsher is about 500 yards west of Nyisäl (SI: Nisālgāon).

District Name	Map page No.	Page Ref.	Survey of India area
DOLPO — Namgung	296–7	77, 83	Nāngung Kholā and Sibu Kholā area (Dābhansār) ;
— Panzang	,,	83, 93	Pānjāng Kholā area;
— Tarap	,,	83, 154	complex of villages and monasteries, including Tarāpgāon, Atāli and other places unmarked;
— Tsharbung	,,	83	Chharkābhotgāon and the Barbung Kholā;[a]
DZAR-DZONG	298	199	valley east of Kāgbeni ascending to Muktināth;
GYASUMDO	299	237	group of villages centring on the junction of the Dudh Kholā and the Marsyandi River, included in Manangbhot;
KUTANG	300	250	Kutang;
LO	298	195	Mustangbhot (Lho);
NAR	299	226	Naurgāon and Phu Kholā;
NUP-RI	300	241	Lārkya;
NYE-SHANG	299	207	villages of the Upper Marsyandi centring on Manang, included in Manangbhot;
PHOKSUMDO	296	59	Phoksumdo Tāl and the surrounding area;
T'HĀK	298	174	Thākkhola;
TICHU-RONG	295	33	Tārakot and surrounding villages;
TSUM	300	257	Shiār;
Upper Bheri	295	24	
Upper Kāli Gandaki	298	163	

[a] The district 'Chharkābhot' on the Survey of India maps seems to include Tsharka Village, Tarap and Panzang, but these represent no unity of any sort. Tsharka and the Barbung villages do represent one however; this is Tsharbung.

Name used in the text	Tibetan name	Sanskrit name
Acme Conqueror Omniscient	rTog-rgyal ye-mkhyen	
Adamantine Being	rDo-rje sems-dpa	Vajrasattva
Adamantine Sagging Belly	rDo-rje grod-lod	
All Good	Kun-tu bzang-po	Samantabhadra
All Unity of Absolute Essence	Yang-snying kun-'dus	
Ancestor King of Phantom Forms	Gong-mdzad 'phrul-gyi rgyal-po	
Banner of Fame	Grags-pa rgyal-mtshan	
Banner of Wisdom	Shes-rab rgyal-mtshan	
Boar-Headed Goddess	rDo-rje phag-mo	Vajravārāhī
Bond-keeper	dam-can	
Boundless Life	Tshe dpa-med	Amitāyus
Boundless Light	'Od dpa-med	Amitābha
Brilliant	rNam-par snang-mdzad	Vairocana
Buddha Master of Medicine	Sangs-rgyas sman-gyi lha	Bhaishajyaguru
Composite Conqueror	rGyal-ba 'dus-pa	
Defender	srung-ma	
Destroyer	rNam-par 'joms-pa	
Dragon-Prince	'Brug-gsas	
Essence of All Joy	Kun-dga snying-po	
Exalted Protector of Living Beings	'Gro-mgon 'phags-pa	
Falcon-Prince	Khra-gsas	
Fierce Blue Master	Gu-ru drag-mthing	
Fierce Lady with Good Things	Legs-ldan drag-mo	
Fierce Master	Gu-ru drag-po	
Fire-Prince	Me-gsas	
Ganacakra[a]	Dam-can ga-na-tsa-kra / lJang-nag dbu brgya phyag stong	
Garuda	mKha-lding	Garuda

[a] 'Ganacakra' is a Sanskrit term meaning 'Circle of Offerings'. It is used by the p'ön-pos as an alternative to the longer name given in the second column. See p. 51.

Name used in the text	Tibetan name	Sanskrit name
Glancing Eye	sPyan-ras gzigs	Avalokiteśvara
of Great Compassion	Thugs-rje chen-po	mahākāruṇa
of the Infallible Noose	Don-yod zhags-pa	amoghapāśa
Glorious Gentle One	'Jam-dpal	Mañjuśrī
Lion of Speech	sMra-ba'i senge	simhanāda
God of the Dart	Phur-pa'i lha	
Goddess of Wisdom	Yum chen-mo	Prajñāpāramitā
Great Black Divinity	Nag-po chen-po	Mahākāla
Great Brilliance	Kun-rig	Mahāvairocana
Guide Master of Medicine	Dran-pa sman-gyi lha	
Gyer-pung	Gyer-spungs	
Heruka	He-ru-ka	Heruka
Hey Vajra	Kye'i-rdo-rje	Hevajra
Holder of the Vajra	rDo-rje 'chang	Vajradhara
Horse-Neck	rTa-mgrin	Hayagrīva
Imperturbable	Mi-bskyod-pa	Akshobhya
Infallible Success	Don-yod grub-pa	Amoghasiddhi
Jambhala	Nor-lha	{Jambhala / Kubera
Jewel-Born	Rin-chen 'byung-ba	Ratnasambhava
Kings of Existence	Srid-rgyal	
Knowledge-Holder	Rig-'dzin	Vidyādhara
Life-Empowering Knowledge-Holder	Tshe-dbang rig-'dzin	
Light-Maker	Mar-me mdzad	Dīpankara
Lightning-Prince	Glog-gsas	
Lion-Headed Ḍākinī	Senge gdong-ma	
Lord of the Dead	gShin-rje	Yama
Lord Spell-Power Victorious	Jo-bo sngags-dbang rnam-rgyal	
Lotus-Born	Pad-ma 'byung-gnas	Padmasambhava
Lotus-in-Hand		Padmapāṇi
Lotus Lord of Dance	Pad-ma gar-gyi dbang-phyug	Padmanarteśvara
{Loving-Kindness / Maitreya, Ch'amba	Byams-pa	Maitreya
Mother with Good Things	A-ma legs-ldan	
One Inseparable	dByer-med-pa	

287

Name used in the text	Tibetan name	Sanskrit name
Precious Master	*Gu-ru rin-po-che* (= Lotus-Born)	
Protectors of the Three Families	*Rigs gsum mgon-po*	
Pure 10,000 times 100,000	*Sang-po 'bum-khri*	
Rāhula	*gZa-lha*	*Rāhula*
Raven-Headed Ḍākinī	*Pho-rog gdong-ma*	
Religion's Defence Glorious and Good	*Chos-skyabs dpal-bzang*	
{ Sage of the Śākyas { Śākyamuni	*Shā-kya thub-pa*	*Śākyamuni*
Satrik	*Sa-trig yer-sangs*	
Saviouress	*sGrol-ma*	*Tārā*
Secret Epitome of Scripture (man of the A-sh'a)[a]	*'A-zha gsang-pa mdo-bsdus*	
Shen-God White Light	*gShen-lha 'od-dkar*	
Shen-rap	*gShen-rab(s)*	
Sky-Gape	*mKha-'gying-kha*	
Sky-Goer	*mKhas-spyod*	
Sky-Guide	*Dran-pa namkha*	
Summit-Prince (Wäl-sä)[b]	*dBal-gsas*	
Supreme Bliss	*bDe-mchog*	*Cakrasamvara*
Supreme Chief Gaping Mouth	*gTso-mchog kha-'gying*	
Supreme Heruka	*Che-mchog he-ru-ka*	
Thunderbolt-in-Hand	*Phyag-na rdo-rje*	*Vajrapāṇi*
Tiger-God	*sTag-lha*	
Torch of Purity	*Thang-ma me-sgron*	
Tranquil and Fierce Divinites	*Zhi-khro*	
Union of the Precious Ones	*dKon-mchog spyi-'dus*	
Unity of All the Blessed	*bDe-gshegs kun-'dus*	
Universal Saviour	*'Gro-ba kun-sgrol*	
Victorious Lady	*rNam-rgyal-ma*	*Vijayā*
Victorious Lady of the Chignon	*gTsug-tor rnam-rgyal-ma*	*Ushnīshavijayā*
Victorious One	*rNam-par rgyal-ba*	
Vile Outcast Mother of those who progress towards bliss	*gTum-mo bde-'gro yum*	
Wäl-sä (Summit Prince)	*dBal-gsas*	
Wild God Topper	*lHa-god thog-pa*	

---

[a] see p. 50 fn. [b] see p. 49 fn.

INDEX

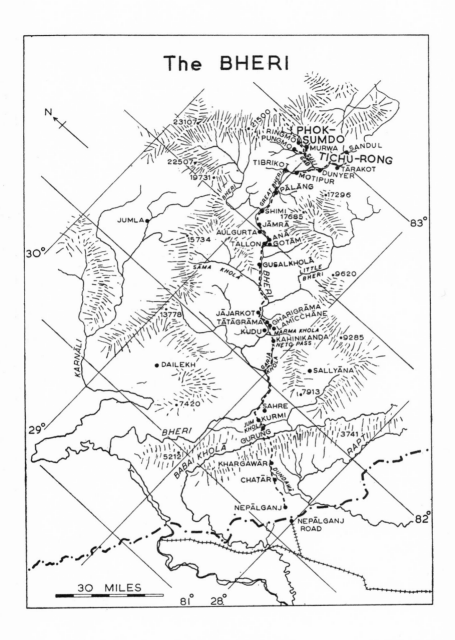

The BHERI

23107

21500

PHOK-
SUMDO

RINGMO
PUNGMO

MURWA SANDUL

TICHU-RONG

22507

TIBRIKOT

TĀRAKOT
DUNYER

19731

MOTIPUR

BHERI

GREAT BHERI

PĀLĀNG

17296

JUMLA

SHIMI
17685

JĀMRĀ

AULGURTA
15734

ANĀ
TALLON GOTĀM

SĀMA KHOLA

GUSALKHOLĀ

BHERI

LITTLE
BHERI

9620

JĀJARKOT
13778 TĀTĀGRĀMA

GHARIGRĀMA
LAMICCHĀNE

KUDU

MARMA KHOLA

KAHINIKANDA
NETO PASS

9285

DAILEKH

GARJA
KHOLA

SALLYĀNA

7913

7420

SAHRE

KURMI

BHERI

JUM
KHOLA

GURUNG

3741

RAPTI

5212

BABAI KHOLA

KHARGAWĀR

DUNDWE

CHATĀR

NEPĀLGANJ

NEPĀLGANJ
ROAD

82°

KARNĀLI

83°

30°

29°

81° 28°

30 MILES

295

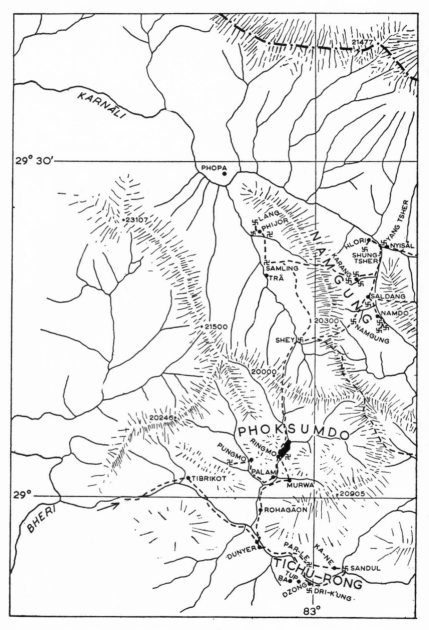

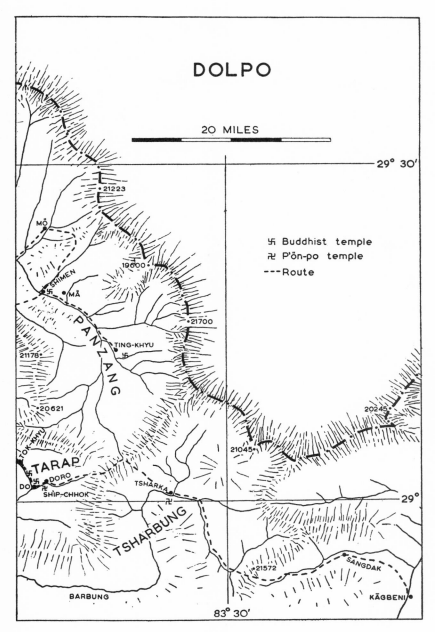

DOLPO

20 MILES

🕉 Buddhist temple
卍 P'ön-po temple
--- Route

29° 30'

21223

MÖ
19600
SHIMEN
MĂ
PANZANG
21700
21178
TING-KHYU
20621
20245
TOK-KHYU
21045
TARAP
DORO
DO
SHIP-CHHOK
TSHARKA
29°
TSHARBUNG
21572
SANGDAK
BARBUNG
KĀGBENI
83° 30'

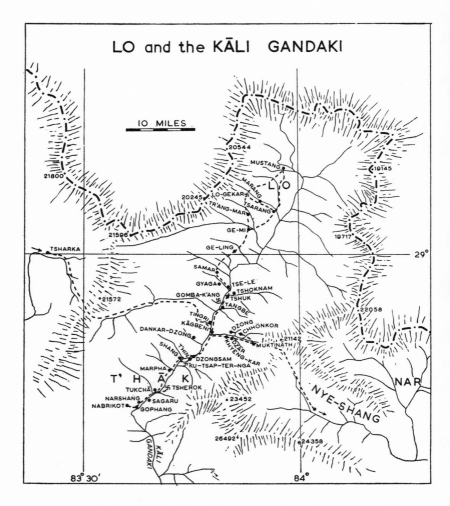

LO and the KĀLI GANDAKI

10 MILES

Except for the map of Dolpo, where all monasteries and temples are represented by a swastika, only isolated monasteries are specially marked on these maps. On the areas covered by the maps on pp. 298–300 there are temples, large or small, in almost all the villages named.

As for the swastika itself, we can only deplore its recent misappropriation for political purposes. It remains an ancient Indian religious symbol, indicating good fortune, still much used in Tibetan lands. Since the Buddhists use it with the bent arms pointing clockwise and the p'ön-pos anti-clockwise (see pp. 42–3), it serves very well as a sign to distinguish Buddhist from p'ön-po temples.

298

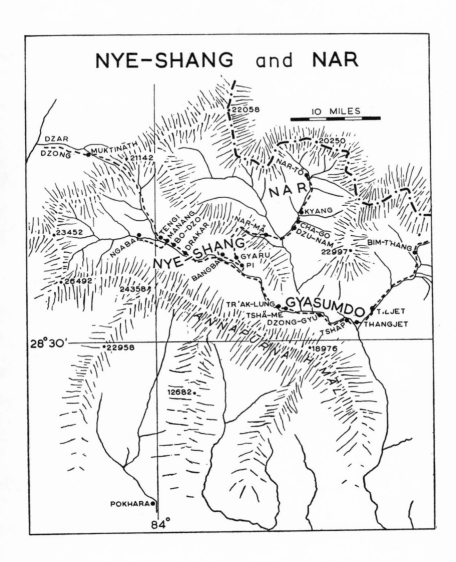

NYE–SHANG and NAR

10 MILES

22058

DZAR
DZONG · MUKTINATH
·21142
20250
NAR-TO

NAR

KYANG
·23452
TENGI
MANANG
BO-DZO
NGABA · DRAKAR
NAR-MĀ
CHA-GO
DZU-NAM
22997·
BIM-T'HANG

NYE-SHANG
GYARU
BANGBA · PI
·26492
·24358

ANNAPURNA
HIMAL

TR'AK-LUNG
GYASUMDO
T·LJET
TSHÄ-ME
DZONG-GYU
THANGJET
TSHAP

28°30'
·22958
·18976

12682·

POKHARA·
84°

299

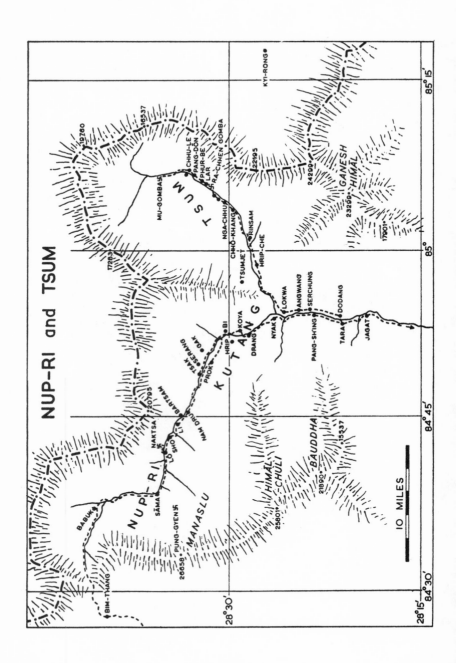

NUP-RI and TSUM

BABUK•

BIM-THANG

NUP-RI

SĀMA

SHO

NAKTSA 20795

BALATSAN

NAM DRU

PUNG-GYEN 26058•

MANASLU

PROK

TSAK SERRANG

BI

HRIP

KOYA

DRANGJE

NYAK

KUTANG

LOKWA

BANGWANG

PANG-SHING

SERCHUNG

TARA

ODANG

JAGAT

HIMAL

CHULI

25801•

21890•

BAUDDHA

15537

19260

16537

MU-GOMBA

CHHU-LE

PANG-DÖN

PHUR-BE

LAR

RA-CHHEN GOMBA

T S U M

NGA-CHHU

CHHÖ-KHANG

TSUMJET

•TSUMJE

RINSAM

HRIP-CHE

17263

22195

24299

GANESH

HIMAL

23260•

17001•

KYI-RONG•

10 MILES

85°15'

85°

84°45'

84°30'

84°15'

28°30'

28°15'

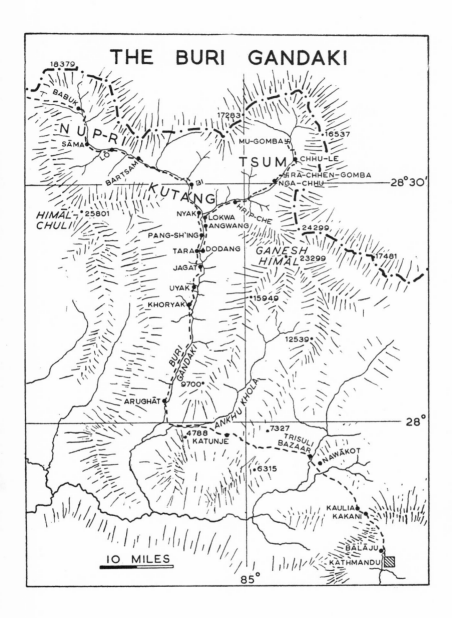

THE BURI GANDAKI

18379

BABUK

NU-P-RI

SĀMA

LŌ

BARTSAM

KUTANG

BI

HIMĀL-
CHULI

25801

NYAK

PANG-SH'ING

TARA

DODANG

JAGAT

UYAK

KHORYAK

LOKWA
ANGWANG

HRIP-CHE

17283

MU-GOMBA

TSUM

TRA-CHHEN-GOMBA
NGA-CHHU

16537

CHHU-LE

28°30'

24299

GANESH
HIMĀL

23299

17481

15949

12539

BURI
GANDAKI

9700

ARUGHĀT

ANKHU KHOLA

28°

4788
KATUNJE

7327

TRISULI
BAZAAR

NAWĀKOT

6315

10 MILES

KAULIA
KAKANI

BĀLĀJU

KATHMANDU

85°

301

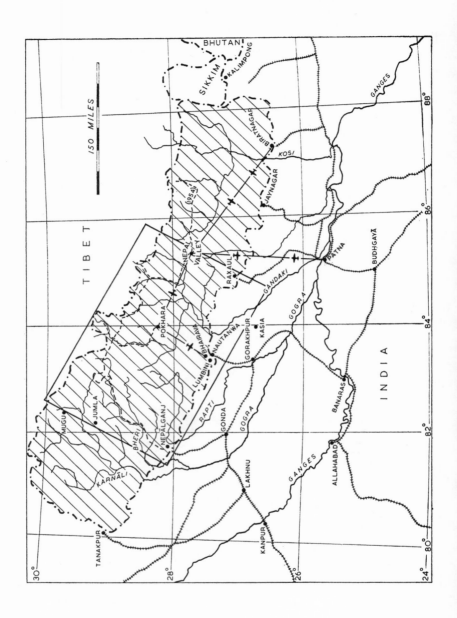

302

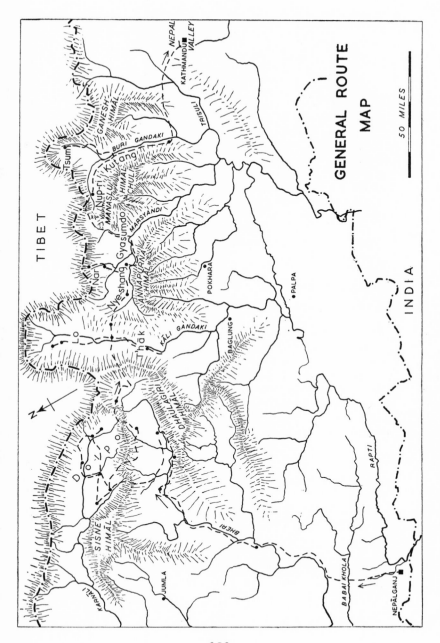

GENERAL ROUTE MAP

50 MILES

TIBET

INDIA

NEPAL

KATHMANDU VALLEY

TRISULI

GANESH HIMAL

BURI GANDAKI

Tsum

Kutang

Nup-ri

MANASLU HIMAL

CHULI

MARSIANDI

Nar

Gyasumdo

We-shang

ANNAPURNA HIMAL

POKHARA

PALPA

Thāk

KĀLI GANDAKI

BAGLUNG

DHAULAGIRI

DHAMĀL

DOLPO

SISNE HIMĀL

KARNĀLI

JUMLA

BHERI

RAPTI

BABAI KHOLA

NEPĀLGANJ

303

BIBLIOGRAPHY

Relevant to Bon:

Helmut Hoffman, *Die Religionen Tibets, Bon und Lamaismus in ihrer geschichtlichen Entwicklung*, Freiburg/München, 1956.
   idem, *Quellen zur Geschichte der tibetischen Bon-Religion*, Wiesbaden, 1950.
   idem, 'Zur Literatur der Bon-po', *Zeitschrift der Deutschen Morgenländischen Gesellschaft*, 94, Leipzig, 1940, pp. 169–88.
René von Nebesky-Wojkowitz, 'Die Tibetische Bon-Religion', *Archiv für Völkerkunde*, II (1947), pp. 26–68.
   idem, *Oracles and Demons of Tibet*, Oxford University Press, London, 1956.
Li An-che, 'Bon: the magico-religious belief of the Tibetan-speaking peoples', *Southwestern Journal of Anthropology*, 4, Albuquerque, 1948, pp. 31–42.

Relevant to the orders of Tibetan Buddhism:

Li An-che, 'A Lamasery in outline', *Journal of the West China Research Society*, xiv, series A, 1942, pp. 35–68.
   idem, 'The Sakya Sect of Lamaism', *Journal of the West China Research Society*, xvi, series A, 1945, pp. 72–86.
   idem, 'rNying-ma-pa: the early form of Lamaism', *Journal of the Royal Asiatic Society*, London, 1948, pp. 142–63.
   idem, 'The bKa'-brgyud-pa Sect of Lamaism', *Journal of the American Oriental Society*, 69, 1949, pp. 51–9.
Hugh Richardson, 'The Karma-pa Sect, A Historical Note', *Journal of the Royal Asiatic Society*, 1958, pp. 139–64, & 1959, pp. 1–18.

Relevant to my travels in West Nepal:

Giuseppe Tucci, *Preliminary Report on Two Scientific Expeditions in Nepal*, Rome, 1956.
   idem, *Tra Giungle e Pagode*, Rome, 1953.
H. W. Tilman, *Nepal Himalaya*, Cambridge, 1952.